FamilyCircle®

ANNUAL RECIPES 2015

CHOCOLATE
RASPBERRY
TRIFLE,
PAGE 46

Meredith® Consumer Marketing
Des Moines, Iowa

**BLT EGGS BENEDICT,
PAGE 113**

A YEAR'S WORTH OF FABULOUS *FAMILY CIRCLE*® RECIPES AT YOUR FINGERTIPS!

Feeding our families well is important to all of us—whether it's a speedy weeknight meal before dashing off to the rest of the day's activities or a once-a-year celebration during which we slow down and savor the specialness of the occasion. At *Family Circle*, we carefully consider the recipes we include in our magazine. Those quick recipes need to be speedy and easy, health- and budget-conscious, and of course, delicious. The celebratory recipes need to be spectacular in some way—but still simple enough to achieve at home. You will find both kinds of recipes—and everything in between—in this one volume, a conveniently bound collection of every recipe that appeared in the 2015 issues of the magazine. It's organized by month, so you can easily find just the kind of recipe you're looking for.

For Valentine's Day, indulge in chocolate treats such as Mini Chocolate Cheesecakes (page 50) or Chocolate Raspberry Trifle (page 46). In summer, gather friends for a backyard barbecue featuring Brown Sugar-Bourbon-Glazed Baby Back Ribs (page 155), Broccoli and Red Cabbage Slaw (page 152), Grilled Potato and Onion Salad with Maytag Blue Cheese (page 152) and Pepper-Studded Cornbread (page 156). When the weather turns cool, warm up with comfort food from around the world, including African Chicken and Peanut Stew (page 275), Moroccan Beef Chili (page 277) and Malaysian Pork Curry Noodle Soup (page 276).

We know that weeknights present cooking challenges, so in every issue—in regular features such as Healthy Family Dinners—we focus on ways to get delicious, nutritious food on your table any night of the week.

Food and family are interconnected. We want to help you enjoy them both around the table every day.

Linda

Linda Fears, Editor in Chief
Family Circle Magazine

Family Circle Annual Recipes 2015

Meredith Consumer Marketing
Consumer Marketing Product Director: Heather Sorensen
Consumer Marketing Product Manager: Wendy Merical
Consumer Marketing Billing/Renewal Manager: Tami Beachem
Business Director: Ron Clingman
Senior Production Manager: Al Rodruck

Waterbury Publications, Inc.
Editorial Director: Lisa Kingsley
Associate Editor: Tricia Bergman
Associate Editor/Food Stylist: Annie Peterson
Assistant Food Stylist: Skyler Myers
Creative Director: Ken Carlson
Associate Design Director: Doug Samuelson
Graphic Designer: Mindy Samuelson
Contributing Copy Editors: Terri Fredrickson, Peg Smith
Contributing Indexer: Mary Williams

Family Circle **Magazine**
Editor in Chief: Linda Fears
Creative Director: Karmen Lizzul
Food Director: Regina Ragone, M.S., R.D.
Executive Food Editor: Julie Miltenberger
Associate Food Editor: Michael Tyrrell
Associate Food Editor: Melissa Knific

Meredith National Media Group
President: Tom Harty

Meredith Corporation
Chairman and Chief Executive Officer: Stephen M. Lacy

In Memoriam: E.T. Meredith III (1933–2003)

Copyright © 2015
Meredith Corporation.
Des Moines, Iowa.
First Edition.
Printed in the United States of America.
ISSN: 1942-7476
ISBN: 978-0-696-30214-5

All of us at Meredith Consumer
Marketing are dedicated to providing
you with information and ideas to
enhance your home. We welcome
your comments and suggestions.
Write to us at: Meredith Consumer
Marketing, 1716 Locust St.,
Des Moines, IA 50309-3023.

LET'S EAT! Coming together around the family table at the end of the day to enjoy a home-cooked meal soothes away the day's stresses and satisfies on so many levels. This collection of recipes from the 2015 issues of *Family Circle* magazine makes it easier than ever to serve tasty food you cook yourself—whether it's a 30-minute dinner, a holiday celebration or a special evening with friends. Recipes are organized by month to take advantage of what's in season and to make it easy to find the perfect recipe for any occasion.

Slow Cooker Mac and Cheese with Bacon (page 55) is part of the "Not Your Everyday Mac" story that appeared in the February issue. Other indulgent comfort-food dishes from that issue include BBQ Mac and Cheese, Organic White Mac and Cheese, and Gluten-Free Mac and Cheese.

MAPLE-PEAR
CHEESECAKE PIE,
PAGE 294

CONTENTS

BAJA FISH TACOS WITH
GRILLED AVOCADO,
PAGE 30

JANUARY

11

16

25

LET THEM EAT CAKE

Celebrate the season with this stunning French dessert.

CLASSIC YULE LOG

The yule log cake is a sweet representation of the large log that was burned in fireplaces on Christmas Eve during European Christmas and solstice celebrations. As long as the log burned, no work would be done—only fun and festivities. The French invented the pastry form of this log, called bûche de Noël.

Classic Yule Log

MAKES 8 servings **PREP** 25 minutes **MICROWAVE** 1 minute **BAKE** at 375° for 14 minutes **REFRIGERATE** 30 minutes

CAKE

- ½ **cup unsweetened cocoa powder**
- ¼ **cup all-purpose flour**
- ½ **teaspoon baking powder**
- 6 **large eggs, separated**
- ¼ **teaspoon cream of tartar**
  Pinch of salt
- ¾ **cup granulated sugar**
- ½ **teaspoon vanilla extract**
- 3 **tablespoons confectioners' sugar**

FILLING AND FROSTING

- 2 **ounces unsweetened baking chocolate, chopped**
- 1 **package (8 ounces) cream cheese, softened**
- 6 **tablespoons unsalted butter, softened**
- 1 **box (16 ounces) confectioners' sugar**
- 1 **teaspoon vanilla extract**
- ¾ **cup heavy cream**
  Pinch of salt
  Chocolate shavings
- 3 **marshmallows**
  Candy Mushrooms (recipe follows; optional)

■ **Cake.** Heat oven to 375°. Coat a 15 x 10 x 1-inch baking pan with nonstick cooking spray. Line bottom of pan with wax paper and coat paper with spray. Set aside.

■ In a small bowl, whisk cocoa powder, flour and baking powder. In a large bowl, whip egg whites, cream of tartar and salt until frothy. Gradually beat in ¼ cup of the granulated sugar until medium shiny peaks form, about 5 minutes. Set aside. With the same beaters, beat egg yolks, remaining ½ cup granulated sugar and the vanilla until pale and thick, about 4 minutes. Fold egg yolk mixture into whipped egg whites. Fold in flour mixture in 2 batches. Spread into prepared pan. Bake at 375° for 12 to 14 minutes, until cake springs back lightly when touched.

■ Dust confectioners' sugar on a clean cotton kitchen towel. Run a thin knife around cake edges and invert onto prepared towel. Remove wax paper. Roll up cake and towel, starting from a short side. Let cool completely.

■ **Filling and Frosting.** While cake cools, heat chocolate in microwave 1 minute, stirring until smooth. Set aside to cool slightly. In a large bowl, beat cream cheese and butter.

Gradually beat in confectioners' sugar and vanilla. Spoon 1½ cups of the cream cheese mixture into a medium bowl. Beat ½ cup of the heavy cream until medium soft peaks form. Fold into first bowl of cream cheese mixture to lighten. Beat melted chocolate, salt and remaining ¼ cup heavy cream into second bowl of mixture.

■ Carefully unroll cake. Spread white filling to within ½ inch of edge of cake. Re-roll cake (without towel) and place seam side down on platter. Refrigerate 30 minutes, if very soft. Spread with chocolate frosting, using a fork to give the ridged appearance of bark. Top with chocolate shavings.

■ To create "knot" on side of cake, place 3 marshmallows in a tight cluster on one side. Cover with frosting, swirling decoratively. Add Candy Mushrooms to platter, if using.

Candy Mushrooms

■ Snip a marshmallow in half with scissors. Unwrap 2 Rolo candies and place a marshmallow half, cut side down, on top of each candy. Dust with a little cocoa powder. Repeat as desired.

PARTY HEARTY

Ring in the New Year with an array of finger foods and drinks that make a meal.

SAUSAGE AND SAGE ARANCINI
(RISOTTO BALLS), PAGE 19

"EVERYTHING"
SALMON BITES,
PAGE 16

WHITE BEAN AND
PROSCIUTTO

KALE WITH
HARISSA

ROASTED GRAPES
WITH RICOTTA

Crostini offer variety and ease. Three very different but simple-to-make toppings are served on tiny toasts that look pretty on a platter and taste wonderful too.

Crostini

Slice a 12-ounce baguette into 24 pieces. Brush with 1 tablespoon olive oil and bake at 400° for 8 to 10 minutes, until lightly toasted. Top with these three options.

Kale with Harissa

MAKES 24 crostini **PREP** 20 minutes

- 8 cups finely sliced kale, tough stems removed
- 3 tablespoons light mayonnaise
- 1 tablespoon harissa paste
- 1 teaspoon lemon juice
- ⅛ teaspoon salt
- 24 pieces crostini

■ Toss kale with mayonnaise, harissa, lemon juice and salt. Set aside for 15 minutes. Mound on crostini.

PER CROSTINO 51 **CAL**; 1 g **FAT** (0 g **SAT**); 2 g **PRO**; 9 g **CARB**; 0 g **FIBER**; 125 mg **SODIUM**; 1 mg **CHOL**

White Bean and Prosciutto

MAKES 24 crostini **PREP** 20 minutes
BAKE at 400° for 18 minutes

- 3 ounces prosciutto
- 2 cans cannelini beans, drained and rinsed
- 6 tablespoons extra-virgin olive oil, plus more for drizzling (optional)
- 1 tablespoon lemon juice
- 1 teaspoon fresh chopped rosemary
- ½ teaspoon salt
- ¼ teaspoon black pepper
- 24 pieces crostini

■ Heat oven to 400°. Place prosciutto on a baking sheet fitted with a rack. Bake at 400° for 15 to 18 minutes, until crispy. Roughly chop.

■ Set aside 1 cup beans. In a food processor, combine remaining beans, the oil, lemon juice, rosemary, salt and pepper. Stir in three-fourths of the prosciutto and the reserved beans. Spread 2 tablespoons on each crostino. Garnish with remaining fourth of the prosciutto. Drizzle with more olive oil, if using.

PER CROSTINO 107 **CAL**; 4 g **FAT** (1 g **SAT**); 4 g **PRO**; 13 g **CARB**; 2 g **FIBER**; 276 mg **SODIUM**; 2 mg **CHOL**

Roasted Grapes with Ricotta

MAKES 24 crostini **PREP** 20 minutes
BAKE at 400° for 50 minutes

- 4 cups red grapes
- 1 tablespoon plus 1 teaspoon fresh thyme, plus more for garnish (optional)
- 1 tablespoon olive oil
- ¼ teaspoon plus ⅛ teaspoon salt
- 1 container (15 ounces) ricotta
- 24 pieces crostini
- 1 tablespoon honey

■ Heat oven to 400°. Toss grapes with 1 tablespoon thyme, the olive oil and ⅛ teaspoon salt. Place on a rimmed baking sheet; roast at 400° for 40 to 50 minutes, shaking a few times, until wilted.

■ Mix ricotta and remaining 1 teaspoon thyme and ¼ teaspoon salt. Spread 1 generous tablespoon on each crostino. Scatter grapes on top and garnish with more thyme, if using. Drizzle with honey.

PER CROSTINO 103 **CAL**; 4 g **FAT** (2 g **SAT**); 4 g **PRO**; 14 g **CARB**; 0 g **FIBER**; 144 mg **SODIUM**; 9 mg **CHOL**

"EVERYTHING" SALMON BITES

Mini Manhattan Crab Chowders

MAKES 24 appetizer servings
PREP 15 minutes **COOK** 19 minutes

- 2 tablespoons olive oil
- ½ cup finely diced carrots
- ½ cup finely diced celery
- ½ cup finely diced onion
- 2 cloves minced garlic
- 2 teaspoons Old Bay seasoning
- 2½ cups chicken broth
- 1½ cups crushed tomatoes
- 1 cup finely diced red potatoes
- 8 ounces crab claw meat packed in water (such as Phillips)
- ½ cup parsley, chopped
- 2 teaspoons lemon juice
- 2 teaspoons Tabasco
- 1 teaspoon sugar

■ Heat oil in a pot over medium heat. Add carrots, celery and onion. Sauté 6 to 8 minutes, stirring often, until softened. Stir in garlic and Old Bay; cook 1 minute. Add broth, tomatoes, potatoes and crab. Bring to a boil, then reduce to a simmer and cover with lid. Cook 10 minutes, until potatoes are tender. Stir in parsley, lemon juice, Tabasco and sugar. Serve warm in 3-ounce shot glasses or small cups. (Note: This also makes 4 dinner portions.)

PER SERVING 36 **CAL**; 1 g **FAT** (0 g **SAT**); 3 g **PRO**; 3 g **CARB**; 1 g **FIBER**; 217 mg **SODIUM**; 11 mg **CHOL**

"Everything" Salmon Bites

MAKES 24 appetizers **PREP** 25 minutes

- ¼ teaspoon poppy seeds
- ¼ teaspoon sesame seeds
- ¼ teaspoon minced garlic
- ¼ teaspoon minced onion
- ¼ teaspoon coarse salt
- 1 package (17.6 ounces) German whole rye bread (such as Mestemacher)
- 24 teaspoons chive-and-onion cream cheese
- 4 ounces smoked salmon, cut into 24 pieces

■ In a small bowl, combine poppy seeds, sesame seeds, garlic, onion and salt.

■ Using a 2-inch round cutter, remove 24 rounds from bread. Spread 1 scant teaspoon of the cream cheese on each round, place a piece of salmon on top and garnish with a bit of the poppy seed mixture.

PER BITE 46 **CAL**; 2 g **FAT** (1 g **SAT**); 4 g **PRO**; 4 g **CARB**; 1 g **FIBER**; 145 mg **SODIUM**; 10 mg **CHOL**

MINI MANHATTAN
CRAB CHOWDERS

Burrata with Arugula Pesto

MAKES 12 servings PREP 15 minutes

- **4** **cups arugula, packed**
- **¼** **cup toasted pine nuts, plus more for garnish**
- **1** **clove garlic**
- **1** **tablespoon lemon juice**
- **⅓** **cup extra-virgin olive oil**
- **⅓** **cup Parmigiano- Reggiano**
- **¼** **teaspoon salt**
- **⅛** **teaspoon black pepper**
- **1** **pound burrata (such as BelGioioso)**
  Crackers, for serving

■ In a food processor, combine arugula, pine nuts, garlic and lemon juice. With processor running, slowly stream in oil until well combined. Transfer to a bowl and stir in Parmigiano-Reggiano, salt and pepper. Spoon 4 tablespoons over burrata (reserve remaining pesto for another use) and garnish with additional pine nuts. Serve with crackers.

PER SERVING 120 **CAL**; 11 g **FAT** (6 g **SAT**); 7 g **PRO**; 0 g **CARB**; 0 g **FIBER**; 136 mg **SODIUM**; 27 mg **CHOL**

SAUSAGE AND SAGE ARANCINI (RISOTTO BALLS)

Sausage and Sage Arancini (Risotto Balls)

MAKES 24 arancini PREP 30 minutes COOK 37 minutes REFRIGERATE 1 hour
FRY 3 minutes per batch

- **2** **links (about 6 ounces) sweet Italian sausage, casings removed**
- **½** **cup diced onion**
- **2** **cloves garlic, minced**
- **2** **tablespoons chopped fresh sage**
- **1** **cup arborio rice**
- **½** **cup dry white wine**
- **2** **cups reduced-sodium chicken broth**
- **½** **teaspoon salt**
- **¼** **teaspoon black pepper**
- **8** **cups vegetable oil**
- **1** **egg, beaten**
- **¾** **cup plain bread crumbs**
- **24** **½-inch cubes Fontina cheese (about 3 ounces)**
  Marinara sauce (optional)

■ Heat a lidded pot over medium-high heat. Add sausage, breaking up with a spoon. Cook 6 minutes, until browned. Reduce heat to medium and stir in onion. Cook 3 to 5 minutes, until softened. Mix in garlic and sage; cook 1 minute. Stir in rice and wine, scraping bottom of pan to release brown bits. Cook until liquid evaporates. Pour in broth and 1½ cups water. Bring to a boil. Cover, reduce to a simmer and cook 25 minutes, until liquid is absorbed and rice is tender. Stir in salt and pepper. Spread rice on a rimmed baking sheet to cool 10 minutes, then refrigerate 1 hour.

■ Heat oil in a large, heavy-bottomed pot to 350° (test with a fry thermometer). Scrape risotto into a large bowl and mix with egg and ¼ cup of the bread crumbs. Using hands, form a ball around a cube of cheese with 2 tablespoons of the mixture. Roll in remaining ½ cup bread crumbs. Place on a baking sheet while continuing to form arancini.

■ Fry arancini in batches (no more than 8 at a time) for 3 minutes each, maintaining temp around 350° (it will drop when arancini are added). Place on a paper-towel-lined plate; allow to cool slightly (cheese will continue to melt inside). Serve hot with marinara on the side for dipping, if using.

PER ARANCINO 100 **CAL**; 7 g **FAT** (2 g **SAT**); 3 g **PRO**; 6 g **CARB**; 0 g **FIBER**; 183 mg **SODIUM**; 15 mg **CHOL**

ROSEMARY
GIN FIZZ

HOLIDAY
GLOGG

MAPLE OLD-
FASHIONED

Offer your guests a special holiday cocktail in the spirit of celebration this season. These selections offer warm and well-spiced options—and something cold and refreshing too.

Maple Old-Fashioned

MAKES 1 serving **PREP** 5 minutes

- ½ **ounce maple syrup**
- 2 **maraschino cherries**
- 2 **to 3 dashes Angostura bitters**
- 2 **ounces rye or bourbon**
  Orange peel

■ In a rocks glass, add maple syrup, cherries and bitters. Pour in rye, then add ice. Stir 1 minute. Run orange peel around rim of glass and place inside.

PER SERVING 206 **CAL**; 0 g **FAT** (0 g **SAT**); 0 g **PRO**; 20 g **CARB**; 0 g **FIBER**; 2 mg **SODIUM**; 0 mg **CHOL**

Rosemary Gin Fizz

MAKES 1 serving **PREP** 5 minutes

- 2 **ounces gin**
- ½ **ounce lemon juice**
- ½ **ounce Rosemary Simple Syrup (recipe below)**
- 2 **ounces seltzer**
  Rosemary sprig

■ Fill a cocktail shaker with ice. Pour in gin, lemon juice and Rosemary Simple Syrup. Shake 1 minute. Pour into a highball glass over ice. Stir 1 minute. Top with seltzer and garnish with rosemary.

PER SERVING 169 **CAL**; 0 g **FAT** (0 g **SAT**); 0 g **PRO**; 11 g **CARB**; 0 g **FIBER**; 2 mg **SODIUM**; 0 mg **CHOL**

Rosemary Simple Syrup

■ Combine 1 cup sugar, 1 cup water and 1 sprig rosemary in a small pot. Bring to a boil and simmer until sugar is dissolved. Cover, remove from heat and steep at least 15 minutes. Let cool until using.

Holiday Glogg

MAKES 14 servings **PREP** 10 minutes
STEEP 1 hour

- 2 **bottles (750 ml each) fruity, full-bodied wine (such as Zinfandel)**
- 1 **bottle (750 ml) port**
- 1 **cup brandy**
- 1 **cup raisins**
- 1 **cup blanched slivered almonds**
- ½ **orange, sliced into half-moons**
- ¼ **cup sugar**
- 4 **cloves**
- 1 **cinnamon stick**
- 1 **bay leaf**

■ Combine all ingredients in a large pot. Heat until steam rises from liquid, but don't bring to a simmer (it will cook off the alcohol). Cover and steep on lowest heat setting for 1 hour. Serve warm.

PER SERVING 283 **CAL**; 5 g **FAT** (0 g **SAT**); 3 g **PRO**; 20 g **CARB**; 2 g **FIBER**; 9 mg **SODIUM**; 0 mg **CHOL**

HEALTHY FAMILY DINNERS

Go RETRO! Serve up these old-school favorites, each redone and slimmed down.

ANCHO MOLE BEEF
STEW, PAGE 25

KOREAN PORK
CHOPS, PAGE 26

**GRASS-FED GROUND
BEEF MEATLOAF**

Grass-Fed Ground Beef Meatloaf

MAKES 6 servings **PREP** 25 minutes
BAKE at 375° for 55 minutes **COOL** 15 minutes

- 1½ **pounds lean grass-fed ground beef**
- 3 **egg whites, lightly beaten**
- ½ **cup bread crumbs**
- 1 **cup tomato sauce**
- 1 **medium zucchini, shredded**
- ½ **medium onion, chopped**
- 1½ **cups chopped red and yellow sweet peppers**
- 3 **cloves garlic, chopped**
- 1 **teaspoon salt**
- ¾ **teaspoon dried sage**
- ¾ **teaspoon dried oregano**
- ½ **teaspoon plus ⅛ teaspoon black pepper**
- 2 **cups reduced-sodium chicken broth**
- 1 **cup red lentils**
- 3 **cups steamed broccoli florets**

■ Heat oven to 375°. Line a 9 x 5-inch loaf pan with foil and coat with nonstick cooking spray.

■ In a large bowl, combine ground beef, egg whites, bread crumbs, ½ cup of the tomato sauce, the zucchini, onion, sweet peppers, garlic, ¾ teaspoon of the salt, the sage, oregano and ½ teaspoon black pepper. Spoon mixture into prepared loaf pan; press flat.

■ Bake at 375° for 30 minutes. Spoon remaining ½ cup tomato sauce over top and bake an additional 25 minutes. Cool 15 minutes before slicing into 6 servings.

■ Meanwhile, in a medium saucepan, combine broth and lentils. Bring to a boil and simmer, covered, 12 to 15 minutes, until tender. Season with remaining ¼ teaspoon salt and ⅛ teaspoon pepper; mash.

■ Serve meatloaf with lentil mash and steamed broccoli.

PER SERVING 369 **CAL**; 9 g **FAT** (3 g **SAT**); 39 g **PRO**; 34 g **CARB**; 8 g **FIBER**; 759 mg **SODIUM**; 70 mg **CHOL**

ANCHO MOLE BEEF STEW

Ancho Mole Beef Stew

MAKES 6 servings **PREP** 25 minutes **COOK** 1 hour, 58 minutes

- ¼ **cup all-purpose flour**
- 1 **teaspoon plus 2 teaspoons ancho chile powder**
- ½ **teaspoon salt**
- 1½ **pounds beef chuck, cut into 1-inch pieces**
- 2 **tablespoons canola oil**
- 1 **onion, chopped**
- 3 **cloves garlic, chopped**
- 2 **tablespoons mole paste (such as La Costeña; see Note)**
- 3 **cups reduced-sodium beef broth**
- 1 **can (14½ ounces) no-salt-added stewed tomatoes**
- 1 **teaspoon dried oregano**
- 1½ **pounds small (1 inch round) red potatoes, halved**
- ½ **pound baby carrots**
- 1 **can (15 ounces) hominy, drained and rinsed**
- **Cilantro, for garnish**

■ Combine flour, 1 teaspoon ancho chile powder and ⅛ teaspoon of the salt. Dredge beef in mixture and reserve leftover mixture.

■ In a large pot, heat 1 tablespoon of the oil over medium-high heat. Add beef and sauté 5 minutes, turning once. Remove to a plate. Add remaining 1 tablespoon oil, the onion and garlic; cook 3 minutes. Stir in reserved flour mixture, mole paste, broth, 1 cup water, tomatoes, oregano and remaining 2 teaspoons chile powder.

■ Return beef to pot. Cover and simmer over medium-low heat 90 minutes, stirring occasionally. Add potatoes, carrots and remaining ⅜ teaspoon salt. Simmer an additional 20 minutes, until vegetables are tender.

■ Add hominy and garnish with cilantro.

PER SERVING 406 **CAL**; 13 g **FAT** (3 g **SAT**); 31 g **PRO**; 44 g **CARB**; 8 g **FIBER**; 807 mg **SODIUM**; 55 mg **CHOL**

Note: Look for mole paste in your supermarket's international foods aisle.

SWISS CHARD AND MUSHROOM LASAGNA

Swiss Chard and Mushroom Lasagna

MAKES 8 servings PREP 30 minutes COOK 17 minutes BAKE at 400° for 50 minutes
COOL 20 minutes

- 2 tablespoons olive oil
- 3 cloves garlic, chopped
- 1 pound Swiss chard, stems removed, cut crosswise into 1-inch slices
- 1 pound baby bella mushrooms, sliced
- ½ teaspoon salt
- ¼ teaspoon black pepper
- 2 tablespoons unsalted butter
- ¼ cup all-purpose flour
- 2½ cups fat-free milk
- ¼ teaspoon ground nutmeg
- ⅛ teaspoon cayenne pepper
- 12 uncooked lasagna noodles
- 1 container (15 ounces) part-skim ricotta cheese
- 1 cup shredded Fontina cheese
- 1 egg, lightly beaten
- 2 cups shredded part-skim mozzarella
- ½ cup grated Grana Padano or Parmigiano-Reggiano cheese

■ Heat oven to 400°. Coat a 13 x 9 x 2-inch baking dish with nonstick cooking spray.

■ In a large nonstick skillet, heat olive oil over medium-high heat. Add garlic, Swiss chard, mushrooms, ¼ teaspoon of the salt and the black pepper. Cook 7 minutes, stirring occasionally. Spoon off any excess liquid.

■ Meanwhile, in a medium saucepan, melt butter over medium heat; stir in flour and cook 1 minute. Gradually whisk in milk. Bring to a simmer; cook, stirring frequently, 3 minutes or until thickened. Add remaining ¼ teaspoon salt, the nutmeg and cayenne.

■ Cook lasagna noodles following package directions, about 10 minutes. Drain. Combine ricotta, Fontina and egg.

■ Spread ¼ cup of white sauce in baking dish. Layer as follows: 3 noodles, ricotta mixture, 3 noodles, 1 cup of the sauce, chard mixture, ½ cup of the mozzarella, 3 noodles, remaining 1½ cups mozzarella and 3 noodles. Spread remaining ¾ cup sauce over noodles and sprinkle Grana Padano over top.

■ Cover and bake at 400° for 30 minutes. Uncover and bake an additional 20 minutes. Cool 20 minutes before serving.

PER SERVING 458 CAL; 20 g FAT (10 g SAT); 29 g PRO; 43 g CARB; 3 g FIBER; 790 mg SODIUM; 87 mg CHOL

Korean Pork Chops

MAKES 4 servings PREP 15 minutes
MARINATE 60 minutes
GRILL OR BROIL 4 minutes COOK 5 minutes

- ⅓ cup orange juice
- ½ cup orange marmalade
- 4 cloves garlic, chopped
- 3 tablespoons reduced-sodium soy sauce
- 2 tablespoons brown sugar
- 2 tablespoons rice vinegar
- 1 tablespoon toasted sesame oil
- 2 teaspoons Asian chili paste
- 4 bone-in rib pork chops (about 7 ounces each)
- 8 ounces sugar snap peas
- 4 ounces angel hair pasta
- 1 teaspoon toasted sesame seeds

■ In a resealable bag, combine orange juice, marmalade, garlic, soy sauce, brown sugar, vinegar, sesame oil and chili paste. Add pork chops, seal bag and marinate in refrigerator 60 minutes.

■ Heat a stovetop grill pan to medium-high or broiler to high. Remove chops from plastic bag, reserving marinade. Grill or broil chops 2 minutes per side or until internal temperature reaches 145°. Place marinade in a small saucepan and boil 5 minutes.

■ Meanwhile, bring a large pot of lightly salted water to a boil. Add snap peas and cook 1 minute. Stir in angel hair and cook 2 minutes. Drain. Place in a bowl, toss with ⅔ cup of the reserved marinade and sprinkle with sesame seeds.

■ Serve pork chops with noodles, snap peas and remaining marinade.

PER SERVING 492 CAL; 15 g FAT (4 g SAT); 36 g PRO; 47 g CARB; 2 g FIBER; 628 mg SODIUM; 85 mg CHOL

KOREAN
PORK CHOPS

SHAWARMA CHICKEN
POT PIE

These homey individual chicken pot pies combine traditional comfort food with a touch of the exotic. Shawarma is the Middle Eastern version of a Greek gyro. The seasoning blend used to flavor the meat usually includes spices such as cumin, cinnamon, cardamom, ginger, cayenne, black pepper and more.

Shawarma Chicken Pot Pie

MAKES 4 servings **PREP** 20 minutes **COOK** 13 minutes **BAKE** at 400° for 25 minutes

- 2 tablespoons canola oil
- 1½ pounds boneless, skinless chicken breast, cut into 1-inch pieces
- 1 medium onion, chopped
- ½ green bell pepper, cored, seeded and chopped
- 4 ounces white mushrooms, stems removed, quartered
- 2 carrots, diced
- 1 rib celery, diced
- ⅓ cup all-purpose flour
- 2 tablespoons shawarma seasoning (see Note)
- ½ teaspoon salt
- ¼ teaspoon black pepper
- 1½ cups reduced-sodium chicken broth
- 1 cup fat-free milk
- 1 cup frozen green peas, thawed
- 2 sheets frozen puff pastry (from a 17.3 ounce package), thawed
- 1 egg, lightly beaten

■ Heat oven to 400°. Coat four 1½-cup ramekins with nonstick cooking spray (see Note).

■ Heat 1 tablespoon of the oil in a large nonstick skillet over medium-high heat. Add chicken and cook 5 minutes, turning once. Remove and place on a plate.

■ Add remaining 1 tablespoon oil, the onion, pepper, mushrooms, carrots and celery. Cook 5 minutes, stirring occasionally. Add flour, shawarma seasoning, salt and pepper. Cook 1 minute. Gradually stir in broth and milk; simmer until thickened, about 2 minutes. Return chicken to skillet and add peas. Stir to combine.

■ Spoon a generous 1½ cups of the mixture into each prepared ramekin.

■ Unroll pastry sheets and cut two 5-inch circles from each (½ inch wider than ramekin). Place a piece of pastry over each ramekin, tuck under and flute. Brush each with egg. Make a vent in center of each with a small knife.

■ Place on a baking sheet and bake at 400° for 25 minutes. Cool slightly.

PER SERVING 487 **CAL**; 19 g **FAT** (4 g **SAT**); 45 g **PRO**; 34 g **CARB**; 6 g **FIBER**; 752 mg **SODIUM**; 148 mg **CHOL**

Note: Look for shawarma seasoning in your supermarket's international foods aisle or in a specialty store.

Note: For one large pie, spoon chicken mixture into an 11 x 8-inch baking dish. Fit pastry over top, vent in a few places and brush with egg. Bake at 400° for 30 to 35 minutes, until browned and bubbly.

SUNDAY ROAST CHICKEN

Baja Fish Tacos with Grilled Avocado

MAKES 4 servings **PREP** 20 minutes
COOK 4 minutes per batch **GRILL** 4 minutes

3	cups cole slaw mix
⅓	cup reduced-fat yogurt
1	scallion, sliced
¾	teaspoon salt
¼	teaspoon black pepper
½	cup all-purpose flour
2	egg whites, lightly beaten
1	cup chipotle-seasoned panko
1	pound tilapia, cut diagonally into 1-inch strips
¼	cup canola oil
1	avocado
16	corn tortillas
	Cilantro, halved grape tomatoes and sliced red onion (optional)
	Lime wedges, chipotle hot sauce and sour cream (optional)

■ In a medium bowl, combine cole slaw mix, yogurt, scallion, ¼ teaspoon of the salt and the black pepper. Cover and refrigerate.

■ Place flour, egg whites and panko in separate shallow dishes. Whisk remaining ½ teaspoon salt into flour. Coat each piece of fish with flour, egg whites and panko.

■ In a large nonstick skillet, heat oil over medium-high heat. Cooking in batches, sauté fish 2 minutes per side, until golden. Place on a wire rack and keep warm.

■ Heat a stovetop grill pan to medium-high. Slice avocado in half; remove skin and pit. Grill 2 minutes per side. Thinly slice, then place on a plate.

■ Gently heat tortillas in microwave.

■ To assemble tacos, double up tortillas and place a few pieces of fish, some slaw and some avocado on each. Garnish with cilantro, tomatoes and onion, if using. Serve with lime wedges, hot sauce and sour cream, if using.

PER SERVING 517 **CAL**; 16 g **FAT** (2 g **SAT**); 33 g **PRO**; 61 g **CARB**; 6 g **FIBER**; 621 mg **SODIUM**; 58 mg **CHOL**

Sunday Roast Chicken

MAKES 6 servings **PREP** 15 minutes **ROAST** at 450° for 30 minutes; 350° for 50 minutes
COOK 4 minutes

1	whole chicken (about 4 pounds), giblets removed
2	teaspoons McCormick Montreal Chicken Seasoning
½	lemon, thinly sliced
3	cloves garlic, sliced
1	pound parsnips, peeled and cut into 1-inch pieces
1	bag (1 pound) peeled baby carrots
1	small head cauliflower, cut into florets
2	tablespoons olive oil
2	tablespoons all-purpose flour
1	can (14½ ounces) reduced-sodium chicken broth

■ Heat oven to 450°.

■ Gently lift skin from breasts and legs and season chicken with 1 teaspoon of the Montreal seasoning. Place lemon and garlic slices under skin.

■ Place chicken on a rack in a large roasting pan. Roast at 450° for 30 minutes. Reduce temperature to 350°. Roast for 50 minutes or until internal temperature registers 165°.

■ Meanwhile, place vegetables on a large rimmed baking sheet and toss with olive oil and remaining 1 teaspoon Montreal seasoning. Place in the 350° oven and roast for about 45 minutes or until tender. Stir after 25 minutes.

■ Pour out all but 3 tablespoons of the pan drippings from roasting pan and whisk in flour. Cook over medium-high heat for 1 minute; whisk in chicken broth and ½ cup water. Simmer 3 minutes, until thickened, scraping browned bits from bottom of pan. Strain.

■ Serve chicken with gravy and vegetables.

PER SERVING 271 cal; 8 g **FAT** (2 g **SAT**); 26 g **PRO**; 23 g **CARB**; 5 g **FIBER**; 514 mg **SODIUM**; 77 mg **CHOL**

BAJA FISH TACOS
WITH GRILLED
AVOCADO

Want to try Meatless Monday—or more? These recipes will please even the pickiest eater.

EGGPLANT
PARMESAN,
PAGE 35

MADRAS CURRY,
PAGE 36

PUMPKIN FARROTTO

EGGPLANT PARMESAN

Pumpkin Farrotto

MAKES 6 servings **PREP** 15 minutes
COOK 6 minutes
SLOW COOK on HIGH for 4 hours

- 4   tablespoons unsalted butter
- 1   medium onion, diced
- 2   cloves garlic, minced
- ¼   cup white wine (optional)
- 1½ cups whole farro (not pearled)
- 4   cups unsalted vegetable stock
- 1   can (15 ounces) pumpkin puree
- 6   tablespoons grated Parmesan
- 1   tablespoon fresh sage, chopped
- 1   box (10 ounces) frozen peas, thawed
- 1   teaspoon salt
- ¼   teaspoon black pepper
- ½   cup toasted walnuts, chopped

■ Melt 3 tablespoons of the butter in a large skillet over medium heat. Add onion and cook, stirring, 3 minutes. Stir in garlic; cook 2 minutes. Add wine and farro; cook 1 minute or until most of the wine evaporates. Transfer to slow cooker.

■ Stir in vegetable stock, pumpkin, 4 tablespoons of the Parmesan and the sage. Cover and cook on HIGH for 4 hours. Uncover and gently stir in peas, remaining 1 tablespoon butter, the salt and pepper. Spoon into bowls and top with walnuts and remaining 2 tablespoons Parmesan.

PER SERVING 436 **CAL**; 17 g **FAT** (6 g **SAT**); 16 g **PRO**; 55 g **CARB**; 14 g **FIBER**; 663 mg **SODIUM**; 24 mg **CHOL**

Eggplant Parmesan

MAKES 8 servings **PREP** 30 minutes **SLOW COOK** on LOW for 6 hours **COOK** 10 minutes

- 3   large eggs
- ⅓   cup prepared pesto
- ¼   cup milk
- 1½ cups plain bread crumbs
- ¼   cup plus 2 tablespoons grated Parmesan
- 4   cups spicy pasta sauce
- 2   medium eggplants (about 2½ pounds total), peeled and cut into ½-inch rounds
- 1   package (8 ounces) Italian cheese blend
- 1   pound spaghetti
- 2   tablespoons olive oil
     Fresh basil (optional)

■ In a medium bowl, whisk eggs, pesto and milk. In a second bowl, toss bread crumbs and ¼ cup of Parmesan.

■ Set aside ½ cup of the sauce. Coat slow cooker bowl with nonstick cooking spray. Spoon ½ cup of the sauce on bottom of slow cooker.

■ Dip each eggplant slice in egg mixture, then bread crumb mixture, and place on a cutting board. Layer one-third of the eggplant slices into slow cooker (about 8 pieces). Top with 1 cup sauce and ⅔ cup Italian cheese blend. Repeat twice. Cover and cook on LOW for 5½ to 6 hours.

■ During last 30 minutes of cooking time, bring a large pot of lightly salted water to a boil. Add spaghetti and cook 10 minutes. Drain and toss with remaining 2 tablespoons Parmesan and the olive oil. Heat reserved sauce gently in microwave or saucepan. Serve alongside eggplant and spaghetti. Garnish with basil, if using.

PER SERVING 606 **CAL**; 25 g **FAT** (8 g **SAT**); 25 g **PRO**; 73 g **CARB**; 10 g **FIBER**; 982 mg **SODIUM**; 108 mg **CHOL**

MADRAS CURRY

Hearty Veggie Chowder

MAKES 6 servings **PREP** 25 minutes
SLOW COOK on HIGH for 6 hours or LOW
for 8 hours

- 2 large leeks (white and light green parts only), cleaned and thinly sliced
- 1 pound diced butternut squash
- ½ pound parsnips, peeled and diced
- ½ pound carrots, sliced
- ⅔ cup barley
- 2 cloves garlic, sliced
- 1 box (32 ounces) vegetable broth
- 1 can (14.5 ounces) petite-cut diced tomatoes
- 1 teaspoon fresh thyme, chopped
- 1 box (10 ounces) frozen corn, thawed
- ½ cup heavy cream
- ¼ cup chopped parsley
- ¾ teaspoon salt
- ¼ teaspoon black pepper
- ⅛ teaspoon cayenne pepper

■ Combine leeks, squash, parsnips, carrots, barley and garlic in slow cooker. Stir in broth, 4 cups water, tomatoes and thyme. Cover and cook on HIGH for 6 hours or LOW for 8 hours.

■ Stir in corn, heavy cream, parsley, salt, black pepper and cayenne. Let sit until corn is heated through.

PER SERVING 309 **CAL**; 8 g **FAT** (5 g **SAT**); 7 g **PRO**; 56 g **CARB**; 10 g **FIBER**; 1,132 mg **SODIUM**; 27 mg **CHOL**

Madras Curry

MAKES 6 servings **PREP** 20 minutes **SLOW COOK** on HIGH for 5½ hours or LOW for 7½ hours

- 1 small head cauliflower (1¾ pounds), trimmed and cut into florets
- 1 pound potatoes, peeled and diced
- 1 bunch red Swiss chard (about ¾ pound), stems trimmed slightly and chopped, or 1 bunch fresh spinach, trimmed
- 1 medium onion, diced
- 1 can (15.5 ounces) chickpeas, drained and rinsed
- 2 tablespoons olive oil
- ½ teaspoon salt
- ¼ teaspoon black pepper
- ⅓ cup mild curry paste
- ½ cup warm water
- 3 tablespoons packed light brown sugar
- 1 can (14.5 ounces) diced tomatoes
- ¾ cup golden raisins
- Cooked basmati rice

Toasted cashews, chopped (optional)

Plain yogurt (optional)

■ Coat slow cooker with nonstick cooking spray. Combine cauliflower, potatoes, stems from Swiss chard, onion and chickpeas. Stir in oil, salt and pepper.

■ In a medium bowl, whisk curry paste, warm water and brown sugar. Add to slow cooker along with tomatoes and raisins. Stir to blend. Cover and cook on HIGH for 5 hours or LOW for 7 hours.

■ Chop Swiss chard leaves or spinach. Add to slow cooker. Re-cover; cook 30 minutes more. Gently stir. Serve curry over basmati rice. Garnish with cashews and a dollop of yogurt, if using.

PER SERVING 542 **CAL**; 13 g **FAT** (1 g **SAT**); 14 g **PRO**; 97 g **CARB**; 12 g **FIBER**; 1,044 mg **SODIUM**; 0 mg **CHOL**

HEARTY VEGGIE
CHOWDER

POTATO-BROCCOLI SOUP

Potato-Broccoli Soup

MAKES 8 servings **PREP** 20 minutes
SLOW COOK on HIGH for 3 hours or LOW
for 7 hours **MICROWAVE** 4 minutes

- 3½ **pounds russet potatoes, peeled and cut into 1½-inch pieces**
- 1 **large onion, cut into wedges**
- 2 **cloves garlic, coarsely chopped**
- 2 **cans (14.5 ounces each) vegetable broth**
- 1 **can (12 ounces) evaporated milk**
- 1 **teaspoon salt**
- ⅛ **teaspoon ground nutmeg**
- 1 **pound broccoli florets, cut into bite-size pieces**
- 8 **ounces sharp cheddar, shredded (white or orange)**
- ½ **cup sour cream**
- ¼ **teaspoon ground black pepper**
  Snipped fresh chives

■ Combine potatoes, onion and garlic in slow cooker. Add 1 can of the broth, the evaporated milk, ½ teaspoon of the salt and the nutmeg. Cover and cook on HIGH for 3 hours or LOW for 7 hours.

■ Place broccoli in a microwave-safe bowl and add ½ cup water. Cover with plastic and microwave 3 to 4 minutes, until tender. Set aside 1½ cups of the broccoli; add remaining broccoli to slow cooker along with remaining can of vegetable broth and 1 cup of the cheddar. Puree with an immersion blender until completely smooth.

■ Stir in remaining ½ teaspoon salt and 1 cup cheddar, reserved broccoli, the sour cream and pepper. Ladle into bowls and sprinkle with chives just before serving.

PER SERVING 385 CAL; 15 g **FAT** (10 g **SAT**); 16 g **PRO**; 47 g **CARB**; 4 g **FIBER**; 988 mg **SODIUM**; 54 mg **CHOL**

WHITE BEAN AND FENNEL SOUP

White Bean and Fennel Soup

MAKES 6 servings **PREP** 25 minutes **SOAK** overnight **SLOW COOK** on HIGH for 6 hours
COOK 9 minutes

- 1 **bag (16 ounces) dry cannellini beans**
- 1 **fennel bulb (about 1½ pounds), trimmed, quartered, cored and sliced**
- 1 **medium onion, chopped**
- 2 **cloves garlic, sliced**
- 1 **teaspoon Italian seasoning**
- 6 **cups vegetable stock**
- 1 **head escarole, cored, rinsed and chopped**
- 1 **can (14.5 ounces) diced tomatoes, drained**
- 1 **cup mini pasta, such as farfellini**
- 1 **teaspoon salt**
  Grated Parmesan and freshly ground black pepper

■ Place cannellini beans in a bowl with 4 cups cold water. Cover with plastic and soak overnight.

■ Drain beans and transfer to a 6-quart slow cooker. Add fennel, onion, garlic and Italian seasoning. Pour in stock and 2 cups water. Cover and cook on HIGH for 5½ hours.

■ Uncover and stir in escarole and diced tomatoes. Re-cover and cook 30 minutes more.

■ Meanwhile, bring a medium saucepan of lightly salted water to a boil. Add pasta and cook 9 minutes or as per package directions. Drain. Stir pasta into soup along with salt. Ladle into bowls and top with Parmesan and black pepper.

PER SERVING 429 CAL; 3 g **FAT** (1 g **SAT**); 28 g **PRO**; 76 g **CARB**; 18 g **FIBER**; 994 mg **SODIUM**; 6 mg **CHOL**

GAME DAY
DOUBLE- BEEF
CHILI, PAGE 72

FEBRUARY

45

49

55

SIMPLY IRRESISTIBLE

Show your affection with these deliciously decadent chocolate desserts.

MINI CHOCOLATE
"DUFFINS", PAGE 45

MINI CHOCOLATE
CHEESECAKES, PAGE 50

OREO BROWNIES

Oreo Brownies

MAKES 9 brownies **PREP** 10 minutes
COOK 5 minutes **BAKE** at 325° for 30 minutes

- ¾ **cup (1½ sticks) unsalted butter**
- 6 **ounces unsweetened chocolate, coarsely chopped**
- 1½ **cups sifted all-purpose flour**
- ¾ **teaspoon baking powder**
- ½ **teaspoon salt**
- 4 **large eggs**
- 2 **cups sugar**
- 1 **teaspoon vanilla extract**
- 1 **cup coarsely chopped Oreo cookies**

■ Heat oven to 325°. Line a 9 x 9-inch baking pan with foil. Coat foil with nonstick cooking spray.

■ In a small heavy saucepan, heat butter and chocolate over low heat, stirring constantly, until chocolate is melted and smooth, about 5 minutes. Set aside to cool. In a small bowl, stir flour, baking powder and salt. Set aside.

■ In a large mixing bowl, beat eggs and sugar with an electric mixer on high speed 5 minutes or until lemon-colored and fluffy, occasionally scraping sides of bowl. Add cooled chocolate mixture and vanilla. Beat on low speed until combined. Add flour mixture. Beat on low speed until combined, scraping sides of bowl. Stir in ½ cup of the Oreo pieces. Spread batter into prepared pan and scatter remaining cookie pieces on top.

■ Bake at 325° for 30 minutes or until brownie appears set. Cool in pan on a wire rack. Once cool, use foil to lift brownie from pan. Cut into 9 squares.

PER BROWNIE 313 **CAL**; 17 g **FAT** (9 g **SAT**); 4 g **PRO**; 41 g **CARB**; 2 g **FIBER**; 143 mg **SODIUM**; 75 mg **CHOL**

MINI CHOCOLATE "DUFFINS"

Mini Chocolate "Duffins"

MAKES 44 duffins **PREP** 20 minutes **BAKE** at 350° for 14 minutes per batch **COOL** 10 minutes
MICROWAVE 30 seconds

DUFFINS

- 2 **cups cake flour (not self-rising)**
- ⅓ **cup cocoa powder**
- 1 **teaspoon baking powder**
- ¼ **teaspoon baking soda**
- ¼ **teaspoon salt**
- 6 **tablespoons unsalted butter, softened**
- ⅔ **cup packed dark brown sugar**
- 1 **large egg**
- ¾ **cup buttermilk**
- 1 **teaspoon vanilla extract**

TOPPING

- 3 **tablespoons unsalted butter**
- ¼ **cup granulated sugar**
- 2 **tablespoons cocoa powder**

■ **Duffins.** Heat oven to 350°. Coat the cups of 2 mini muffin pans with nonstick cooking spray (22 per batch).

■ In a medium bowl, whisk cake flour, cocoa powder, baking powder, baking soda and salt. In a large bowl, beat softened butter and brown sugar until smooth. Add egg and beat until creamy, 2 minutes. On low speed, beat in half the flour mixture, then the buttermilk, followed by remaining flour mixture. Stir in vanilla. Divide batter into prepared pans, about 1 tablespoon batter per cup.

■ Bake at 350° for 12 to 14 minutes. Cool 10 minutes in pans on wire racks, then remove directly to racks to cool. Repeat with a second batch of 22.

■ **Topping.** While duffins cool, melt butter in microwave, 30 seconds. Combine granulated sugar and cocoa in a small bowl. Dip duffin tops in melted butter, followed by cocoa sugar. Serve slightly warm.

PER DUFFIN 64 **CAL**; 3 g **FAT** (2 g **SAT**); 1 g **PRO**; 9 g **CARB**; 0 g **FIBER**; 37 mg **SODIUM**; 11 mg **CHOL**

The combination of chocolate and raspberry is a classic—and so is this lovely English dessert that features alternating layers of cake, chocolate mousse, fruit and whipped cream.

Chocolate Raspberry Trifle

MAKES 24 servings **PREP** 15 minutes **BAKE** at 350° for 35 minutes **COOK** 7 minutes **REFRIGERATE** at least 1 hour, then up to overnight

- 1 **box (16.25 ounces) chocolate cake mix**
- 2 **large eggs**
- ½ **cup vegetable oil**
- 4 **large egg yolks**
- ½ **cup plus 5 tablespoons sugar**
- ¼ **cup (½ stick) unsalted butter, cut up**
- 4 **ounces bittersweet chocolate, chopped**
- 2½ **cups heavy cream**
- 1 **teaspoon vanilla extract**
- 2 **packages (6 ounces each) fresh raspberries**

  Chocolate curls or cocoa powder, for garnish

■ Heat oven to 350°. Coat a 13 x 9 x 2-inch baking pan with nonstick cooking spray. Line bottom with wax paper; coat paper with spray. Prepare cake mix as per package directions with eggs, oil and 1¼ cups water. Bake at 350° for 35 minutes or until cake springs back when pressed. Cool 10 minutes in pan on a wire rack; invert directly onto rack, remove paper and cool completely.

■ While cake cools, in a large metal bowl, combine egg yolks, ½ cup sugar, ¼ cup water and butter. Place bowl over a pot of simmering water. Cook, whisking constantly, until mixture is pale and thickened and registers 160° on an instant-read thermometer, about 7 minutes. Remove bowl from saucepan and whisk in chocolate until smooth. In a separate bowl, beat 1 cup of the cream with 2 tablespoons of the sugar and the vanilla until medium-firm peaks form. Fold whipped cream into chocolate mixture until no white remains. Cover surface directly with plastic and refrigerate at least 1 hour.

■ Once cake has cooled, cut into 1½-inch cubes. Whip remaining 1½ cups cream with remaining 3 tablespoons sugar to medium-firm peaks. Begin layering trifle: Spoon half the cake cubes into a 4-quart glass bowl or dish. Compress slightly. Spread half the chocolate mousse (about 1½ cups) over cake cubes. Top mousse with 1 package of the raspberries and half the whipped cream (about 1½ cups). Repeat layering and garnish with chocolate curls or cocoa powder. Serve immediately or refrigerate up to overnight until serving.

PER SERVING 292 **CAL**; 21 g **FAT** (9 g **SAT**); 3 g **PRO**; 27 g **CARB**; 2 g **FIBER**; 146 mg **SODIUM**; 91 mg **CHOL**

CHOCOLATE
RASPBERRY TRIFLE

WHITE CHOCOLATE PIE

The sweet hearts on the top of this pretty pie are easy to make. Raspberry sauce is piped in dots all over the top of the pie, then a thin knife or toothpick is dragged through the drops in one direction to create the heart shapes.

White Chocolate Pie

MAKES 12 servings **PREP** 25 minutes **COOK** 3 minutes **COOL** 30 minutes **REFRIGERATE** at least 4 hours or up to overnight

18   Oreo cookies

3   tablespoons unsalted butter, melted

5   tablespoons sugar

3   tablespoons cornstarch

1   bag (12 ounces) frozen raspberries, thawed

1½   teaspoons gelatin

⅛   teaspoon salt

2   cups whole milk

6   ounces white chocolate, finely chopped

1   cup whipped coconut topping (such as SoDelicious) or frozen whipped topping, thawed if frozen

■ Place cookies in food processor and pulse until finely chopped. Add melted butter and pulse until evenly blended. Press into bottom and up sides of a 9-inch pie plate. Refrigerate while making filling.

■ Combine 2 tablespoons of the sugar and 1 tablespoon of the cornstarch in a small saucepan. Stir in thawed raspberries and 2 tablespoons water. Bring to a boil over medium heat. Cook 3 minutes, until dark red and thickened. Strain out seeds and cool completely.

■ Whisk remaining 3 tablespoons sugar and 2 tablespoons cornstarch, the gelatin and salt in a saucepan. Gradually whisk in milk until smooth. Cook over medium heat, stirring constantly with a wooden spoon or silicone spatula, until pudding thickens and begins to bubble around edges, about 5 minutes. Continue to cook, stirring, for 2 minutes. Remove from heat and stir in white chocolate. Let cool 30 minutes at room temperature, then stir in whipped topping. Pour into prepared crust, smoothing top.

■ Transfer raspberry sauce to a small piping bag. Snip off tip. Pipe dots of raspberry sauce (in a continuous spiral) all over top of pie. Starting in the center, run a thin knife or toothpick through the drops in one direction, to create hearts (alternately, you can do this after pie is chilled). Refrigerate pie for at least 4 hours or overnight, until firm. Cut into wedges and serve.

PER SERVING 264 **CAL**; 14 g **FAT** (7 g **SAT**); 3 g **PRO**; 32 g **CARB**; 2 g **FIBER**; 147 mg **SODIUM**; 15 mg **CHOL**

There's no need for a fancy mold to make these mini cheesecakes. They're baked in a jumbo muffin tin with paper liners so they slip easily out of the pan.

Mini Chocolate Cheesecakes

MAKES 6 mini cakes **PREP** 25 minutes **BAKE** at 350° for 30 minutes **MICROWAVE** 2½ minutes **COOL** 30 minutes **REFRIGERATE** 1 hour + 10 minutes

CRUST

18	Nabisco Famous chocolate wafers, finely crushed
2	tablespoons unsalted butter, melted

CHEESECAKES

4	ounces semisweet chocolate, chopped
1	large egg, separated
1	large egg white
⅓	cup plus 2 teaspoons sugar
1½	packages cream cheese, softened
⅓	cup sour cream
1	tablespoon cornstarch
½	teaspoon vanilla extract

TOPPING

1	cup strawberries, chopped
½	teaspoon sugar
½	cup heavy cream
4	ounces semisweet chocolate, chopped

■ **Crust.** Combine crushed wafers and butter in a bowl. Set aside.

■ **Cheesecakes.** Heat oven to 350°. Line 6 indents of a jumbo muffin tin with jumbo muffin liners.

■ Microwave chocolate 1 minute. Stir until smooth, microwaving more if there are lumps. Set aside to cool slightly. Beat egg whites with 2 teaspoons sugar until stiff peaks form. Set aside.

■ Beat cream cheese until smooth. Add remaining ⅓ cup sugar, the sour cream and cornstarch; beat until sugar is almost dissolved, 2 minutes. Beat in melted chocolate, egg yolk and vanilla until smooth and no white streaks remain, scraping sides of bowl. Fold in beaten egg whites. Divide evenly among indents in prepared muffin tin, ⅓ to ½ cup batter in each.

■ Top each cheesecake with 3 tablespoons of the crumb mixture, patting slightly to adhere. Bake at 350° for 20 to 30 minutes, until puffed and set in the center. Remove from oven and cool 30 minutes in pan on a wire rack. Refrigerate at least 1 hour.

■ Once cheesecakes are cool, remove from pan, invert them and remove liners (some crumbs will fall off). Place on a wire rack set over wax paper.

■ **Topping.** Stir strawberries and sugar. Let stand to blend flavors. Microwave heavy cream 30 seconds. Pour over chopped chocolate and whisk until chocolate is melted and mixture is smooth and shiny. Refrigerate 10 minutes. Spoon over cheesecakes and spread with a small spatula. Top each cake with 1 heaping tablespoon of the strawberry mixture and serve.

PER ½ MINI CAKE 339 **CAL**; 24 g **FAT** (14 g **SAT**); 4 g **PRO**; 27 g **CARB**; 2 g **FIBER**; 170 mg **SODIUM**; 73 mg **CHOL**

MINI CHOCOLATE
CHEESECAKES

NOT YOUR EVERYDAY MAC

Fun takes on an iconic American dish that include organic, gluten-free—even fried.

BBQ MAC AND CHEESE,
PAGE 56

FRIED MAC AND
CHEESE BITES,
PAGE 59

SLOW COOKER
MAC AND CHEESE
WITH BACON

GLUTEN-FREE
MAC AND CHEESE

Slow Cooker Mac and Cheese with Bacon

MAKES 6 servings **PREP** 15 minutes
SLOW COOK on LOW for 3 hours

- 12 ounces (about 4 cups) uncooked radiatore pasta (or your favorite shape)
- 8 slices bacon, cooked
- 2 cups milk
- 1 can (12 ounces) evaporated milk
- 2 teaspoons Dijon mustard
- 1 teaspoon onion powder
- ¼ teaspoon salt
- ¼ teaspoon black pepper
- 6 ounces thinly sliced deli American cheese, cut into thin strips
- 1 cup (4 ounces) grated Gouda cheese

■ Coat a 4- to 5-quart slow cooker bowl with nonstick cooking spray.

■ Bring a pot of lightly salted water to a boil and cook pasta 2 minutes less than package directions. Drain. Crumble 6 slices of the bacon and add to slow cooker with milk, evaporated milk, mustard, onion powder, salt and pepper. Whisk until blended, then stir in pasta. Cover and cook on LOW for 2½ hours.

■ Stir in cheeses and cook an additional 30 minutes. Crumble remaining 2 slices bacon and sprinkle on top.

PER SERVING 516 **CAL**; 22 g **FAT** (14 g **SAT**); 26 g **PRO**; 52 g **CARB**; 3 g **FIBER**; 813 mg **SODIUM**; 66 mg **CHOL**

Gluten-Free Mac and Cheese

MAKES 8 servings **PREP** 15 minutes **COOK** 14 minutes **BAKE** at 350° for 20 minutes

- 1 package (16 ounces) gluten-free elbow macaroni (see tip, right)
- 3 tablespoons unsalted butter
- 2 cups milk
- 1 package (8 ounces) Neufchâtel cheese, cut into pieces
- 1 package (8 ounces) sharp cheddar, shredded
- 2 teaspoons cornstarch
- ½ teaspoon salt
- ¼ teaspoon black pepper
- 1 cup frozen peas, thawed
- ⅔ cup crushed gluten-free crackers

■ Heat oven to 350°. Bring a large pot of lightly salted water to a boil. Cook pasta 2 minutes less than package directions (about 13 minutes). Drain.

■ Meanwhile, combine 2 tablespoons of the butter and the milk in a medium saucepan over medium heat. Bring just to a simmer and stir in Neufchâtel. Toss cheddar with cornstarch and stir into saucepan along with salt and pepper until melted and smooth. Simmer 2 minutes, stirring frequently. Remove from heat and stir in peas and pasta.

■ Melt remaining 1 tablespoon butter in a small skillet over medium-high heat. Add cracker crumbs and stir to mix. Brown 1 minute.

■ Coat 8 individual baking dishes with nonstick cooking spray. Divide macaroni mixture among prepared dishes. Top each with about 1 tablespoon cracker crumbs. Bake at 350° for 20 minutes.

PER SERVING 499 **CAL**; 24 g **FAT** (13 g **SAT**); 18 g **PRO**; 56 g **CARB**; 2 g **FIBER**; 527 mg **SODIUM**; 68 mg **CHOL**

Gluten-Free Pasta Picks

When wheat-free pasta first appeared on health food store shelves, the cooked texture was like wet cardboard. Not anymore. Many brands now available in mainstream supermarkets stand up well to their traditional counterparts. Three of our favorites: Tinkyada, a blend of brown rice and rice bran, comes in 18 shapes, with elbows and spaghetti most readily available. Ronzoni, made from a combination of white and brown rice, corn and quinoa, is available in rotini, penne and spaghetti. For the best texture, cook until al dente and rinse afterward. Barilla, made from a mixture of corn flour and rice flour, is available in elbows, penne, rotini and spaghetti.

BBQ MAC AND CHEESE

Organic White Mac and Cheese

MAKES 6 servings **PREP** 15 minutes
COOK 7 minutes **BAKE** at 350° for 20 minutes

- 1 **pound organic pipe rigate pasta (or rigatoni)**
- 3 **tablespoons organic unsalted butter**
- 3 **tablespoons organic whole wheat flour**
- 2½ **cups organic milk**
- ¾ **teaspoon sea salt**
- ¼ **teaspoon black pepper**
- 1 **package (6 ounces) shredded organic mild white cheddar**
- 1 **package (6 ounces) shredded organic mozzarella**
- 1 **package (4 ounces) organic goat cheese**
- 3 **tablespoons grated organic Parmesan**

■ Heat oven to 350°. Coat 6 individual oven-proof dishes with nonstick cooking spray. Bring a large pot of salted water to a boil. Add pasta and cook 1 minute less than package directions (7 minutes for pipe rigate). Drain.

■ Meanwhile, heat butter in a medium saucepan over medium heat. Whisk in flour until smooth and beginning to bubble (about 1 minute). While whisking, add milk in a thin stream. Stir in salt and pepper and bring to a simmer. Cook, simmering and stirring, for 2 minutes.

■ Toss ½ cup each of the cheddar and mozzarella in a bowl. Add remaining cheddar and mozzarella to sauce. Stir in goat cheese. Combine cheese sauce with pasta and stir to coat. Divide mac and cheese among dishes. Top each with about 2 tablespoons of the cheddar-mozzarella mixture, followed by ½ tablespoon of the Parmesan. Bake at 350° for 20 minutes, until browned on top.

PER SERVING 673 **CAL**; 31 g **FAT** (18 g **SAT**); 32 g **PRO**; 66 g **CARB**; 4 g **FIBER**; 812 mg **SODIUM**; 89 mg **CHOL**

BBQ Mac and Cheese

MAKES 6 servings **PREP** 15 minutes **COOK** 6 minutes **MICROWAVE** 6 minutes
BAKE at 350° for 20 minutes

- 1 **pound cavatappi pasta**
- 2 **tablespoons unsalted butter**
- 2 **tablespoons all-purpose flour**
- 1¾ **cups 2% milk**
- ½ **teaspoon smoked paprika**
- ¼ **teaspoon salt**
- ¼ **teaspoon black pepper**
- 3 **cups shredded cheddar**
- 1 **package (16 ounces) pulled chicken or pork**

■ Bring a large pot of lightly salted water to a boil. Add cavatappi and return to a boil. Cook 6 minutes; drain.

■ Meanwhile, melt butter in a medium saucepan. Whisk in flour. While whisking, add milk in a thin stream. Whisk in paprika, salt and pepper. Bring to a simmer; cook 2 minutes.

■ Remove from heat and whisk in 2 cups of the cheddar. Fold cheese sauce into pasta.

■ Place half the macaroni and cheese in a baking dish. Microwave pulled chicken per package directions, about 6 minutes. Spoon over pasta in dish and top with remaining mac and cheese and 1 cup cheddar. Bake at 350° for 20 minutes, until melted and bubbly.

PER SERVING 678 **CAL**; 27 g **FAT** (16 g **SAT**); 32 g **PRO**; 77 g **CARB**; 4 g **FIBER**; 740 mg **SODIUM**; 85 mg **CHOL**

ORGANIC WHITE
MAC AND CHEESE

FRIED MAC AND
CHEESE BITES

Crispy on the outside and creamy on the inside, these tasty treats are a popular appetizer menu item at restaurants and a tempting snack at outdoor fairs.

Fried Mac and Cheese Bites

MAKES 30 bites **PREP** 30 minutes **COOK** 7 minutes **REFRIGERATE** overnight **FRY** 4 minutes per batch

- 12 ounces (about 4 cups) elbow macaroni
- 2 tablespoons unsalted butter
- 2 tablespoons all-purpose flour
- 1½ cups milk
- ½ teaspoon salt
- ¼ teaspoon black pepper
  Pinch cayenne pepper
- 2 cups shredded cheddar
- 4 ounces thinly sliced deli American cheese, cut into thin strips
- 1 cup shredded mozzarella
- 2 large eggs
- 1 box (8 ounces) Italian seasoned panko bread crumbs
- 6 cups peanut or vegetable oil, for frying

■ Bring a large pot of lightly salted water to a boil. Add macaroni and cook 7 minutes or per package directions; drain.

■ Meanwhile, melt butter in a saucepan over medium heat. Whisk in flour, cooking until bubbly. While whisking, add 1¼ cups of the milk in a thin stream. Season with salt, black pepper and cayenne. Bring to a simmer and cook 2 minutes. Remove from heat and mix in 1 cup of the cheddar and the American cheese. Fold into macaroni in a large bowl. Let cool slightly, then stir in mozzarella and remaining 1 cup cheddar. Spread mac and cheese onto a rimmed sheet. Cover with plastic and refrigerate overnight.

■ Use a scoop to spoon out about ¼ cup of the mixture at a time and shape into 2- to 3-inch balls, compressing slightly.

■ Whisk eggs with remaining ¼ cup milk. Dip balls in egg mixture, then coat in panko.

■ Heat oil in a deep 4-quart pot to 360° on a deep-fry thermometer. Fry 6 or 7 mac and cheese bites at a time for 3 to 4 minutes per batch, until golden. Serve immediately.

PER BITE 200 **CAL**; 14 g **FAT** (5 g **SAT**); 6 g **PRO**; 13 g **CARB**; 0 g **FIBER**; 255 mg **SODIUM**; 31 mg **CHOL**

HEALTHY FAMILY DINNERS

Hold the gluten—here are five hearty wheat-free meals!

CHICKEN AND WAFFLES,
PAGE 64

BUTTERNUT SQUASH–
SWISS CHARD FRITTATA, PAGE 67

TURKEY-QUINOA
MEATBALLS WITH
MUSHROOM GRAVY

The recent interest in gluten-free eating—and not just for those who have medical issues—has greatly increased access to gluten-free products. Good quality gluten-free flours are now readily available in the baking aisle of most supermarkets.

Turkey-Quinoa Meatballs with Mushroom Gravy

MAKES 4 servings **PREP** 35 minutes **COOK** 25 minutes **LET STAND** 5 minutes **BAKE** at 400° for 15 minutes

- 1 **cup uncooked red quinoa, rinsed**
- 1½ **pounds baking potatoes, peeled and cut into 2-inch pieces**
- ½ **cup 1% milk**
- ½ **cup light sour cream**
- 2 **tablespoons unsalted butter**
- ¾ **teaspoon salt**
- ½ **teaspoon black pepper**
- 1 **package (10 ounces) cremini mushrooms**
- ½ **pound ground turkey**
- 1 **egg, beaten**
- ¼ **cup shredded Parmesan**
- ⅓ **cup parsley, chopped**
- 2 **tablespoons gluten-free flour**
- 1½ **cups unsalted beef stock**

■ In a small pot, add quinoa to 1 cup boiling water. Cover, reduce heat and cook 15 minutes. Let stand, covered, 5 minutes.

■ Heat oven to 400°. In a sided skillet, cover potatoes with 1 inch cold water. Bring to a boil. Reduce to a simmer, cover and cook 10 minutes, until fork-tender. Drain potatoes and return to pot. Mash and stir in milk, sour cream, 1 tablespoon of the butter, ¼ teaspoon of the salt and ⅛ teaspoon of the pepper. Cover and set aside.

■ Finely chop 1 cup of the mushrooms. Combine with cooked quinoa, turkey, egg, Parmesan, parsley, ¼ teaspoon plus ⅛ teaspoon of the salt and ¼ teaspoon of the pepper. Form into twenty 2-inch meatballs and place on a rimmed sheet coated with nonstick cooking spray. Bake at 400° for 15 minutes, until cooked through.

■ Meanwhile, slice remaining mushrooms. Add to remaining 1 tablespoon butter in a saucepan over medium heat; cook 8 minutes, stirring several times. Stir in flour; cook 1 minute. Whisk in stock and bring to a boil. Reduce to a simmer; cook 3 minutes, until thickened. Season with remaining ⅛ teaspoon salt and ⅛ teaspoon pepper.

■ Serve meatballs and gravy over mashed potatoes.

PER SERVING 545 **CAL**; 18 g **FAT** (8 g **SAT**); 28 g **PRO**; 71 g **CARB**; 6 g **FIBER**; 833 mg **SODIUM**; 129 mg **CHOL**

CHICKEN AND WAFFLES

Chicken and Waffles

MAKES 4 servings PREP 15 minutes COOK 6 minutes BAKE at 400° for 10 minutes

- ¼ **cup honey**
- ⅛ **teaspoon red pepper flakes**
- ⅓ **cup gluten-free flour**
- 1 **teaspoon salt**
- ⅛ **teaspoon black pepper**
- 1 **egg**
- ½ **cup gluten-free cornflake crumbs**
- 1½ **pounds boneless, skinless chicken breasts (4 breasts)**
- 2 **tablespoons unsalted butter**
- 1 **teaspoon vegetable oil**
- 4 **gluten-free waffles (such as Van's), toasted**
- **Broccoli slaw (optional)**

■ Heat oven to 400°. Combine honey and red pepper flakes; set aside.

■ In a small bowl, combine flour, ¾ teaspoon of the salt and the black pepper. In a second bowl, beat egg. In a third bowl, combine cornflake crumbs and remaining ¼ teaspoon salt. Dredge chicken in flour, then egg and finally cornflakes.

■ Heat butter and oil in a large saucepan over medium-high heat. Sear chicken 3 minutes per side, until golden. Transfer chicken to a baking sheet and bake at 400° for 10 minutes, until cooked through.

■ Place chicken on toasted waffles. Drizzle with spicy honey and serve with broccoli slaw, if using.

PER SERVING 456 **CAL**; 14 g **FAT** (5 g **SAT**); 35 g **PRO**; 46 g **CARB**; 1 g **FIBER**; 663 mg **SODIUM**; 97 mg **CHOL**

Sesame Soba and Steak

MAKES 6 servings PREP 10 minutes
COOK 13 minutes LET REST 5 minutes

- 1 **package (12.8 ounces) soba noodles**
- 1 **tablespoon olive oil**
- 1 **pound flank steak**
- ¾ **teaspoon salt**
- ⅛ **teaspoon black pepper**
- 3 **tablespoons tahini paste**
- 3 **tablespoons fresh lemon juice**
- 2 **tablespoons harissa**
- 2 **tablespoons honey**
- 2 **teaspoons sesame oil**
- 1 **pint grape tomatoes, halved**
- ½ **English cucumber, halved and sliced**
- ½ **cup fresh mint, roughly chopped**
- 2 **tablespoons sesame seeds**
- **Crumbled feta (optional)**

■ Bring a large pot of lightly salted water to a boil. Add soba; cook 3 minutes. Drain and rinse in cold water.

■ Add olive oil to a large skillet over medium-high heat. Pat steak dry and season with ¼ teaspoon of the salt and the pepper. Cook 5 minutes per side, until medium-rare (145°). Let rest 5 minutes, then thinly slice against the grain.

■ In a large bowl, whisk ½ cup water, tahini, lemon juice, harissa, honey, sesame oil and remaining ½ teaspoon salt. Toss with cooked soba, sliced steak, tomatoes, cucumber, mint and sesame seeds. Garnish with crumbled feta, if using.

PER SERVING 457 **CAL**; 15 g **FAT** (3 g **SAT**); 27 g **PRO**; 55 g **CARB**; 3 g **FIBER**; 537 mg **SODIUM**; 25 mg **CHOL**

SESAME SOBA
AND STEAK

SHRIMP FRIED RICE

Shrimp Fried Rice

MAKES 4 servings **PREP** 10 minutes
COOK 1 hour, 3 minutes

- 1 **cup brown rice**
- 4 **slices thick-cut bacon, diced**
- 1 **pound peeled and deveined shrimp**
- 2 **cloves garlic, chopped**
- 1 **head bok choy (about 1 pound), chopped**
- 2 **tablespoons unsalted butter**
- 2 **eggs, beaten**
- 4 **scallions, sliced**
- 5 **teaspoons low-sodium tamari (gluten-free soy sauce, such as San-J)**
  Sriracha (optional)

■ In a medium pot, combine rice and 2 cups water. Bring to a boil. Reduce to a simmer, cover and cook 45 minutes. Set aside.

■ Add bacon to a large skillet over medium heat. Sauté 10 minutes, until just crispy. Remove to a plate with a slotted spoon.

■ Increase heat to medium-high. Add shrimp and garlic. Sauté 2 to 3 minutes, until shrimp is just cooked. Remove with slotted spoon to plate with bacon. Stir in bok choy; cook 2 minutes, until wilted and slightly tender. Remove to plate with slotted spoon. Pour off any liquid.

■ Return pan to stove. Over medium heat, add 1 tablespoon of the butter. Pour in eggs; scramble 1 minute. Add remaining 1 tablespoon butter, the cooked rice and scallions. Fry 1 to 2 minutes, stirring a few times. Stir in cooked bacon, shrimp, bok choy and tamari. Serve with sriracha, if using.

PER SERVING 446 **CAL**; 18 g **FAT** (8 g **SAT**); 30 g **PRO**; 40 g **CARB**; 4 g **FIBER**; 819 mg **SODIUM**; 302 mg **CHOL**

BUTTERNUT SQUASH–SWISS CHARD FRITTATA

Butternut Squash–Swiss Chard Frittata

MAKES 4 servings **PREP** 15 minutes **MICROWAVE** 5 minutes **COOK** 11 minutes
BAKE at 400° for 10 minutes **LET REST** 5 minutes

- 12 **ounces butternut squash, peeled and cut into ½-inch cubes**
- 6 **large eggs**
- 4 **egg whites**
- ¾ **teaspoon salt**
- ⅛ **teaspoon black pepper**
- 2 **tablespoons olive oil**
- ¼ **cup diced shallots**
- 2 **cloves garlic, sliced**
- 8 **ounces Swiss chard, chopped**
- 2 **ounces plain goat cheese**

■ Heat oven to 400°. Microwave squash and ¼ cup water in a dish, covered and vented, for 5 minutes. In a large bowl, whisk eggs, egg whites, salt and pepper. Heat oil in a 10-inch cast-iron skillet over medium heat. Sauté shallots and garlic 2 minutes. Add Swiss chard. Increase heat to high; cook 5 minutes, until water is mostly absorbed. Carefully stir in cubed squash; cook 2 minutes. Pour in eggs. Reduce heat to medium. Dot cheese on top. Cook 2 minutes.

■ Place skillet in oven and bake at 400° for 10 minutes, until set. Let rest 5 minutes, then loosen edges with a nonstick spatula. Slice into 4 pieces.

PER SERVING 271 **CAL**; 17 g **FAT** (5 g **SAT**); 18 g **PRO**; 13 g **CARB**; 3 g **FIBER**; 764 mg **SODIUM**; 324 mg **CHOL**

WINTER WARMERS

Cozy up with these flavor-packed slow cooker chili suppers.

GAME DAY
DOUBLE-BEEF
CHILI, PAGE 72

White Bean Chicken Chili

MAKES 6 servings **PREP** 15 minutes **COOK** 10 minutes **SLOW COOK** on HIGH for 3 hours or LOW for 5 hours

- 2 **tablespoons canola oil**
- 2 **pounds boneless, skinless chicken thighs, cut into 1½-inch pieces**
- 1 **large onion, chopped**
- 4 **cloves garlic, chopped**
- 2 **cups chicken broth**
- 2 **Cubanelle peppers, seeded and sliced**
- 1 **jalapeño, seeded and chopped**
- 2 **teaspoons ancho chile powder**
- 1 **teaspoon dried oregano**
- 1 **teaspoon ground cumin**
- ½ **teaspoon salt**

- 2 **cans (15 ounces each) pinto beans, drained and rinsed**
- 1 **can (15¼ ounces) white shoepeg corn, drained**
- 2 **tablespoons lime juice**
- ½ **cup cilantro leaves**
   Cornbread (optional)

■ Coat slow cooker bowl with nonstick cooking spray.

■ Heat oil in a large skillet over medium-high heat. Add chicken, onion and garlic. Cook 10 minutes, stirring occasionally, until lightly browned. Add to slow cooker.

■ Stir in broth, Cubanelle peppers, jalapeño, ancho chile powder, oregano, cumin and salt. Mash 1 can of the beans and stir in with remaining can of beans and the corn.

■ Cover and cook on HIGH for 3 hours or LOW for 5 hours.

■ Stir in lime juice and cilantro. Serve with cornbread, if using.

PER SERVING 440 **CAL**; 15 g **FAT** (3 g **SAT**); 40 g **PRO**; 39 g **CARB**; 11 g **FIBER**; 1,020 mg **SODIUM**; 147 mg **CHOL**

WHITE BEAN CHICKEN CHILI

**FAJITA-STYLE
CHICKEN CHILI**

CARIBBEAN PORK AND MANGO CHILI

Fajita-Style Chicken Chili

MAKES 6 servings PREP 15 minutes
COOK 6 minutes SLOW COOK on HIGH for
3 hours or LOW for 6 hours

- 1 tablespoon canola oil
- 2½ pounds boneless, skinless chicken breasts, thinly sliced diagonally
- 2 large onions, cut into ¼-inch slices
- 2 large sweet red peppers, seeded and cut into ¼-inch-thick slices
- 1 can (15½ ounces) pink beans, drained and rinsed
- 2 cans (14½ ounces each) diced tomatoes
- 2 tablespoons chili powder
- 1 teaspoon ground cumin
- 1 teaspoon dried oregano
- 1 teaspoon salt
  Shredded cheddar, sour cream, guacamole and flour tortillas (optional)

■ Coat slow cooker bowl with nonstick cooking spray.

■ In a large nonstick skillet, heat oil over medium-high heat. Add chicken and cook 6 minutes, until lightly browned. Cook in 2 batches, if necessary.

■ In slow cooker bowl, layer onions, peppers, cooked chicken and beans. Combine tomatoes, chili powder, cumin, oregano and salt. Pour over beans.

■ Cover and cook on HIGH for 3 hours or LOW for 6 hours.

■ Serve with shredded cheddar, sour cream, guacamole and flour tortillas, if using.

PER SERVING 353 CAL; 8 g FAT (2 g SAT); 44 g PRO; 24 g CARB; 8 g FIBER; 920 mg SODIUM; 104 mg CHOL

Caribbean Pork and Mango Chili

MAKES 6 servings PREP 20 minutes COOK 10 minutes SLOW COOK on HIGH for 5½ hours

- 2 tablespoons canola oil
- 2 pounds pork shoulder, cut into 1½-inch pieces
- 2 cups seeded and diced plum tomatoes (about 6)
- 1 can (8 ounces) tomato sauce
- 1 tablespoon chili powder
- 1 teaspoon ground cumin
- ½ teaspoon salt
- 1 teaspoon smoked paprika
- ½ teaspoon cinnamon
- ¼ teaspoon allspice
- 1 can (15 ounces) black beans, drained and rinsed
- 1 mango, peeled and diced
  Lime wedges and additional diced mango, for garnish (optional)
  Coconut Rice (optional)

■ Coat slow cooker bowl with nonstick cooking spray.

■ Heat oil in a large nonstick skillet over medium-high heat. Add pork

and cook 10 minutes, stirring occasionally, until lightly browned. Cook in 2 batches, if necessary. Drain and add to slow cooker.

■ Stir in tomatoes, tomato sauce, chili powder, cumin, salt, paprika, cinnamon and allspice.

■ Cover and cook on HIGH for 5½ hours. Stir in beans and mango during last 15 minutes.

■ Garnish with lime and mango, if using. Serve with Coconut Rice, if using.

PER SERVING 350 CAL; 14 g FAT (3 g SAT); 34 g PRO; 21 g CARB; 6 g FIBER; 629 mg SODIUM; 91 mg CHOL

Coconut Rice

In a medium saucepan, combine 2 cups rice, 1 can (13½ ounces) coconut milk, 1½ cups water, ½ teaspoon sugar and ¼ teaspoon salt. Bring to a boil and cover. Simmer over low heat 15 minutes, until liquid is absorbed. Makes 6 cups.

GAME DAY DOUBLE-BEEF CHILI

Game Day Double-Beef Chili

MAKES 12 servings **PREP** 20 minutes **COOK** 18 minutes
SLOW COOK on HIGH for 5 hours or LOW for 8 hours

- 2 **tablespoons canola oil**
- 2 **pounds ground beef**
- 2 **large onions, chopped**
- 8 **cloves garlic, roughly chopped**
- 2 **pounds beef brisket, cut into 1-inch pieces**
- 2 **large green bell peppers, seeded and diced**
- 1 **can (28 ounces) fire-roasted diced tomatoes**
- 2 **cans (8 ounces each) tomato sauce**
- ¼ **cup chili powder**
- 1 **tablespoon sweet paprika**
- 2 **teaspoons ground cumin**
- 1½ **teaspoons salt**
- ¼ **teaspoon cayenne pepper**
- 6 **cups cooked Texmati rice**
- 1½ **cups shredded Cotija cheese**
  Chopped scallion and red onion for garnish (optional)

■ Coat slow cooker bowl with nonstick cooking spray.

■ Heat 1 tablespoon of the oil in a large nonstick skillet over medium-high heat. Add ground beef, onions and garlic; cook 8 minutes, stirring occasionally. Place in slow cooker. Add remaining 1 tablespoon oil and the brisket to skillet; cook 4 to 5 minutes per side, until browned. Place in slow cooker.

■ Stir in green peppers, tomatoes, tomato sauce, chili powder, paprika, cumin, salt and cayenne.

■ Cover and cook on HIGH for 5 hours or LOW for 8 hours.

■ Serve with rice and Cotija. Garnish with scallion and red onion, if using.

PER SERVING 451 CAL; 14 g FAT (6 g SAT); 41 g PRO; 38 g CARB; 4 g FIBER; 865 mg SODIUM; 92 mg CHOL

Spicy Vegetable and Barley Chili

MAKES 6 servings **PREP** 20 minutes
SLOW COOK on HIGH for 4 hours or LOW for 6 hours

- 4 **cups low-sodium spicy vegetable juice**
- 2 **tablespoons chili powder**
- 1¼ **teaspoons salt**
- 1 **teaspoon dried oregano**
- 1 **teaspoon ground cumin**
- 1 **large onion, chopped**
- 4 **cloves garlic, chopped**
- 4 **cups cauliflower florets (about half a head)**
- 2 **cups frozen corn, thawed**
- 1 **large zucchini, cut into 1-inch dice**
- 1 **large summer squash, cut into 1-inch dice**
- 1 **sweet orange pepper, seeded and cut into 1-inch dice**
- 2 **ribs celery, sliced**
- 1 **cup pearled barley**
- 1 **can (15 ounces) kidney beans, drained and rinsed**
- 1 **package frozen chopped spinach, thawed**
- ¼ **cup cilantro, chopped**

■ Coat slow cooker bowl with nonstick cooking spray.

■ Stir in 3 cups of the vegetable juice, the chili powder, salt, oregano, cumin, onion and garlic. Stir in cauliflower, corn, zucchini, squash, sweet pepper, celery and barley.

■ Cover and cook on HIGH for 4 hours or LOW for 6 hours. During last 30 minutes of cooking time, stir in remaining 1 cup vegetable juice, the beans and spinach. Garnish with cilantro and serve.

PER SERVING 341 CAL; 2 g FAT (0 g SAT); 15 g PRO; 72 g CARB; 19 g FIBER; 791 mg SODIUM; 0 mg CHOL

SPICY VEGETABLE AND BARLEY CHILI

MOROCCAN STEAK
SALAD, PAGE 85

MARCH

77

85

91

GOOD-MOOD FOOD

The secret ingredient in these recipes is happiness—in the form of mood-boosting foods.

ROASTED BRUSSELS SPROUTS AND SPINACH SALAD, PAGE 79

Poached Pears with Crème Fraîche

MAKES 4 servings **PREP** 10 minutes **COOK** 48 minutes

- **4** **firm Bosc pears**
- **1½** **cups pomegranate juice**
- **½** **cup port wine**
- **½** **cup toasted walnuts**
- **½** **cup crème fraîche**
-   **Mint, for garnish**

■ Peel pears. Cut a small slice from bottom of each pear so it will stand upright.

■ Place pomegranate juice and port in a large covered skillet and bring to a boil. Place pears in skillet on their sides. Cover and simmer 40 to 45 minutes, until tender. Turn pears a few times so all sides color evenly.

■ Remove pears to serving plates. Cook poaching liquid over high heat 3 minutes, until thick and syrupy.

■ Spoon sauce over pears. Garnish with walnuts, crème fraîche and mint.

PER SERVING 392 **CAL**; 21 g **FAT** (8 g **SAT**); 4 g **PRO**; 46 g **CARB**; 6 g **FIBER**; 26 mg **SODIUM**; 40 mg **CHOL**

POACHED PEARS WITH CRÈME FRAÎCHE

Seared Wild Salmon with Pistachio Gremolata

MAKES 4 servings **PREP** 25 minutes **COOK** 49 minutes

FARRO PILAF

- 3 tablespoons olive oil
- 8 ounces sliced wild mushrooms
- 1 large shallot, sliced
- ¾ cup farro
- ¼ cup dry white wine
- 2 cups chicken broth
- ¼ teaspoon salt
- ⅛ teaspoon black pepper

GREMOLATA

- ⅓ cup shelled pistachios, finely chopped
- ¼ cup parsley, chopped
- ¼ cup mint, chopped
- 1 tablespoon lemon zest
- 1 tablespoon olive oil
- 1 garlic clove, finely chopped
- Pinch of salt

SALMON

- 2 tablespoons olive oil
- 1 pound salmon fillet, cut into 4 squares
- Pinch of salt and pepper

■ **Farro Pilaf.** In a large skillet, heat 2 tablespoons of the olive oil over medium-high heat. Add mushrooms and sauté 5 minutes, until lightly browned. Transfer to a bowl. Heat remaining 1 tablespoon of the oil in a medium saucepan over medium heat. Add shallot and cook 3 minutes. Stir in farro and wine; cook 1 minute. Add broth, salt and pepper; bring to a simmer. Cover and simmer 35 to 40 minutes, until tender. Stir in sautéed mushrooms.

■ **Gremolata.** In a small bowl, combine pistachios, parsley, mint, lemon zest, oil, garlic and salt. Set aside.

■ **Salmon.** Meanwhile, heat oil in same skillet over medium-high heat. Season salmon with salt and pepper and place in skillet, skin side down. Cook 3 minutes, turn and cook an additional 3 minutes.

■ Spoon gremolata over salmon and serve with farro.

PER SERVING 587 **CAL**; 35 g **FAT** (5 g **SAT**); 34 g **PRO**; 33 g **CARB**; 4 g **FIBER**; 755 mg **SODIUM**; 72 mg **CHOL**

ROASTED BRUSSELS SPROUTS AND SPINACH SALAD

CHICKPEA, WHITE BEAN AND ESCAROLE STEW

Roasted Brussels Sprouts and Spinach Salad

MAKES 6 servings **PREP** 15 minutes
ROAST at 400° for 22 minutes

- 3 tablespoons red wine vinegar
- 1 teaspoon Dijon mustard
- ⅛ teaspoon salt
- ⅛ teaspoon black pepper
- ⅓ cup extra-virgin olive oil
- 1¼ pounds Brussels sprouts, trimmed and cut into quarters
- 6 scallions, cut into 1-inch pieces
- 12 cups baby spinach
- 1 cup red grapes, halved
- 3 tablespoons sunflower seeds
- 2 tablespoons crumbled Gorgonzola cheese
  Additional salt and pepper (optional)

■ In a small bowl, whisk vinegar, mustard, salt and pepper until combined. Gradually whisk in olive oil until thickened.

■ Place Brussels sprouts and scallions on a large baking sheet and toss with 2 tablespoons of the dressing. Roast at 400° for 22 minutes, turning once, until tender. Cool slightly.

■ In a large bowl, combine spinach, grapes and sunflower seeds. Toss with 4 tablespoons of the remaining dressing. Add Brussels sprouts and scallions.

■ Top with cheese. Serve with remaining dressing and, if using, additional salt and pepper.

PER SERVING 224 **CAL**; 16 g **FAT** (3 g **SAT**); 6 g **PRO**; 19 g **CARB**; 7 g **FIBER**; 201 mg **SODIUM**; 2 mg **CHOL**

Chickpea, White Bean and Escarole Stew

MAKES 12 servings **PREP** 15 minutes **SOAK** overnight **COOK** 1 hour, 40 minutes

- 1½ cups dry white beans
- 1½ cups dry chickpeas
- 2 tablespoons olive oil
- 2 onions, chopped
- 3 carrots, diced
- 2 ribs celery, diced
- 6 cloves garlic, sliced
- 6 plum tomatoes, seeds removed, chopped
- 1 sprig rosemary
- 4 sprigs thyme
- 2 bay leaves
- 1 package (10 ounces) frozen lima beans, thawed
- 4 ounces sliced prosciutto, cut into ribbons
- 1 teaspoon salt
- ¼ teaspoon black pepper
- 1 large bunch escarole (about 1 pound), sliced
  Shaved Parmesan (optional)
  Extra-virgin olive oil, for drizzling (optional)

■ Place beans and chickpeas in a large pot and cover with cold water. Soak overnight.

■ Heat olive oil in a large pot over medium-high heat. Add onions, carrots, celery and garlic; cook 8 minutes, stirring occasionally. Add tomatoes, rosemary, thyme and bay leaves. Stir in drained beans and 6 cups water. Bring to a boil. Lower heat and simmer, covered, 90 minutes.

■ Add lima beans, prosciutto, salt and pepper. Return to a simmer and gradually add escarole. Cook 2 minutes, until escarole is tender.

■ Ladle into bowls. Top with shaved Parmesan and drizzle with olive oil, if using.

PER SERVING 257 **CAL**; 4 g **FAT** (1 g **SAT**); 15 g **PRO**; 42 g **CARB**; 12 g **FIBER**; 415 mg **SODIUM**; 0 mg **CHOL**

SHRIMP AND FENNEL

Shrimp and Fennel

MAKES 4 servings **PREP** 15 minutes **COOK** 13 minutes

- 4 **tablespoons olive oil**
- 4 **cups thinly sliced fennel**
- 1¼ **pounds large shrimp, shelled and deveined**
- 1 **orange sweet pepper, seeded and thinly sliced**
- 6 **cloves garlic, finely chopped**
- ¼ **teaspoon red pepper flakes**
- 2 **tablespoons capers**
- 2 **tablespoons dry vermouth**
- 2 **tablespoons lemon juice**
- 2 **tablespoons chopped parsley**
- ⅛ **teaspoon salt**
  Spaghetti Cacio e Pepe (optional; recipe follows)

■ In a large skillet, heat 2 tablespoons of the olive oil over medium-high heat. Add fennel and cook 8 minutes, stirring occasionally. Remove to a plate.

■ Add remaining 2 tablespoons olive oil to skillet; stir in shrimp, sweet pepper, garlic and red pepper flakes. Cook 4 minutes, stirring occasionally. Return fennel to skillet; stir in capers, vermouth and lemon juice. Cook 1 minute.

■ Garnish with parsley and season with salt. If desired, serve with Spaghetti Cacio e Pepe.

PER SERVING 258 **CAL**; 15 g **FAT** (2 g **SAT**); 24 g **PRO**; 6 g **CARB**; 1 g **FIBER**; 480 mg **SODIUM**; 210 mg **CHOL**

Spaghetti Cacio e Pepe

Cook ½ pound whole wheat thin spaghetti following package directions; drain. Stir in ½ cup grated Parmesan and 1 teaspoon coarsely ground black pepper or to taste. Drizzle with 2 tablespoons extra-virgin olive oil.

Mediterranean Gratin

MAKES 4 servings **PREP** 20 minutes
BAKE at 400° for 1 hour, 15 minutes
COOL 10 minutes

- 1½ **pounds plum tomatoes, cut into ¼-inch slices**
- 1 **pound zucchini, cut into ¼-inch slices**
- 1 **pound small eggplant, cut into ¼-inch slices**
- ½ **medium red onion, cut into ¼-inch half-moons**
- 4 **cloves garlic, coarsely chopped**
- 6 **tablespoons extra-virgin olive oil**
- ¾ **teaspoon coarse sea salt**
- ¼ **teaspoon black pepper**
- 1 **tablespoon marjoram leaves**
- ¾ **cup ricotta**
- 3 **tablespoons grated Asiago cheese**
- 3 **tablespoons whole-grain panko**

■ Heat oven to 400°. Grease a 2-quart oval baking dish.

■ Around edge of dish, alternately fan tomato and zucchini slices. They will be standing up on edge once finished. In middle of dish, fan eggplant slices so that they overlap. Randomly tuck in onion slices and sprinkle garlic over top. Drizzle 4 tablespoons of the olive oil over gratin and season with salt and pepper. Sprinkle marjoram leaves over top.

■ Cover with foil and bake at 400° for 60 minutes. Dollop ricotta over top and sprinkle with Asiago and panko. Bake, uncovered, for an additional 15 minutes or until vegetables are tender.

■ Cool 10 minutes. Drizzle with remaining 2 tablespoons olive oil and serve.

PER SERVING 375 **CAL**; 29 g **FAT** (8 g **SAT**); 11 g **PRO**; 23 g **CARB**; 8 g **FIBER**; 555 mg **SODIUM**; 28 mg **CHOL**

MEDITERRANEAN
GRATIN

HEALTHY FAMILY DINNERS

These 20-minute meals go from prep to plate in record time.

THAI RICE NOODLE
BOWL, PAGE 89

ASIAN LETTUCE
WRAPS, PAGE 86

CHICKEN AND
TORTELLINI

Chicken and Tortellini

MAKES 6 servings **PREP** 3 minutes
COOK 15 minutes

- 1 **package (9 ounces) refrigerated spinach tortellini**
- 1 **package (9 ounces) refrigerated cheese tortellini**
- 1½ **pounds boneless, skinless chicken breasts**
- 2 **tablespoons olive oil**
- ⅛ **teaspoon plus ½ teaspoon salt**
- 1 **bag (5 ounces) baby spinach**
- 1 **pint grape or cherry tomatoes, halved (2 cups)**
- ⅓ **cup heavy cream**
- 2 **tablespoons grated Parmesan**
  Freshly ground black pepper

■ Bring a large pot of lightly salted water to a boil. Add tortellini and cook 7 minutes (or as per package directions).

■ Meanwhile, dice chicken into 1-inch pieces. Drain tortellini, reserving ¼ cup of the cooking water.

■ Heat oil in a large skillet over medium-high heat. Sprinkle chicken with ⅛ teaspoon of the salt. Add to skillet and brown on all sides, 5 minutes. Stir in spinach, tomatoes, heavy cream and remaining ½ teaspoon salt. Simmer 1 minute. Add tortellini and reserved pasta water, if needed; cook 2 minutes. Remove from heat and toss with Parmesan. Grind black pepper over top.

PER SERVING 492 **CAL**; 17 g **FAT** (7 g **SAT**); 40 g **PRO**; 45 g **CARB**; 4 g **FIBER**; 784 mg **SODIUM**; 123 mg **CHOL**

MOROCCAN STEAK SALAD

Moroccan Steak Salad

MAKES 4 servings **PREP** 10 minutes **COOK** 8 minutes

- ¾ **cup dry pearl couscous**
- 2 **ounces dried apricots (about ¼ to ⅓ cup)**
- ¾ **pound beef filet mignon**
- ¾ **teaspoon garam masala**
- ¾ **teaspoon salt**
- ¼ **teaspoon ground black pepper**
- ¼ **cup sliced almonds**
- 2 **tablespoons olive oil**
- 1 **can (15 ounces) chickpeas, drained and rinsed**
- 2½ **cups packed arugula**
- 3 **tablespoons cider vinegar**
- 2 **teaspoons honey**

■ Bring a medium saucepan of lightly salted water to a boil. Add couscous and cook 7 minutes. Stir apricots into couscous and cook 1 minute more.

■ Meanwhile, cut steak into ¾-inch pieces. Toss with ½ teaspoon of the garam masala, ¼ teaspoon of the salt and ⅛ teaspoon of the pepper. Heat a large stainless steel skillet over medium heat. Add almonds and toast 3 minutes, shaking pan frequently. Transfer to a plate. Increase heat to medium-high and add 1 tablespoon of the oil, swirling to coat pan. Add beef and sear on all sides, 2 to 3 minutes.

■ Drain couscous and transfer to a large serving bowl. Add beef and any drippings, chickpeas and arugula to bowl. In a small bowl, whisk vinegar, honey and remaining 1 tablespoon olive oil, ¼ teaspoon garam masala, ½ teaspoon salt and ⅛ teaspoon pepper. Add to large bowl and toss. Stir in toasted almonds and serve.

PER SERVING 505 **CAL**; 22 g **FAT** (5 g **SAT**); 27 g **PRO**; 50 g **CARB**; 8 g **FIBER**; 809 mg **SODIUM**; 55 mg **CHOL**

ASIAN LETTUCE WRAPS

Asian Lettuce Wraps

MAKES 4 servings **PREP** 7 minutes **COOK** 12 minutes

- 2 **medium carrots, thinly sliced, or ¾ cup shredded**
- 2 **heads Boston lettuce**
- 1 **tablespoon canola oil**
- 1 **package (8 ounces) sliced mushrooms**
- 1 **sweet yellow pepper, cored, seeded and cut into ½-inch pieces**
- 2 **cloves garlic, sliced**
- 1¼ **pounds lean ground beef**
- 1 **package (8.8 ounces) fully cooked brown rice**
- 1 **large egg**
- 3 **scallions, sliced**
- 3 **tablespoons low-sodium soy sauce**
- 3 **tablespoons rice vinegar**
- 2 **teaspoons sugar**
- 1 **teaspoon toasted sesame oil**
- 1 **teaspoon ground ginger**
  Mint leaves, for serving
  Steamed broccoli

■ Combine carrots and ¼ cup water in a large lidded skillet over medium-high heat. Cover and cook 4 minutes.

■ Meanwhile, remove 16 leaves from lettuce; rinse and pat dry. Set aside.

■ Stir canola oil into skillet with carrots. Add mushrooms, sweet pepper and garlic. Cook 2 minutes. Crumble in ground beef and cook 3 minutes. Add brown rice and cook 2 minutes. Lightly beat egg; push skillet contents to one side of pan. Add egg to skillet and scramble, 1 minute. Stir in scallions, soy sauce, vinegar, sugar, sesame oil and ginger. Remove from heat.

■ Serve meat mixture with lettuce leaves (spoon a scant ⅓ cup into each leaf). Sprinkle with mint leaves and serve with steamed broccoli on the side.

PER SERVING 503 **CAL**; 22 g **FAT** (7 g **SAT**); 38 g **PRO**; 35 g **CARB**; 6 g **FIBER**; 624 mg **SODIUM**; 145 mg **CHOL**

Schnitzel and Salad

MAKES 4 servings **PREP** 14 minutes **COOK** 6 minutes

- 8 **small thinly sliced boneless pork chops (about 1½ pounds)**
- ¾ **cup plain bread crumbs**
- ½ **teaspoon plus ¼ teaspoon salt**
- 1 **large egg**
- ½ **cup all-purpose flour**
- 1 **package (11 ounces) mixed salad greens**
- 2 **medium oranges**
- 2 **lemons**
- 2 **teaspoons honey**
- 1 **teaspoon Dijon mustard**
- ⅛ **teaspoon ground black pepper**
- 2 **tablespoons olive oil**
- 3 **tablespoons vegetable oil**

■ If needed, pound pork chops to ¼-inch thickness. Place bread crumbs and ½ teaspoon of the salt in a shallow bowl. Whisk egg plus 2 tablespoons water in a second bowl. Place flour in a third bowl.

■ Coat 1 pork chop in flour. Dip into egg mixture, allowing excess to drip back into bowl. Coat with bread crumbs and transfer to a large cutting board. Repeat with remaining pork chops.

■ Place salad greens in a large bowl. Peel oranges and slice into half-moons. Add to greens. Juice 1 lemon to yield ¼ cup juice; cut second lemon into wedges. Whisk lemon juice with honey, mustard, remaining ¼ teaspoon salt and the pepper. Whisk in olive oil and toss with salad greens.

■ Heat 1½ tablespoons of the vegetable oil in a large skillet over medium-high heat. Add 4 pork chops; cook 3 minutes, turning once. Repeat with remaining 1½ tablespoons vegetable oil and 4 pork chops.

■ Divide salad among 4 plates. Top each with 2 pieces pork schnitzel. Serve with lemon wedges on the side.

PER SERVING 402 **CAL**; 18 g **FAT** (3 g **SAT**); 31 g **PRO**; 28 g **CARB**; 3 g **FIBER**; 804 mg **SODIUM**; 115 mg **CHOL**

SCHNITZEL AND SALAD

SAUSAGE, PEPPERS
AND BROCCOLI RABE

Try Thai one night and Italian the next. With fresh ingredients and a few smart strategies, quick weeknight meals are anything but monotonous.

THAI RICE NOODLE BOWL

Sausage, Peppers and Broccoli Rabe

MAKES 4 servings **PREP** 7 minutes
COOK 13 minutes

- 1 **bunch broccoli rabe, tough stems trimmed**
- 1½ **pounds russet potatoes, scrubbed and cut into 2-inch pieces**
- 1 **package (12 ounces) fully cooked roasted pepper and Asiago or Italian-style chicken sausage links**
- 2 **tablespoons olive oil**
- 1 **sweet red pepper, cored, seeded and cut into 1-inch pieces**
- 2 **cloves garlic, sliced**
- ½ **teaspoon salt**
- ½ **cup milk**
- ½ **cup part-skim ricotta**

■ Bring a large pot of lightly salted water to a boil. Add broccoli rabe and cook 1 minute. Remove to a strainer with a slotted spoon. Add potatoes to boiling water and cook 12 minutes.

■ Meanwhile, cut sausages on the bias into ¼-inch-thick slices and heat oil in a large skillet over medium-high heat. Add sausage, pepper and garlic and sauté 4 minutes. Squeeze liquid from broccoli rabe. Cut into 2-inch pieces and add to skillet. Sauté 2 minutes and season mixture with ⅛ teaspoon of the salt.

■ Drain potatoes; smash with milk and remaining ¼ teaspoon plus ⅛ teaspoon of the salt. Divide potatoes among 4 shallow bowls. Top with sausage mixture and spoon 2 tablespoons ricotta cheese on each serving.

PER SERVING 419 **CAL**; 18 g **FAT** (6 g **SAT**); 27 g **PRO**; 38 g **CARB**; 3 g **FIBER**; 772 mg **SODIUM**; 83 mg **CHOL**

Thai Rice Noodle Bowl

MAKES 4 servings **PREP** 16 minutes
COOK 2 minutes **GRILL OR BROIL** 6 minutes

- 7 **ounces (half a 14-ounce box) thin stir-fry rice noodles**
- ⅓ **cup rice vinegar**
- 3 **tablespoons low-sodium soy sauce**
- 3 **tablespoons creamy peanut butter**
- 2 **tablespoons fish sauce**
- 2 **tablespoons warm water**
- 1 **tablespoon plus 1 teaspoon sugar**
- ¼ **teaspoon red pepper flakes**
- ½ **seedless cucumber**
- ¾ **pound small chicken breast halves, boneless pork chops or steak (see Note)**
- ¾ **teaspoon cornstarch**
- 1 **cup sweet pepper strips**
- ½ **cup shredded carrot**
- 3 **scallions, trimmed and sliced**
- ⅓ **cup cilantro leaves, sliced, plus more for serving**
- ½ **cup chopped peanuts**
  Lime wedges

■ Bring a large saucepan of water to a boil. Add noodles, turn off heat and let soak 6 to 8 minutes.

■ Meanwhile, in a small bowl, whisk vinegar, soy sauce, peanut butter, fish sauce, warm water, sugar and red pepper flakes until smooth. Peel, halve and slice cucumber into half-moons.

■ Heat grill pan or broiler. Place chicken in a resealable plastic bag or a glass dish. Add 3 tablespoons of the dressing, turning to coat.

■ Place remaining dressing in a small saucepan with cornstarch. Bring to a boil; boil 2 minutes. Remove from heat.

■ Grill or broil chicken 6 minutes, turning once, until cooked through.

■ Drain and rinse noodles and transfer to a large bowl. Add sweet pepper, shredded carrot, cucumber, scallions and sliced cilantro. Drizzle dressing into bowl and toss to combine. Divide among 4 bowls. Slice chicken and divide among bowls. Sprinkle with cilantro leaves and chopped peanuts. Serve each bowl with a lime wedge.

PER SERVING 468 **CAL**; 16 g **FAT** (3 g **SAT**); 32 g **PRO**; 51 g **CARB**; 4 g **FIBER**; 763 mg **SODIUM**; 49 mg **CHOL**

Note: To save even more time, buy precooked chicken from the deli counter, slice and serve over noodle mixture. Swap in a reduced-calorie bottled Asian sesame salad dressing or peanut sauce for the dressing made here.

LIGHTEN UP!

This veggie-packed meatless lasagna warms you up but won't weigh you down.

EASY VEGGIE LASAGNA

Broiling thin strips of zucchini before layering in the lasagna helps them to release some of their water so that the finished dish has a nice firm—not soggy—texture.

Easy Veggie Lasagna

MAKES 10 servings **PREP** 30 minutes **BROIL** 10 minutes **BAKE** at 375° for 1 hour, 5 minutes

- 12 traditional lasagna noodles
- 4 zucchini (about 1¾ pounds), trimmed and sliced lengthwise (24 slices total)
- 1 tablespoon olive oil
- ¼ teaspoon salt
- ¼ teaspoon black pepper
- 2 containers (16 ounces each) 2% cottage cheese
- 2 egg yolks
- ¼ cup fresh basil, chopped
- 1 jar (24 ounces) marinara sauce
- 1 can (14.5 ounces) diced tomatoes, drained
- 1 box (9 ounces) frozen artichoke hearts, thawed and chopped
- 3 cups shredded part-skim mozzarella

Chopped parsley (optional)

■ Place dry noodles in a large bowl and add the hottest tap water you can. Soak 20 minutes.

■ Meanwhile, heat broiler. Toss zucchini with oil and ⅛ teaspoon each of the salt and pepper. Spread onto 1 large or 2 small baking sheets. Broil 5 minutes; flip slices over and broil an additional 5 minutes. Set aside. Lower oven temp to 375°.

■ In a medium bowl, beat cottage cheese, egg yolks, basil and remaining ⅛ teaspoon each salt and pepper.

■ Coat a 13 x 9 x 2-inch baking dish with nonstick cooking spray. Spread ½ cup of the marinara on bottom of dish. Top with 3 of the soaked noodles. Top noodles with 2 cups of the cottage cheese mixture. Add 3 more noodles to dish. Top noodles with half the zucchini slices. Combine remaining marinara sauce, the diced tomatoes and chopped artichoke hearts. Spread half over zucchini. Top with 3 noodles. Layer with remaining 2 cups cottage cheese mixture, remaining zucchini slices and 1 cup of the mozzarella. Add remaining 3 noodles, remaining marinara mixture and top with remaining 2 cups mozzarella.

■ Cover with nonstick foil and bake at 375° for 35 minutes. Uncover dish and bake an additional 30 minutes, until cheese is melted, edges are bubbly and noodles are tender when pierced with a knife. Sprinkle lasagna with chopped parsley, if using, and let stand 20 minutes before slicing.

PER SERVING 390 **CAL**; 13 g **FAT** (6 g **SAT**); 26 g **PRO**; 42 g **CARB**; 5 g **FIBER**; 965 mg **SODIUM**; 74 mg **CHOL**

FLOWER CAKE,
PAGE 103

POP CHICKS,
PAGE 103

BUTTERFLY
CUPCAKES,
PAGE 104

EASTER THUMBPRINTS,
PAGE 104

DIPPED STRAWBERRY
"CARROTS", PAGE 103

98

101

109

HONEY CAKE, PAGE 101

STANDING RIB
ROAST, PAGE 96

ORANGE-
INFUSED
HEIRLOOM
CARROTS,
PAGE 98

SAUTÉED BABY
SPINACH AND
OYSTER
MUSHROOMS,
PAGE 97

ROASTED RED-SKINNED
POTATOES WITH CRISPY
SHALLOTS, PAGE 97

Standing Rib Roast

MAKES 8 servings PREP 20 minutes ROAST at 450° for 20 minutes; at 375° for 1 hour 10 minutes LET REST 15 minutes

- **1** standing rib roast (3 ribs, about 6 pounds total)
- **1** tablespoon olive oil
- **4** cloves garlic, chopped
- **1** plus ⅛ teaspoon salt
- **½** teaspoon plus ⅛ teaspoon black pepper
- **1½** cups parsley leaves
- **¼** cup oregano leaves
- **3** tablespoons red wine vinegar
- **2** cloves garlic, chopped
- **⅛** teaspoon red pepper flakes
- **⅓** cup olive oil

■ Heat oven to 450°. Place a rack in a large roasting pan.

■ Rub roast with oil, then rub with garlic. Season with 1 teaspoon of the salt and ½ teaspoon of the pepper. Place roast on rack in pan, rib side down.

■ Roast at 450° for 20 minutes. Reduce oven temperature to 375° and continue to roast for 70 minutes or until temperature reaches 120°. Tent with foil and let rest 15 minutes.

■ Meanwhile, make chimichurri. Place parsley, oregano, vinegar, garlic, red pepper flakes and remaining ⅛ teaspoon each salt and pepper in a blender; pulse until chopped. Gradually add oil and process until combined. Cover until serving.

■ Thinly slice and serve with chimichurri.

PER SERVING 547 **CAL**; 21 g **FAT** (7 g **SAT**); 82 g **PRO**; 1 g **CARB**; 0 g **FIBER**; 515 mg **SODIUM**; 230 mg **CHOL**

STANDING RIB ROAST

ROASTED RED-SKINNED POTATOES WITH CRISPY SHALLOTS

A beef roast is so elegant and essentially hands-off to prepare. An array of sides featuring spring vegetables brings color and freshness to the table.

Roasted Red-Skinned Potatoes with Crispy Shallots

MAKES 8 servings **PREP** 20 minutes
ROAST at 375° for 1 hour 5 minutes

- 8 **large red-skinned potatoes (about 8 ounces each)**
- 8 **cloves garlic, thinly sliced**
- 3 **tablespoons olive oil**
- ¾ **teaspoon salt**
- ⅛ **teaspoon black pepper**
- 3 **shallots, sliced**

■ Heat oven to 375°.

■ Vertically slice each potato into ¼-inch slices, about ¼ inch from the bottom. Place on a baking sheet; gently press garlic between slices. Drizzle with 2 tablespoons of the olive oil and season with ½ teaspoon of the salt and the pepper.

■ Roast at 375° for 65 minutes or until tender.

■ Meanwhile, heat remaining 1 tablespoon oil in a small skillet. Add shallots and cook, stirring, 6 to 8 minutes or until crispy.

■ To serve, season with remaining salt and spoon shallots over potatoes.

PER SERVING 189 **CAL**; 5 g **FAT** (1 g **SAT**); 4 g **PRO**; 30 g **CARB**; 3 g **FIBER**; 250 mg **SODIUM**; 0 mg **CHOL**

SAUTÉED BABY SPINACH AND OYSTER MUSHROOMS

Sautéed Baby Spinach and Oyster Mushrooms

MAKES 8 servings **PREP** 15 minutes **COOK** 9 minutes

- 2 **tablespoons extra-virgin olive oil**
- 4 **cloves garlic, sliced**
- ½ **pound oyster mushrooms, separated from stem**
- ½ **sweet yellow pepper, sliced**
- ½ **sweet red pepper, sliced**
- 1 **pound baby spinach**
- ½ **teaspoon salt**
- ¼ **teaspoon black pepper**
- 1 **teaspoon fresh thyme leaves**
- 1 **teaspoon fresh marjoram leaves**
  Lemon slices, for squeezing

■ Heat oil in a large skillet over medium-high heat. Add garlic and cook 1 minute. Stir in mushrooms and peppers; cook 4 minutes, stirring occasionally.

■ Gradually add spinach and stir until wilted, about 4 minutes. Stir in salt, pepper, thyme and marjoram. Serve with lemon for squeezing over the top.

PER SERVING 61 **CAL**; 3 g **FAT** (0 g **SAT**); 2 g **PRO**; 8 g **CARB**; 3 g **FIBER**; 236 mg **SODIUM**; 0 mg **CHOL**

ORANGE-INFUSED
HEIRLOOM CARROTS

Small, sweet carrots are one of the harbingers of spring. Leave just a little of the green tops on each carrot for color and interest.

Charred Asparagus and Tomato Salad

MAKES 8 servings **PREP** 10 minutes
COOK 20 minutes

- 2 tablespoons red wine vinegar
- 1 teaspoon mustard
- ⅛ teaspoon salt
- ⅛ teaspoon black pepper
- ¼ cup extra-virgin olive oil
- 1 tablespoon minced shallots
- 2 pounds asparagus, woody ends trimmed
- 16 cups mixed spring salad greens
- 2 cups red and yellow grape tomatoes, halved

■ In a small bowl, whisk vinegar, mustard, salt and pepper. Gradually whisk in oil; stir in shallots. Set aside.

■ Heat a large nonstick skillet over medium-high heat. Add asparagus and cook 7 to 10 minutes, until nicely darkened on each side. Cook in 2 batches. Place in a large bowl and toss with 2 tablespoons of the dressing. Set aside.

■ In a large bowl, toss greens and tomatoes with remaining dressing. Arrange asparagus on top and serve.

PER SERVING 114 **CAL**; 7 g **FAT** (1 g **SAT**); 4 g **PRO**; 12 g **CARB**; 6 g **FIBER**; 94 mg **SODIUM**; 0 mg **CHOL**

Orange-Infused Heirloom Carrots

MAKES 8 servings **PREP** 10 minutes **COOK** 10 minutes

- 2½ pounds heirloom carrots, peeled
- 2¼ cups orange juice
- ¼ cup (½ stick) butter or margarine
- ¼ cup honey
- ¼ teaspoon salt
- ⅛ teaspoon black pepper
- 1 tablespoon chopped parsley

■ Place carrots in a large skillet with 2 cups of the orange juice and water to cover. Bring to a boil; reduce heat and simmer 5 minutes. Drain.

■ Add butter, honey, remaining ¼ cup orange juice, salt and pepper. Cook over medium-low heat, covered, 5 minutes, stirring occasionally, until carrots are tender and glazed.

■ Place carrots on a serving plate and drizzle with glaze from skillet. Sprinkle with parsley.

PER SERVING 153 **CAL**; 6 g **FAT** (4 g **SAT**); 2 g **PRO**; 25 g **CARB**; 3 g **FIBER**; 149 mg **SODIUM**; 15 mg **CHOL**

**CHARRED ASPARAGUS
AND TOMATO SALAD**

PASSOVER CHOCOLATE CHIP MANDELBREAD

Passover Chocolate Chip Mandelbread

MAKES 18 pieces **PREP** 15 minutes
BAKE at 350° for 30 minutes **COOL** 15 minutes
BROIL 2 minutes

4	**eggs**
1	**cup Passover cake meal**
1	**cup sugar**
1	**cup semisweet Passover chocolate chips**
½	**cup canola oil**
½	**cup chopped walnuts**
¼	**cup Passover potato starch**
1	**teaspoon vanilla (imitation for Passover)**
⅓	**cup cinnamon sugar**

■ Heat oven to 350°. Grease a 13 x 9 x 2-inch baking dish.

■ In a large bowl, beat eggs until foamy. Add cake meal, sugar, chocolate chips, oil, walnuts, potato starch and vanilla. Stir until well combined.

■ Spoon into baking dish and spread evenly. Sprinkle with 2 tablespoons of the cinnamon sugar. Bake at 350° for 30 minutes.

■ Remove from oven and cool 15 minutes on a wire rack. Heat broiler.

■ Slice bread vertically into thirds, then slice each third horizontally into six 1-inch pieces. Place slices on their sides on a baking sheet. Sprinkle with half the remaining cinnamon sugar; broil 1 minute. Turn and sprinkle with remaining cinnamon sugar; broil 1 minute. Cool before serving.

PER PIECE 53 **CAL**; 13 g **FAT** (3 g **SAT**); 4 g **PRO**; 26 g **CARB**; 1 g **FIBER**; 19 mg **SODIUM**; 50 mg **CHOL**

CHOCOLATE MERINGUE COOKIES

HONEY CAKE

Chocolate Meringue Cookies

MAKES 18 cookies **PREP** 20 minutes
BAKE at 325° for 12 minutes

- 2 **egg whites**
- ½ **cup sugar**
- 1 **cup semisweet Passover chocolate chips, melted and slightly cooled**
- ¾ **cup chopped pecans**
- ½ **teaspoon vanilla (imitation for Passover)**

■ Heat oven to 325°. Coat a baking sheet with vegetable spray.

■ In a large bowl, beat egg whites until foamy. Gradually add sugar and continue to beat until glossy stiff peaks form, about 4 minutes.

■ Add cooled chocolate, pecans and vanilla, mixing until incorporated.

■ Drop tablespoonfuls of mixture onto prepared baking sheet, 2 inches apart.

■ Bake at 325° for 12 minutes, until set. Cool on baking sheet 2 minutes. Transfer cookies to a wire rack to cool completely.

PER COOKIE 24 **CAL**; 7 g **FAT** (2 g **SAT**); 2 g **PRO**; 13 g **CARB**; 1 g **FIBER**; 6 mg **SODIUM**; 0 mg **CHOL**

Honey Cake

MAKES 12 servings **PREP** 20 minutes **BAKE** at 350° for 40 minutes **COOL** 15 minutes
COOK 5 minutes **REFRIGERATE** 4 hours

CAKE
- ¾ **cup granulated sugar**
- ¼ **cup packed dark brown sugar**
- ¼ **cup vegetable oil**
- 3 **eggs**
- 1 **cup finely chopped walnuts**
- ½ **cup Passover cake meal**
- ½ **cup chopped almonds**
- 3 **tablespoons orange juice**
- ½ **teaspoon ground cinnamon**
- ⅛ **teaspoon salt**

SYRUP
- ⅓ **cup granulated sugar**
- ⅓ **cup orange juice**
- ¼ **cup honey**
- 2 **tablespoons lemon juice**
- ½ **cup sliced almonds**

■ **Cake.** Heat oven to 350°. Line bottom of an 8-inch cake pan with wax paper. Grease paper and pan.

■ In a large bowl, beat sugars, oil and eggs until smooth. Add walnuts, cake meal, almonds, orange juice, cinnamon and salt. Stir until combined. Spoon into prepared pan.

■ Bake at 350° for 40 minutes, until cake is set. Cool on a wire rack 15 minutes.

■ **Syrup.** In a small saucepan, combine sugar, orange juice, ⅓ cup water, honey and lemon juice. Simmer 5 minutes, stirring frequently until mixture reduces slightly. Let cool.

■ Using a fork, poke holes in cake and pour syrup over the top. Refrigerate 4 hours. Invert onto platter. Remove wax paper and top with sliced almonds.

PER SERVING 78 **CAL**; 16 g **FAT** (2 g **SAT**); 6 g **PRO**; 32 g **CARB**; 2 g **FIBER**; 48 mg **SODIUM**; 56 mg **CHOL**

SPRING SWEETS

Ring in spring with these charming treats that sing of the season.

FLOWER CAKE

POP CHICKS

BUTTERFLY
CUPCAKES,
PAGE 104

DIPPED STRAWBERRY
"CARROTS"

EASTER THUMBPRINTS, PAGE 104

Flower Cake

MAKES 12 servings **PREP** 25 minutes
BAKE at 350° for 35 minutes **COOL** 15 minutes

CAKE

- 2½ cups cake flour (not self-rising)
- 1⅓ cups sugar
- 1 tablespoon plus ½ teaspoon baking powder
- ½ teaspoon salt
- 1 cup milk
- ⅔ cup solid vegetable shortening
- 2 tablespoons lemon juice
- 2 teaspoons lemon zest
- 2 large eggs

BUTTERCREAM FROSTING

- 1 cup (2 sticks) unsalted butter, softened
- 1 box (16 ounces) confectioners' sugar
- 3 tablespoons half-and-half or milk
- 1 teaspoon vanilla extract
- Pink gel food coloring
- Generous ½ cup assorted-colored M&M's (makes 15 flowers)

■ **Cake.** Heat oven to 350°. Coat two 8-inch round cake pans with nonstick cooking spray. Line pans with wax paper; coat paper with spray.

■ Combine flour, sugar, baking powder, salt, ½ cup of the milk and the shortening in a large bowl. Beat at low speed until blended, then beat on high speed 2 minutes.

■ Combine remaining ½ cup milk, the lemon juice, lemon zest and eggs in a small bowl. Gradually add to batter and beat on high speed 2 minutes longer, scraping down sides of bowl occasionally. Divide batter between pans.

■ Bake at 350° for 33 to 35 minutes or until a toothpick inserted in center tests clean. Cool cakes in pans on racks 15 minutes. Remove cakes from pans to racks and remove paper. Let cool completely.

■ **Buttercream Frosting.** While cake cools, with an electric mixer, beat butter until smooth. Add confectioners' sugar, half-and-half and vanilla and beat until smooth. Tint frosting pink with food coloring. Set aside.

■ Place 1 cake layer on a serving plate. Spread top with 1 cup of the frosting. Gently press second cake layer on top. Spread remaining frosting on side and top of cake. Press M&M's into cake to resemble flowers, alternating colors of centers and petals.

Dipped Strawberry "Carrots"

MAKES about 16 berries **PREP** 15 minutes
MICROWAVE at 50% power for 2 minutes

- 1 container (16 ounces) large strawberries (about 15 or 16 berries)
- 2 cups orange candy melts (such as Wilton)
- 2 teaspoons canola oil

■ Line a large baking sheet with wax paper. Rinse strawberries and dry completely with paper towels.

■ Microwave candy melts and oil in a glass bowl or measuring cup at 50% power for 1 minute. Stir. Continue melting at 50% power in 30-second increments (stirring after each) until smooth.

■ Holding a strawberry by the green part, dip into melted candy to cover. Shake off excess and place on wax paper. Repeat with remaining strawberries.

■ Transfer remaining melted candy to a piping bag or quart-size resealable plastic bag. Snip off a small corner and drizzle crosswise over berries. Refrigerate to firm.

Pop Chicks

MAKES 12 servings **PREP** 15 minutes
MICROWAVE at 50% power for 2 minutes
REFRIGERATE 5 minutes

- 12 Double Stuf golden Oreo cookies
- 1½ cups bright yellow candy melts (such as Wilton)
- 2 teaspoons canola oil
- 12 white paper treat sticks
- 3 orange jelly beans
- 12 pairs Wilton candy eyeballs
- 1 tablespoon white nonpareils
- 1 piece Styrofoam (to hold sticks while they dry) or wax paper

■ Place cookies on a baking sheet. Microwave candy melts and oil in a glass bowl or measuring cup at 50% power for 1 minute. Stir. Continue melting at 50% power in 30-second increments (stirring after each) until smooth.

■ Dip a treat stick into melted candy, then insert into cookie filling, pressing down to sandwich. Refrigerate 5 minutes to firm.

■ Carefully cut jelly beans in half lengthwise, then cut each half in half crosswise (for a total of 4 pieces from each; these will become the beaks).

■ At any time, return melted candy to microwave for 15 seconds to keep fluid. Dip a cookie into melted candy, then shake off excess. Scrape back of cookie along bowl edge to keep from dripping. Add eyes and jelly bean beak. Hold cookie over a bowl and use a small spoon to add nonpareils at the bottom to resemble an eggshell. Secure stick in Styrofoam or place flat on a sheet of wax paper and continue with remaining chicks.

Easter Thumbprints

MAKES about 3½ dozen cookies
PREP 15 minutes
BAKE at 375° for 12 minutes per batch

COOKIES

   2   cups all-purpose flour
   1   teaspoon baking soda
   ¼   teaspoon salt
   ½   cup (1 stick) unsalted butter, softened
   ½   package (4 ounces) cream cheese, softened
  1¼   cups granulated sugar
   1   large egg
   1   teaspoon vanilla extract

FILLING

   ¾   cup (1½ sticks) unsalted butter, softened
   3   cups confectioners' sugar
   2   tablespoons half-and-half or milk
       Gel food coloring
       Assorted sparkling sugars (optional)

■ **Cookies.** Heat oven to 375°. In a medium bowl, whisk flour, baking soda and salt.

■ In a large bowl, with an electric mixer, beat butter and cream cheese until smooth. Add 1 cup of the sugar and beat until pale and fluffy, about 2 minutes. Beat in egg, followed by vanilla. On low speed, beat in flour mixture.

■ Place remaining ¼ cup sugar in a small bowl. Scoop scant tablespoonfuls of dough into your hand. Roll into balls, then roll balls in sugar. Place on an ungreased baking sheet and continue shaping dough.

■ Bake at 375° for 12 minutes per batch. Remove from oven and press down centers with your thumb or the reverse end of an ice cream scoop or other kitchen tool (we used a citrus reamer). Repeat with all remaining dough. Cool cookies on a wire rack.

■ **Filling.** Meanwhile, with an electric mixer, beat butter until smooth. Add confectioners' sugar and half-and-half and beat until smooth. Divide among 4 bowls and tint yellow, pink, blue and green or your desired colors. Spoon into piping bags and snip a ½-inch opening. Pipe filling into cooled cookies; sprinkle with sparkling sugar, if using. Refrigerate until filling is firm before stacking.

For Easter, a baby or wedding shower, or simply for fun, these sweets in the form of flowers, birds and butterflies are simple to make—and impressive to see. The clever use of candies and a few convenience products make creating them a breeze.

Butterfly Cupcakes

MAKES 24 servings   PREP 20 minutes

   1   cup (2 sticks) unsalted butter, softened
   1   box (16 ounces) confectioners' sugar
   3   tablespoons milk
   2   tablespoons corn syrup
   1   teaspoon vanilla extract
       Turquoise, lime green and pink food coloring
  24   baked cupcakes
       Assorted-colored Sixlets, jelly beans, M&M's and/or mini Gobstoppers
  48   mini pretzels
       Black licorice whips

■ With an electric mixer, beat butter until smooth. Add confectioners' sugar, milk, corn syrup and vanilla and beat until smooth. Divide frosting among 3 bowls and tint turquoise, green and pink with food coloring.

■ Smoothly spread each color of frosting onto 8 cupcakes. Transfer frostings to 3 resealable plastic bags and snip off a corner on each bag.

■ Pipe frosting in contrasting colors onto cupcakes for butterfly bodies. Insert candies into some of the frosting bodies. Make heads using mini Gobstoppers in a contrasting color. Insert a pretzel on either side of each body for wings. Cut 2-inch pieces of licorice and insert above heads to resemble antennae.

BUTTERFLY CUPCAKES

EASTER THUMBPRINTS

Skip the dinner scramble—eggs make everything easier.

SPANISH TORTILLA,
PAGE 110

ISRAELI POACHED
EGGS (SHAKSHUKA),
PAGE 113

HUEVOS RANCHEROS

Huevos Rancheros

MAKES 4 servings **PREP** 10 minutes
COOK 12 minutes

- 1 tablespoon olive oil
- ½ cup chopped onion
- 3 cloves garlic, chopped
- ½ teaspoon chili powder
- ¼ teaspoon ground cumin
- ¼ teaspoon salt
- 1 can (15 ounces) black beans, drained and rinsed
- ½ cup chicken broth or water
- 8 small (6-inch) corn tortillas
- 2 tablespoons unsalted butter
- 8 eggs
- ½ cup shredded Monterey Jack
  Sliced avocado, salsa and cilantro (optional)

■ Heat oven to 200°. In a skillet, heat oil over medium heat. Stir in onion; cook 3 minutes. Add garlic, chili powder, cumin and ⅛ teaspoon of the salt; cook another 2 minutes. Stir in beans and broth; bring to a simmer and cook 3 minutes. Smash half the beans with the back of a fork and stir. Place tortillas on a baking sheet and spread 2 tablespoons of the beans on each tortilla. Place in a 200° oven.

■ Wipe out skillet, then add 1 tablespoon of the butter. Fry 4 of the eggs 2 minutes, until cooked. Transfer to tortillas in oven. Add remaining 1 tablespoon butter and repeat with remaining 4 eggs.

■ Remove tortillas from oven, season with remaining ⅛ teaspoon salt and top each with 1 tablespoon Monterey Jack. Garnish with avocado, salsa and cilantro, if using.

PER SERVING 444 **CAL**; 20 g **FAT** (7 g **SAT**); 25 g **PRO**; 41 g **CARB**; 10 g **FIBER**; 702 mg **SODIUM**; 436 mg **CHOL**

CHICKEN-AND-EGG BURGERS

Chicken-and-Egg Burgers

MAKES 4 servings **PREP** 15 minutes **COOK** 15 minutes

- 1 pound ground chicken breast
- 3 cups packed spinach, chopped
- 1 large shallot, grated
- 1 clove garlic, grated
- 1 tablespoon Dijon mustard
- ½ teaspoon salt
- ¼ teaspoon plus ⅛ teaspoon black pepper
- 1 tablespoon vegetable oil
- 4 ounces thinly sliced sharp cheddar
- 1 tablespoon unsalted butter
- 4 eggs
- 4 whole wheat hamburger buns, split
- 1 teaspoon white wine vinegar

■ In a bowl, combine chicken, 2 cups of the spinach, the shallot, garlic, mustard, salt and ¼ teaspoon of the pepper. Form into 4 patties.

■ Heat oil in a large nonstick skillet over medium heat. Cook burgers 6 minutes per side or until cooked through, adding cheese after flipping. (To help cheese melt, cover with a lid or tent loosely with aluminum foil.) Set burgers on a plate.

■ Add butter to skillet. Fry eggs 2 minutes, until cooked, and sprinkle with remaining ⅛ teaspoon pepper. Top each burger with an egg. Add buns to pan cut sides down; toast 1 minute. Transfer burgers to bottom halves of buns. Toss remaining 1 cup spinach with vinegar. Top each burger with some spinach and remaining bun halves.

PER SERVING 438 **CAL**; 21 g **FAT** (7 g **SAT**); 37 g **PRO**; 27 g **CARB**; 4 g **FIBER**; 833 mg **SODIUM**; 297 mg **CHOL**

SPANISH TORTILLA

Spring Carbonara

MAKES 6 servings PREP 15 minutes
COOK 17 minutes

- 4 ounces pancetta, diced
- 1 cup sliced leeks
- 3 cloves garlic, sliced
- 6 eggs
- 1 cup grated Pecorino cheese, plus more for garnish (optional)
- 1 teaspoon freshly cracked black pepper, plus more for garnish (optional)
- ½ teaspoon salt
- 1 pound linguine
- 2 cups shelled fresh peas
- 1 pound asparagus, trimmed and sliced into ½-inch pieces
- ⅓ cup roughly chopped parsley

■ Bring a large pot of lightly salted water to a boil. In a large skillet over medium heat, cook pancetta 4 minutes. Remove to a plate with a slotted spoon. Add leeks and garlic; cook 3 minutes. Turn off heat and set aside.

■ In a bowl, whisk eggs, Pecorino, pepper and salt. Set aside.

■ Cook linguine in boiling salted water 9 minutes. (Add peas and asparagus to water after 7 minutes.) Drain, reserving ½ cup of the pasta water.

■ Return pan to medium heat. Add linguine, peas, asparagus and pancetta to leeks and garlic. Cook 1 minute, stirring well. Vigorously mix in egg mixture, making sure not to scramble. Stir in reserved pasta water, if needed, and parsley. Serve immediately, garnishing with more Pecorino and pepper, if using. (If pan isn't large enough, pasta can be tossed in the pot once linguine is drained.)

PER SERVING 525 CAL; 16 g FAT (7 g SAT); 27 g PRO; 68 g CARB; 6 g FIBER; 785 mg SODIUM; 237 mg CHOL

Spanish Tortilla

MAKES 4 servings PREP 10 minutes ROAST at 400° for 25 minutes COOK 47 minutes

- 1 bag (28 ounces) small red-skinned potatoes, cut into 1-inch pieces
- 2 tablespoons extra-virgin olive oil
- ¾ teaspoon salt
- ¼ teaspoon plus ⅛ teaspoon black pepper
- 2 ounces (½ cup) cured Spanish chorizo, casing removed, diced
- 1 yellow onion, thinly sliced
- 7 eggs
- Fresh parsley, for garnish

■ Heat oven to 400°. On a rimmed baking sheet, toss potatoes with 1 tablespoon of the oil, ¼ teaspoon of the salt and ⅛ teaspoon of the pepper. Roast at 400° for 15 minutes, flip and roast another 10 minutes.

■ In a 10-inch nonstick skillet, cook chorizo 5 minutes over medium heat.

Remove to a plate with a slotted spoon. Pour in remaining 1 tablespoon oil. Add onion; cook 5 to 7 minutes, until softened. Stir in potatoes and chorizo. Reduce heat to medium-low.

■ In a bowl, beat eggs with remaining ½ teaspoon salt and ¼ teaspoon pepper. Pour over mixture in skillet. Cook 10 minutes, then cover with foil. Cook 20 minutes, then loosen with a silicone spatula, place a plate on top of skillet and carefully flip tortilla onto plate. Slide tortilla back into skillet, uncooked side down. Cook another 5 minutes.

■ Flip onto a new plate, garnish with parsley and slice into 4 pieces.

PER SERVING 425 CAL; 22 g FAT (6 g SAT); 19 g PRO; 39 g CARB; 4 g FIBER; 823 mg SODIUM; 383 mg CHOL

SPRING CARBONARA

BLT EGGS BENEDICT

BLT Eggs Benedict

MAKES 4 servings **PREP** 15 minutes
BAKE at 400° for 25 minutes **COOK** 11 minutes

- 8 slices bacon
- ¾ cup fat-free buttermilk
- 8 eggs plus 1 yolk
- 1 tablespoon cornstarch
- ¼ teaspoon plus ⅛ salt
  Pinch of cayenne
- 2 tablespoons fresh lemon juice
- 2 tablespoons chopped chives
- 1 tablespoon unsalted butter
- 2 tomatoes on the vine, sliced
- 8 slices whole wheat bread, toasted
- 2 cups arugula

■ Heat oven to 400°. Place bacon on a rimmed baking sheet fitted with a wire rack. Bake at 400° for 20 to 25 minutes, until crispy.

■ Fill a large, deep-sided skillet three-fourths full with water. Bring water to barely simmering and cover. Meanwhile, in a small pot, whisk buttermilk, egg yolk, cornstarch, ¼ teaspoon of the salt and the cayenne over medium heat until smooth. Cook, stirring constantly, until liquid barely simmers and is thickened, about 3 minutes, being careful not to scramble egg. Remove from heat and stir in lemon juice, chives and butter. Cover with lid to keep warm.

■ Sprinkle tomatoes with remaining ⅛ teaspoon salt. Place 2 slices toasted bread on each plate. Top with some sliced tomatoes, ½ cup of the arugula and 2 slices bacon (each slice broken in half). Crack 4 of the eggs into separate cups. Pour into skillet of simmering water one by one. Poach eggs 3 to 4 minutes, until whites are set. Remove with a slotted spoon and place 1 on each slice. Repeat with remaining 4 eggs. Spoon sauce over eggs.

PER SERVING 421 **CAL**; 22 g **FAT** (8 g **SAT**); 27 g **PRO**; 30 g **CARB**; 5 g **FIBER**; 971 mg **SODIUM**; 498 mg **CHOL**

ISRAELI POACHED EGGS (SHAKSHUKA)

Israeli Poached Eggs (Shakshuka)

MAKES 4 servings **PREP** 10 minutes **COOK** 25 minutes **LET STAND** 5 minutes

- 1 tablespoon olive oil
- 1 cup diced yellow onion
- 3 cloves garlic, sliced
- 1 teaspoon harissa paste
- 1 teaspoon ground cumin
- 1 teaspoon ground turmeric
- 1 can (28 ounces) Cento crushed tomatoes
- 1 jar (12 ounces) roasted red peppers, drained and diced
- ¼ teaspoon salt
- ½ cup cilantro, chopped, plus more for garnish
- ½ cup crumbled feta
- 8 eggs
- 4 whole wheat pitas, warmed (optional)

■ Heat olive oil in a deep-sided skillet over medium heat. Add onion; cook 3 minutes. Stir in garlic, harissa, cumin and turmeric. Cook 2 more minutes. Mix in tomatoes, roasted peppers and salt. Simmer 10 minutes.

■ Stir in cilantro and two-thirds of the feta. Crack eggs, one by one, into a small dish and carefully pour them into sauce. Simmer 10 minutes. Cover and remove from heat. Let stand about 5 minutes, depending on desired doneness. Sprinkle with remaining feta. Garnish with additional cilantro and serve in a bowl with pita, if using.

PER SERVING 395 **CAL**; 18 g **FAT** (6 g **SAT**); 23 g **PRO**; 35 g **CARB**; 9 g **FIBER**; 807 mg **SODIUM**; 440 mg **CHOL**

SLICE IT UP

Liven up your daily bread with these flavor-packed combos.

Master Cornbread Recipe

- 1¼ **cups cornmeal**
- ¾ **cup all-purpose flour**
- ¼ **cup golden (or regular) flaxseed meal**
- 1½ **teaspoons baking powder**
- ½ **teaspoon salt**
- ½ **cup vegetable oil**
- ½ **cup plain yogurt or sour cream**
- 2 **large eggs**

■ Heat oven to 350°. Line a 9 x 5 x 3-inch loaf pan with nonstick foil. Set aside. In a medium bowl, whisk cornmeal, flour, flaxseed meal, baking powder and salt. In a large bowl, whisk oil, yogurt and eggs. Add other ingredients as directed in each variation that follows.

■ Mix dry ingredients into wet ingredients. Fold in any extras. Transfer batter to prepared pan and bake as directed. Cool completely on a wire rack.

Sun-Dried Tomato–Basil Cornbread

MAKES 1 loaf; 12 servings **PREP** 15 minutes **SOAK** 3 minutes **BAKE** at 350° for 50 minutes

■ Soak ½ cup chopped sun-dried tomatoes in 1 cup boiling water for 3 minutes. Drain, reserving ⅓ cup of the soaking liquid. Add ⅓ cup grated Parmesan, ¼ cup cornmeal, 2 tablespoons flaxseed meal, 1½ tablespoons sugar, 1½ teaspoons baking powder, ½ teaspoon crushed fennel seeds and ¼ teaspoon salt to dry ingredients. Whisk ¼ cup oil, ¼ cup sour cream, 1 large egg and the ⅓ cup soaking liquid into wet ingredients. Fold softened tomatoes and ⅓ cup chopped basil into mixed batter. Transfer to prepared pan and bake at 350° for 50 minutes.

PER SLICE 316 **CAL**; 19 g **FAT** (4 g **SAT**); 6 g **PRO**; 28 g **CARB**; 2 g **FIBER**; 312 mg **SODIUM**; 68 mg **CHOL**

MAPLE
BACON

Maple Bacon Cornbread

MAKES 1 loaf; 12 servings **PREP** 15 minutes **BAKE** at 350° for 48 minutes

■ Add ½ teaspoon baking powder to dry ingredients. Whisk ½ cup maple syrup into wet ingredients. Fold 8 slices cooked and crumbled bacon into mixed batter. Transfer to prepared pan and bake at 350° for 48 minutes.

PER SLICE 272 **CAL**; 15 g **FAT** (3 g **SAT**); 5 g **PRO**; 29 g **CARB**; 1 g **FIBER**; 246 mg **SODIUM**; 47 mg **CHOL**

SUN-DRIED
TOMATO-BASIL

SCALLION
AND HERB

LEMON
BLUEBERRY

Scallion and Herb Cornbread

MAKES 1 loaf; 12 servings **PREP** 15 minutes
BAKE at 350° for 50 minutes

■ Add ¼ cup cornmeal, 2 tablespoons flaxseed meal, 1½ tablespoons sugar, 1½ teaspoons baking powder and ¼ teaspoon salt to dry ingredients. Whisk ¼ cup sour cream, ¼ cup oil, 1 large egg and ⅓ cup milk into wet ingredients. Fold in ½ cup chopped scallions, 3 tablespoons chopped cilantro and 3 tablespoons chopped chives. Transfer to prepared pan and bake at 350° for 50 minutes.

PER SLICE 300 **CAL**; 19 g **FAT** (3 g **SAT**); 5 g **PRO**; 26 g **CARB**; 2 g **FIBER**; 259 mg **SODIUM**; 67 mg **CHOL**

Lemon Blueberry Cornbread

MAKES 1 loaf; 12 servings **PREP** 15 minutes
BAKE at 350° for 1 hour 5 minutes

■ Add ¼ cup all-purpose flour and ¼ teaspoon baking soda to dry ingredients. Whisk ½ cup agave syrup, ⅓ cup packed light brown sugar, ¼ cup lemon juice and 2 teaspoons lemon zest into wet ingredients. Toss 1 package (6 ounces) blueberries with 1 tablespoon all-purpose flour and fold into mixed batter. Transfer to prepared pan and bake at 350° for 60 to 65 minutes.

PER SLICE 301 **CAL**; 13 g **FAT** (2 g **SAT**); 4 g **PRO**; 42 g **CARB**; 2 g **FIBER**; 190 mg **SODIUM**; 43 mg **CHOL**

Master Whole Wheat Recipe

1¾ cups whole wheat flour

⅓ cup wheat germ

2 teaspoons baking powder

½ teaspoon salt

2 large eggs

¼ cup vegetable oil

■ Heat oven to 350°. Line a 9 x 5 x 3-inch loaf pan with nonstick foil. Set aside. In a medium bowl, whisk flour, wheat germ, baking powder and salt. In a large bowl, whisk eggs and oil. Add other ingredients as directed in each variation that follows.

■ Mix dry ingredients into wet ingredients. Fold in any extras. Transfer batter to prepared pan and bake as directed. Cool completely on a wire rack.

SPINACH FETA

BANANA ALMOND

Spinach Feta Whole Wheat Bread

MAKES 1 loaf; 12 servings **PREP** 15 minutes
BAKE at 350° for 58 minutes

■ Add ½ teaspoon salt to dry ingredients. Add 1 cup milk and ⅓ cup oil to wet ingredients. Once blended, fold in ¾ cup crumbled feta cheese, ½ cup thawed frozen spinach (squeezed dry) and 2 tablespoons chopped dill. Transfer to prepared pan and bake at 350° for 55 to 58 minutes.

PER SLICE 220 **CAL**; 15 g **FAT** (3 g **SAT**); 7 g **PRO**; 16 g **CARB**; 3 g **FIBER**; 329 mg **SODIUM**; 48 mg **CHOL**

Banana Almond Whole Wheat Bread

MAKES 1 loaf; 12 servings **PREP** 15 minutes
BAKE at 350° for 60 minutes

■ Add 2 tablespoons wheat germ to dry ingredients. Add 3 very ripe bananas, peeled and mashed; ¼ cup milk; ½ cup packed light brown sugar; ⅓ cup almond butter and ¼ cup apple butter to wet ingredients. Transfer to prepared pan and top with ¼ cup sliced almonds. Bake at 350° for 60 minutes.

PER SLICE 260 **CAL**; 12 g **FAT** (1 g **SAT**); 7 g **PRO**; 35 g **CARB**; 4 g **FIBER**; 200 mg **SODIUM**; 38 mg **CHOL**

MILLET
SUNFLOWER
CHIP

Millet Sunflower Chip Whole Wheat Bread

MAKES 1 loaf; 12 servings **PREP** 15 minutes
BAKE at 350° for 60 minutes

■ Add 1 cup coconut palm sugar,
¾ cup milk, ¼ cup oil and 1 teaspoon
vanilla extract to wet ingredients.
Once blended, fold in ½ cup each
millet, sunflower seeds and miniature
chocolate chips. Transfer to prepared
pan and bake at 350° for 60 minutes.

PER SLICE 343 **CAL**; 17 g **FAT** (3 g **SAT**); 8 g
PRO; 44 g **CARB**; 5 g **FIBER**; 213 mg **SODIUM**;
39 mg **CHOL**

Cherry Tangerine Whole Wheat Bread

MAKES 1 loaf; 12 servings **PREP** 15 minutes
BAKE at 350° for 60 minutes

■ Add ¼ teaspoon ground cardamom
to dry ingredients, if desired. Add
½ cup orange or tangerine juice,
½ cup oil, ⅓ cup honey, ⅓ cup packed
light brown sugar and 2 teaspoons
tangerine or orange zest to wet
ingredients. Once blended, fold in
1¼ cups fresh or thawed frozen pitted
cherries, quartered. Transfer to
prepared pan and bake at 350° for
60 minutes.

PER SLICE 288 **CAL**; 16 g **FAT** (1 g **SAT**); 5 g
PRO; 36 g **CARB**; 3 g **FIBER**; 181 mg **SODIUM**;
38 mg **CHOL**

CHERRY
TANGERINE

CHOCOLATE-COCONUT
BARS, PAGE 145

123

137

144

MORE, POR FAVOR!

Celebrate Cinco De Mayo with these south-of-the-border slow cooker recipes.

BEEF TACOS WITH
CHUNKY GUACAMOLE,
PAGE 127

SALSA VERDE PORK
RIBS, PAGE 124

ANCHO PORK AND
BLACK BEAN
TOSTADAS

A slow-cooked pork shoulder makes perfect party food—it feeds a lot of people for not a lot of money—and it can be seasoned and served in so many ways.

Ancho Pork and Black Bean Tostadas

MAKES 10 tostadas, plus 5 cups pork mixture for another meal PREP 30 minutes SLOW COOK on HIGH for 6 hours or LOW for 8 hours
COOK 10 minutes

3½	pounds boneless pork shoulder or butt
1	teaspoon salt
½	teaspoon black pepper
2	teaspoons ancho chile powder
1	teaspoon ground cumin
1	teaspoon dried oregano
¼	teaspoon cinnamon
1	onion, chopped
4	cloves garlic, chopped
8	plum tomatoes, seeded and chopped
1	cup chicken broth
1	can (15 ounces) black beans, drained and rinsed
2	cups vegetable oil
10	corn tortillas
3	cups shredded iceberg lettuce
	Pineapple-Habanero Salsa (recipe follows)

■ Coat slow cooker bowl with nonstick cooking spray. Season pork with salt and pepper. Place in slow cooker. Sprinkle with ancho chile powder, cumin, oregano and cinnamon.

■ Place onion, garlic and tomatoes around pork. Pour broth down sides of bowl.

■ Cover and cook on HIGH for 6 hours or LOW for 8 hours.

■ Remove pork to a cutting board and shred with 2 forks. Return to slow cooker; stir in beans and heat through.

■ Heat oil in a skillet to 375°. Cook tortillas in batches 1 minute per side or until crisp. Place on a paper-towel-lined baking sheet.

■ Top each tortilla with ½ cup of the pork, some shredded lettuce and Pineapple-Habanero Salsa.

PER TOSTADA 255 CAL; 16 g FAT (2 g SAT); 11 g PRO; 20 g CARB; 4 g FIBER; 312 mg SODIUM; 24 mg CHOL

Pineapple-Habanero Salsa

■ Combine 2½ cups diced fresh pineapple; ¼ cup finely chopped sweet pepper; 1 habanero pepper, seeded and chopped; 2 tablespoons chopped cilantro; and 1 tablespoon each lime and olive oil. Season with ⅛ teaspoon salt.

SALSA VERDE PORK RIBS

Triple-Cheese Chicken Enchiladas

MAKES 10 servings **PREP** 20 minutes
COOK 10 minutes
SLOW COOK on LOW for 4 hours
COOL 30 minutes

- 2 **tablespoons olive oil**
- 1½ **pounds ground chicken**
- 1 **cup chopped onion**
- 2 **Cubanelle peppers, seeded and chopped**
- 3 **cloves garlic, chopped**
- 1 **can (8 ounces) tomato sauce**
- 1 **can (15 ounces) kidney beans, drained and rinsed**
- 1 **can (15 ounces) pinto beans, drained and rinsed**
- 2 **teaspoons chili powder**
- ½ **teaspoon ground cumin**
- ½ **teaspoon salt**
- 2 **cups shredded Monterey Jack**
- 2 **cups shredded cheddar**
- 1 **cup shredded Swiss cheese**
- 13 **corn tortillas**

■ Heat oil in a large skillet over medium-high heat. Add chicken, onion, peppers and garlic. Cook 8 minutes, stirring occasionally.

■ Stir in tomato sauce, beans, chili powder, cumin and salt. Simmer 2 minutes. In a large bowl, combine cheeses.

■ Line a round 4-quart slow cooker bowl with a slow cooker liner. Coat liner with nonstick cooking spray.

■ Fit 2½ tortillas into bottom of slow cooker; top with 1½ cups of the chicken mixture and ¾ cup of the cheese mixture. Repeat layering 3 times. For the final layer, fit 3 tortillas into slow cooker. Top with remaining chicken mixture and cheese.

■ Cook on LOW for 4 hours. Let cool at least 30 minutes before cutting into wedges.

PER SERVING 468 **CAL**; 26 g **FAT** (11 g **SAT**); 30 g **PRO**; 30 g **CARB**; 7 g **FIBER**; 1,002 mg **SODIUM**; 94 mg **CHOL**

Salsa Verde Pork Ribs

MAKES 8 servings **PREP** 10 minutes **SLOW COOK** on HIGH for 6 hours or LOW for 8 hours
BROIL 4 minutes

- 1 **jar (16 ounces) tomatillo salsa**
- ½ **red onion, diced**
- 2 **jalapeños, seeded and diced**
- ½ **cup cilantro leaves**
- 3 **cloves garlic, chopped**
- 1 **teaspoon salt**
- ¾ **teaspoon black pepper**
- 4 **pounds pork ribs, cut into 2 sections**
- ¾ **teaspoon ground coriander**
- ½ **teaspoon ground cumin**
  Pepitas and chopped scallion, for garnish (optional)

■ Coat slow cooker bowl with nonstick cooking spray. In a large bowl, combine tomatillo salsa, onion, jalapeños, cilantro, garlic and ½ teaspoon each of the salt and pepper.

■ Season ribs with remaining ½ teaspoon salt and ¼ teaspoon pepper, the coriander and cumin. Place in slow cooker; pour tomatillo mixture over top.

■ Cook on HIGH for 6 hours or LOW for 8 hours.

■ Heat broiler to high. Cut ribs apart; place on a broiler pan and spoon some sauce over top. Broil 3 to 4 minutes, until browned and slightly crispy.

■ Serve ribs garnished with pepitas and scallion, if using.

PER SERVING 336 **CAL**; 24 g **FAT** (8 g **SAT**); 27 g **PRO**; 3 g **CARB**; 0 g **FIBER**; 666 mg **SODIUM**; 99 mg **CHOL**

TRIPLE-CHEESE
CHICKEN ENCHILADAS

**MEXICAN MEATBALLS
IN CHIPOTLE SAUCE**

BEEF TACOS WITH
CHUNKY GUACAMOLE

Mexican Meatballs in Chipotle Sauce

MAKES 24 meatballs **PREP** 20 minutes
SLOW COOK on HIGH for 3 hours

- 1½ **pounds ground beef, pork and veal mixture or ground chuck**
- 1 **cup bread crumbs**
- ¼ **cup milk**
- 2 **eggs, lightly beaten**
- 2 **teaspoons chili powder**
- 1 **teaspoon garlic powder**
- 1 **teaspoon salt**
- 1 **teaspoon ground cumin**
- 1 **can (28 ounces) fire-roasted crushed tomatoes**
- ½ **cup chicken broth**
- 3 **cloves garlic, chopped**
- 1 **teaspoon dried oregano**
- 3 **chipotles in adobo, chopped**
- 2 **tablespoons chopped cilantro**

■ In a large bowl, combine ground meat, bread crumbs, milk, eggs, chili powder, garlic powder and ½ teaspoon each of the salt and cumin. Form mixture into 24 meatballs, using about 1 tablespoonful for each.

■ Coat slow cooker bowl with nonstick cooking spray. Stir in tomatoes, broth, garlic, oregano, remaining ½ teaspoon each salt and cumin, and the chipotles. Add meatballs.

■ Cook on HIGH for 3 hours. Stir in cilantro before serving.

PER MEATBALL 88 **CAL**; 4 g **FAT** (1 g **SAT**); 7 g **PRO**; 6 g **CARB**; 1 g **FIBER**; 265 mg **SODIUM**; 34 mg **CHOL**

Beef Tacos with Chunky Guacamole

MAKES 12 tacos, plus 3 cups beef mixture for another meal **PREP** 15 minutes **COOK** 12 minutes
SLOW COOK on HIGH for 6 hours or LOW for 8 hours

- 1 **beef chuck roast (about 3½ pounds)**
- 1 **teaspoon salt**
- ½ **teaspoon black pepper**
- 2 **tablespoons vegetable oil**
- 2 **teaspoons chili powder**
- 1 **teaspoon ground cumin**
- ½ **teaspoon cayenne pepper**
- 1 **onion, chopped**
- 1 **sweet red pepper, seeded and chopped**
- 4 **cloves garlic, sliced**
- 1 **cup beef broth**
- 12 **fajita-size flour tortillas, heated gently**
  Chunky Guacamole (recipe follows)

■ Season roast with salt and pepper. Heat oil in a large skillet over medium-high heat; add roast and brown on all sides, about 12 minutes total. Remove and discard strings if roast is tied.

■ Coat slow cooker bowl with nonstick cooking spray. Place roast in slow cooker and season with chili powder, cumin and cayenne. Top with onion, sweet pepper and garlic. Pour broth over top.

■ Cook on HIGH for 6 hours or LOW for 8 hours.

■ Remove roast to a cutting board and shred with 2 forks. Stir meat back into liquid in slow cooker.

■ Wrap ¼ cup beef mixture in each warmed tortilla and top with Chunky Guacamole.

PER TACO 386 **CAL**; 24 g **FAT** (6 g **SAT**); 19 g **PRO**; 24 g **CARB**; 6 g **FIBER**; 517 mg **SODIUM**; 57 mg **CHOL**

Chunky Guacamole

■ Coarsely mash 4 ripe avocados in a medium bowl. Stir in ½ cup finely chopped red onion, ½ cup quartered grape tomatoes, 1 seeded and chopped jalapeño, 2 tablespoons lime juice, 2 tablespoons chopped cilantro, 1 tablespoon olive oil and ¼ teaspoon salt.

HOUSE SPECIAL

Foodie moms and bloggers offer these kid-friendly weeknight meals.

SWEET POTATO AND TURKEY
SHEPHERD'S PIE,
PAGE 131

SPAGHETTI SQUASH AND BLACK BEAN
TACOS WITH QUESO FRESCO, PAGE 132

SHRIMP UN-FRIED RICE

Fried rice and shepherd's pie—two traditional favorites—get a nutrition boost with ingredients such as whole grain brown rice, sweet potatoes and lean ground turkey.

SWEET POTATO AND TURKEY SHEPHERD'S PIE

Shrimp Un-Fried Rice

MAKES 4 servings **PREP** 10 minutes
COOK 11 minutes

- 1 tablespoon + 2 teaspoons vegetable oil
- 4 eggs, whisked
- 1 sweet red pepper, diced
- ½ cup shelled edamame
- 1 clove garlic, minced
- ½ pound peeled and deveined shrimp
- ¼ teaspoon salt
- 4 cups cooked brown rice
- 4 teaspoons low-sodium soy sauce
- 1 tablespoon sesame seeds
- 1 tablespoon diced scallions

■ Heat 1 teaspoon of the oil in a skillet over medium heat. Add whisked eggs and scramble 1 minute. Remove to a plate.

■ Heat remaining 2 teaspoons oil. Add sweet pepper and cook 3 to 4 minutes, until soft. Add edamame and garlic; cook 1 more minute. Add shrimp and salt. Cook 3 more minutes, until shrimp are pink.

■ Stir in cooked eggs, rice, soy sauce and sesame seeds. Cook 2 minutes, until just heated through. Top with scallions and serve.

PER SERVING 410 CAL; 12 g FAT (3 g SAT); 24 g PRO; 50 g CARB; 5 g FIBER; 830 mg SODIUM; 275 mg CHOL

Sweet Potato and Turkey Shepherd's Pie

MAKES 10 servings **PREP** 15 minutes **COOK** 38 minutes **BAKE** at 350° for 1 hour

- 2½ pounds sweet potatoes, peeled and cut into 2-inch pieces
- ¼ cup light brown sugar
- 4 tablespoons unsalted butter
- 1½ teaspoons salt
- 3 tablespoons olive oil
- 2 cups diced yellow onion
- 3 cups quartered button mushrooms
- 2 pounds ground turkey
- 1 tablespoon minced garlic
- 2 teaspoons smoked paprika
- 2 teaspoons turmeric
- 2 teaspoons ground cumin
- ½ teaspoon ground chipotle pepper
- 8 ounces tomato sauce
- 10 ounces frozen spinach, thawed
- ⅔ cup grated Parmesan

■ Heat oven to 350°. Place sweet potatoes in a medium pot and cover with water. Bring to a boil, reduce to a simmer and cook until fork-tender, about 10 minutes. Drain and return to pot over low heat. Add sugar, butter and ½ teaspoon of the salt. Mash sweet potatoes and mix until ingredients are incorporated.

■ Heat 1 tablespoon of the oil in a large skillet over medium heat. Add onion and ½ teaspoon of the remaining salt; cook 5 minutes. Push onion to edge of pan. Pour in another 1 tablespoon of the oil and add mushrooms. Cook 2 minutes without stirring, allowing mushrooms to brown. Mix with onion; cook 2 minutes more. Transfer to a plate.

■ Add remaining 1 tablespoon oil to pan. Stir in turkey, breaking up meat with a spatula. Season with remaining ½ teaspoon salt, the garlic, smoked paprika, turmeric, cumin and chipotle. Cook 4 minutes. Stir in onion and mushrooms, tomato sauce, spinach and 1 cup water. Bring to a simmer and cook 10 to 15 minutes, until mixture thickens.

■ Spread turkey mixture into a 9 x 13-inch baking dish. Spread mashed sweet potatoes over the top in an even layer. Sprinkle with Parmesan. Bake at 350° for 1 hour, uncovered.

PER SERVING 360 CAL; 18 g FAT (6 g SAT); 23 g PRO; 28 g CARB; 4 g FIBER; 670 mg SODIUM; 85 mg CHOL

SPAGHETTI SQUASH AND BLACK BEAN TACOS WITH QUESO FRESCO

Carroty Mac and Cheese

MAKES 6 servings **PREP** 15 minutes
COOK 7 minutes **BAKE** at 375° for 40 minutes

2	**cups whole wheat macaroni**
2½	**cups coarsely grated carrots (about 8 small)**
2½	**cups grated reduced-fat sharp cheddar**
2	**tablespoons unsalted butter, cut into pieces**
½	**cup sour cream**
½	**cup milk**
3	**eggs**
¾	**teaspoon salt**
¾	**teaspoon mustard powder**
¼	**teaspoon freshly cracked black pepper**
¼	**cup finely grated Parmesan**

■ Heat oven to 375°. Arrange a rack in top third of oven. Grease an 8-inch-square or 2-quart oval baking pan.

■ Cook macaroni as per package directions (about 7 minutes) in a large pot of salted boiling water. Add carrots 1 minute before pasta is finished cooking; drain well in a fine-mesh strainer.

■ While pasta is hot, stir in all but ½ cup of the cheddar and the butter. In a bowl, whisk sour cream, milk, eggs, salt, mustard powder and pepper. Fold mixture into pasta.

■ Scrape mixture into prepared pan. Sprinkle remaining ½ cup cheddar and the Parmesan over the top. Bake at 375° until firm to touch and golden-brown, 30 to 40 minutes.

PER SERVING 410 **CAL**; 21 g **FAT** (12 g **SAT**); 23 g **PRO**; 34 g **CARB**; 4 g **FIBER**; 810 mg **SODIUM**; 155 mg **CHOL**

Spaghetti Squash and Black Bean Tacos with Queso Fresco

MAKES 4 servings **PREP** 15 minutes **MICROWAVE** 17 minutes **COOK** 16 minutes

3	**pounds spaghetti squash (1 large)**
2	**tablespoons lime juice**
1	**tablespoon chili powder**
½	**teaspoon ground cumin**
½	**teaspoon ground coriander**
½	**teaspoon coarse salt**
16	**6-inch corn tortillas**
1	**can (15 ounces) black beans, drained and rinsed**
4	**ounces queso fresco, feta or Cotija cheese, crumbled**
¼	**cup finely diced red or white onion**
¼	**cup chopped cilantro**
	Hot sauce and lime wedges (optional)

■ Pierce squash (about 1-inch deep) all over with a knife. Place in a microwave-safe dish and microwave on HIGH for 7 minutes. Turn squash over and microwave another 8 to 10 minutes, until slightly soft. Cool 5 minutes. (Alternatively, you can roast squash. Cut in half lengthwise, scoop out seeds and roast cut sides down in an oiled baking pan at 375° for 40 minutes.)

■ Scoop squash flesh into a bowl, discarding seeds and skin. In a small bowl, whisk lime juice, chili powder, cumin, coriander and salt. Pour over squash and gently toss.

■ Heat a skillet over medium-high heat. Warm and slightly blister tortillas, about 30 seconds per side. Transfer to a platter and top each tortilla with 2 tablespoons each beans and squash and 2 teaspoons cheese. Garnish with onion and cilantro and, if using, hot sauce and lime wedges.

PER SERVING 430 **CAL**; 10 g **FAT** (4 g **SAT**); 17 g **PRO**; 69 g **CARB**; 15 g **FIBER**; 814 mg **SODIUM**; 20 mg **CHOL**

Chicken in Dijon Cream

MAKES 4 servings **PREP** 20 minutes **COOK** 11 minutes

- **4 boneless, skinless chicken breast halves (about 2 pounds)**
- **½ teaspoon plus ⅛ teaspoon kosher salt**
- **1 tablespoon extra-virgin olive oil**
- **½ tablespoon unsalted butter**
- **½ small onion, minced**
- **¼ cup dry white wine**
- **1 cup chicken stock**
- **1 tablespoon Dijon mustard**
- **¼ cup heavy cream**
- **1½ teaspoons chopped fresh thyme**
- **1½ teaspoons chopped fresh tarragon**

■ On a large cutting board, place chicken between sheets of wax paper. Pound with a meat mallet, rolling pin or heavy skillet until meat is an even ½ inch in thickness. Season chicken with ½ teaspoon salt (¼ teaspoon on each side).

■ Heat a large skillet over medium-high heat. Coat with oil, then add butter. When butter is foamy but not brown, add half the chicken. Cook until browned, about 3 minutes. Flip chicken and cook until browned but not cooked through, about 2 additional minutes. Transfer to a plate. Repeat with remaining chicken.

■ Add onion to skillet. Cook 1 minute, scraping brown bits from pan. Add wine and cook until reduced by half, about 1 minute, then add stock. Simmer 1 minute.

■ Whisk in mustard and cook 1 minute. Stir in cream and remaining ⅛ teaspoon salt. Bring to a boil; reduce heat to a simmer, then add chicken back to pan with its juices. Simmer until chicken is cooked through, about 2 minutes. Stir in thyme and tarragon.

PER SERVING 390 **CAL**; 17 g **FAT** (6 g **SAT**); 52 g **PRO**; 2 g **CARB**; 0 g **FIBER**; 730 mg **SODIUM**; 190 mg **CHOL**

SWEET SWAPS

Indulge your sweet tooth with something new—desserts made with a variety of alternative natural sweeteners.

MAPLE AND VANILLA-ROASTED FRUIT, PAGE 138

Raspberry Lemonade Yogurt Pops

MAKES about ten 2½-ounce pops
PREP 15 minutes **FREEZE** at least 6 hours

- 12 ounces fresh or thawed frozen raspberries
- ⅔ cup light agave nectar or honey
- 1 vanilla bean, split lengthwise
- 1 tablespoon freshly squeezed lemon juice
- 1 teaspoon finely grated lemon zest
- ⅛ teaspoon fine sea salt
- 1 cup 2% Greek yogurt

■ In a medium saucepan, combine raspberries, agave nectar, ½ cup water, vanilla bean, lemon juice, lemon zest and salt. Set saucepan over medium-high heat and stir gently until mixture comes to a full boil. Remove saucepan from heat and let cool completely. Pull vanilla pod from saucepan. Using the back of a knife, scrape any remaining vanilla seeds into saucepan and discard pod.

■ Pour raspberry mixture into a blender or the bowl of a food processor fitted with the steel blade. Puree until smooth. Add yogurt and 3 tablespoons water and process until well blended. Transfer mixture to a large spouted measuring cup for easy pouring, and pour into Popsicle molds. Insert wooden sticks. Freeze until firm.

**ALL-PURPOSE CUPCAKES
WITH SOFT, FLUFFY MERINGUE**

Nondairy milk (coconut, soy or almond) and honey, maple syrup or agave nectar stand in for cow's milk and processed white sugar in these tender-crumb cupcakes.

All-Purpose Cupcakes

MAKES 1 dozen cupcakes **PREP** 15 minutes **BAKE** at 350° for 20 minutes

- 2 **cups unbleached all-purpose flour, spooned and leveled**
- 1 **teaspoon baking powder**
- ½ **teaspoon baking soda**
- ½ **teaspoon fine sea salt**
- 1 **cup full-fat coconut, soy or almond milk (see Note)**
- ¾ **cup honey, pure maple syrup or agave nectar**
- ⅓ **cup grapeseed, vegetable or coconut oil**
- 1 **tablespoon freshly squeezed lemon juice**
- 1 **tablespoon pure vanilla extract**

■ Position a rack in center of oven and heat oven to 350˚. Line a 12-cup muffin tin with paper liners.

■ In a large bowl, whisk flour, baking powder, baking soda and salt.

■ In a medium bowl, whisk milk, honey, oil, lemon juice and vanilla. Pour wet ingredients into dry. Beat with a handheld electric mixer on medium-high speed until smooth and slightly aerated, about 2 minutes.

■ Divide batter among wells of muffin tin, filling them about three-quarters full. Bake at 350° until lightly golden, a toothpick inserted into center of cupcakes comes out clean and tops spring back when lightly touched, 18 to 20 minutes. Rotate pan 180° halfway through baking time. Let cakes cool in pan on a wire rack 3 minutes before removing from pan to cool completely.

Note: You have many mix-and-match options when it comes to the nondairy milks and sweeteners here. An ideal pairing is full-fat coconut milk, for richness, plus honey—or agave if you want to make a truly vegan cake. But any combination of the sweeteners, milks and oils listed in the recipe works just fine. This is a great basic cake that can be flavored with any variety of zests, spices and extracts.

Soft, Fluffy Meringue

MAKES about 5 cups **PREP** 25 minutes **COOK** 3 minutes

- 3 **large egg whites, at room temperature**
- 2 **teaspoons cornstarch**
- ⅔ **cup honey or pure maple syrup**
- ¼ **teaspoon fine sea salt**
- 2 **teaspoons pure vanilla extract**

■ Into the bowl of an electric mixer fitted with the whisk attachment, add egg whites. Whip on medium-high speed until soft peaks form. Add cornstarch and continue whipping until firm peaks form, about 1 minute more. Stop mixer.

■ In a medium saucepan, combine honey, 2 tablespoons water and salt. Set saucepan over high heat. Stir mixture gently to combine as it heats to a boil. When syrup has begun to bubble, clip a candy thermometer onto side of saucepan. Cook syrup until temperature reaches 248˚. Remove saucepan from heat, and with a mitted hand, carefully carry it over to mixer. Restart mixer on medium speed. Slowly drizzle syrup into whipping egg whites—just a tablespoon or two at a time at first to avoid scrambling egg whites. When all the syrup has been added, increase mixer speed to high and whip meringue until it is stiff and glossy and bowl is cool to the touch, about 5 minutes. Beat in vanilla during the last minute.

■ Use immediately as a frosting or filling.

CHOCOLATE CHIP OATMEAL RAISIN TREATS

Maple and Vanilla-Roasted Fruit

MAKES 3 to 4 cups, depending on the type of fruit **PREP** 10 minutes
ROAST at 375° for 50 minutes

- ⅓ **cup maple sugar**
- 1 **vanilla bean**
- 1 **teaspoon finely grated lemon zest**
- 2 **pounds seasonal fruit, peeled, halved, cored and/or pitted**
- 1 **tablespoon freshly squeezed lemon juice**
- 1 **tablespoon unsalted butter, cut into small bits**

   Ice cream, yogurt or crème fraîche, for serving (optional)

- Position a rack in center of oven and heat oven to 375°.

- Place sugar in a small bowl. With a sharp knife, split vanilla bean in half lengthwise and scrape seeds into sugar (reserve the vanilla pod). Work sugar, vanilla seeds and lemon zest together with your fingertips until sugar is fragrant and moist-looking.

- Arrange fruit in a 9 x 13-inch metal baking dish, cut side up. Drizzle with lemon juice and sprinkle with sugar. Dot butter bits all over fruit. Add vanilla pod and 2 tablespoons water to dish.

- Roast at 375° for 30 minutes, occasionally spooning pan juices over fruit. Turn fruit and continue to roast, basting once or twice, until tender, 15 to 20 minutes more.

- Serve with ice cream, yogurt or crème fraîche, if using.

Chocolate Chip Oatmeal Raisin Treats

MAKES 40 servings **PREP** 15 minutes **LET STAND** 10 minutes **REFRIGERATE** 30 minutes

- 1 **cup pitted Medjool dates, tightly packed (see Note)**
- 1¾ **cups old-fashioned rolled oats**
- ¾ **cup raisins**
- ⅓ **cup bittersweet chocolate chips (60% to 70% cacao)**
- 1 **generous tablespoon natural peanut, almond or sunflower seed butter**
- 1 **teaspoon chia seeds**
- ½ **teaspoon ground cinnamon**
- ¾ **teaspoon pure vanilla extract**
- ⅛ **teaspoon fine sea salt**

- Place dates in a medium bowl. Fill bowl with hot water to cover dates by about an inch. Let stand 10 minutes. Drain.

- Combine all ingredients in the bowl of a food processor. Process continuously until mixture comes together, forming a dough of sorts.

You want the oats to be pretty much completely broken down, with a few bits of raisins and little chips of chocolate still visible.

- Using a teaspoon-size scoop, portion out small pieces of dough, using your hands to roll them into balls about 1 inch in diameter. Place balls on a cookie sheet. Refrigerate until firm, about 30 minutes. Once chilled, transfer to an airtight container to store in the fridge for up to 10 days.

Note: The dates should be nice and tacky here, more like a delicious edible "glue" than a soft fruit puree, so you should soak them less than you would if you were making baked goods. Medjool dates work best in this recipe because they're extra sticky, but Deglet Noor dates work too—they may require about 10 minutes more soaking time.

MAPLE AND
VANILLA–
ROASTED FRUIT

PARTY PEOPLE

Your next get-together just got a little better thanks to this all-purpose crowd-pleasing menu.

Buffalo Deviled Eggs

MAKES 18 servings **PREP** 10 minutes **COOK** 10 minutes **LET STAND** 10 minutes

- **9 large eggs**
- **2 tablespoons bottled blue cheese dressing**
- **2 tablespoons light mayonnaise**
- **2 tablespoons Frank's hot sauce, plus more for drizzling**
- **1 celery rib, finely diced**
- **2 tablespoons crumbled blue cheese**
- **2 tablespoons celery leaves, chopped (optional)**

■ Place eggs in a medium saucepan. Add cold water to cover by 1 inch. Bring to a boil, then reduce heat to medium and simmer 10 minutes. Drain and run under cool water. Let stand in cool water 10 minutes.

■ Peel eggs and cut in half lengthwise. If making ahead, refrigerate peeled eggs in a resealable bag overnight. Place yolks in a medium bowl and whites on a platter. Add dressing, mayonnaise and hot sauce to yolks and mash with a fork until smooth. Stir in celery and blue cheese; transfer to a quart-size resealable plastic bag. Snip off a ¾-inch corner and pipe mixture into egg whites. Garnish with chopped celery leaves, if desired, and drizzle with more hot sauce.

PER EGG HALF 56 **CAL**; 4 g **FAT** (1 g **SAT**); 3 g **PRO**; 1 g **CARB**; 0 g **FIBER**; 120 mg **SODIUM**; 95 mg **CHOL**

BUFFALO DEVILED EGGS

**BLACK BEAN AND
AVOCADO DIP, PAGE 143**

**PIMENTO CHEESE
CROSTINI, PAGE 142**

ASPARAGUS ORZO SALAD

Pimiento Cheese Crostini

MAKES 40 crostini PREP 15 minutes
REFRIGERATE 1 hour TOAST 4 minutes

- 8 **ounces sharp cheddar, shredded**
- 4 **ounces cream cheese**
- ¼ **cup light mayonnaise**
- 1 **small jar (4 ounces) pimientos, drained and chopped**
- 2 **scallions, trimmed and sliced**
- 1 **teaspoon garlic powder**
  Pinch cayenne pepper
- 1 **large baguette, cut into forty ¼-inch slices**
- 3 **tablespoons olive oil**

■ In a bowl, combine cheddar, cream cheese and mayonnaise. Beat with a hand mixer on medium speed until blended and fairly smooth. Stir in pimientos, scallions, garlic powder and cayenne. Cover and refrigerate at least 1 hour or overnight.

■ Heat broiler to high. Place baguette slices on 2 small baking sheets. Brush on both sides with oil. Toast under broiler (4 inches from heat) 2 minutes. Flip over and broil another 1 to 2 minutes.

■ Spread 1 heaping tablespoon pimento cheese on each toast.

PER CROSTINO 95 CAL; 5 g FAT (2 g SAT); 3 g PRO; 10 g CARB; 1 g FIBER; 163 mg SODIUM; 10 mg CHOL

PIMIENTO CHEESE CROSTINI

Asparagus Orzo Salad

MAKES 12 servings PREP 15 minutes COOK 11 minutes

- 1 **bunch thin asparagus, trimmed and cut into 1-inch pieces**
- 1 **box (16 ounces) orzo pasta**
- 1 **cup crumbled feta cheese**
- ⅔ **cup flat Italian parsley leaves, chopped**
  Zest of 1 lemon (about 1 tablespoon)
- ⅓ **cup fresh lemon juice**
- 1 **tablespoon plain yogurt or sour cream**
- 1½ **teaspoons sugar**
- ¾ **teaspoon salt**
- ¼ **teaspoon black pepper**
- ½ **cup extra-virgin olive oil**

■ Bring a large pot of lightly salted water to a boil. Blanch asparagus in boiling water for 2 minutes. Remove to a bowl with a slotted spoon and run under cold water to stop cooking. Return water to boiling. Add orzo and cook according to package directions, about 9 minutes. Drain and rinse with cold water.

■ In a large serving bowl, combine orzo, asparagus, feta, parsley and lemon zest. In a medium bowl, whisk lemon juice, yogurt, sugar, ¼ teaspoon of the salt, the pepper and oil. Set aside ¼ cup of the dressing; add remaining dressing to salad along with remaining ½ teaspoon salt. Toss to combine; refrigerate until serving.

■ Immediately before serving, toss salad with reserved ¼ cup dressing. Serve chilled or at room temperature.

PER SERVING 268 CAL; 13 g FAT (3 g SAT); 7 g PRO; 31 g CARB; 2 g FIBER; 263 mg SODIUM; 12 mg CHOL

KOREAN-STYLE FRIED WINGS

Korean-Style Fried Wings

MAKES 24 pieces **PREP** 20 minutes **FRY** 36 minutes (12 minutes per batch)

- 6 **cups peanut oil**
- ¼ **cup cornstarch**
- 1 **teaspoon salt**
- ½ **teaspoon ground black pepper**
- ¼ **teaspoon cayenne pepper**
- ¾ **cup all-purpose flour**
- ¾ **cup cold water**
- 3 **cups panko bread crumbs, crushed**
- 24 **chicken wing pieces (about 3½ pounds)**

  Bottled Korean BBQ sauce, for dipping

■ Place oil in a medium saucepan fitted with a deep-fry thermometer. Heat to 350°.

■ In a large bowl, whisk cornstarch, ½ teaspoon of the salt, the pepper and cayenne. In a second bowl, whisk flour and cold water. Place panko in a third bowl and season with remaining ½ teaspoon salt. Toss wing pieces in cornstarch mixture to coat.

■ Working in batches, dip wing pieces in flour batter, turning with tongs to coat completely. Lift from batter, allowing excess to drip back into bowl. Toss in panko and place on a wire rack set over a baking sheet.

■ Fry 8 wings at a time in hot oil for 6 minutes. Return to rack and repeat with remaining wings, allowing oil to return to 350° before adding next batch. Fry 6 more minutes per batch, until wings are golden, crispy and cooked through. Place on a paper-towel-lined baking sheet. Serve with BBQ sauce on the side, for dipping.

PER PIECE 149 **CAL**; 8 g **FAT** (2 g **SAT**); 8 g **PRO**; 12 g **CARB**; 0 g **FIBER**; 143 mg **SODIUM**; 40 mg **CHOL**

Black Bean and Avocado Dip

MAKES 5 cups (20 servings) **PREP** 20 minutes

- 1 **can (15.5 ounces) black beans, drained and rinsed**
- ½ **seedless cucumber, peeled and diced**
- 1 **orange, peeled, sections cut into ½-inch pieces**
- ¼ **cup chopped scallions**
- 2 **firm-ripe avocados, peeled, pitted and diced**
- 2 **tablespoons white wine vinegar**
- 2 **tablespoons olive oil**
- ½ **teaspoon salt**

  Ground black pepper

  Pita chips

■ In a medium bowl, toss black beans, cucumber, orange and scallions. If making in advance, do not cut up avocado until just before serving.

■ Add diced avocado to bowl and drizzle with vinegar and oil. Season with salt and pepper and gently stir, trying to keep avocado from getting smashed. Serve with chips.

PER ¼ CUP 120 **CAL**; 6 g **FAT** (1 g **SAT**); 3 g **PRO**; 14 g **CARB**; 4 g **FIBER**; 254 mg **SODIUM**; 0 mg **CHOL**

BLACK BEAN AND AVOCADO DIP

ROASTED TOMATO
PANZANELLA

Shrimp Salad Sliders

MAKES 12 servings **PREP** 25 minutes
COOK 3 minutes

- ½ **lemon**
- 1 **pound peeled and cleaned shrimp**
- 2 **ribs celery, finely diced**
- ⅓ **cup light mayonnaise**
- 1 **small shallot, minced (about 2 tablespoons)**
- 1 **tablespoon chopped fresh dill**
- 1 **tablespoon Dijon mustard**
- ¼ **teaspoon salt**
  Pinch cayenne pepper
- 12 **small soft dinner or slider rolls**
- 1 **cup packed arugula, chopped**

■ Bring a pot of water to a boil. Add juice from ½ lemon. Drop in shrimp and reduce heat to medium. Poach shrimp 2 to 3 minutes, until white. Drain and run under cold water until cool to the touch.

■ Finely chop shrimp and combine with celery, mayonnaise, shallot, dill, mustard, salt and cayenne. Cover and chill until serving.

■ Split rolls. Divide shrimp mixture evenly among them. Top each with a few tablespoons chopped arugula.

PER SLIDER 179 **CAL**; 4 g **FAT** (0 g **SAT**); 12 g **PRO**; 24 g **CARB**; 1 g **FIBER**; 413 mg **SODIUM**; 63 mg **CHOL**

Roasted Tomato Panzanella

MAKES 8 to 12 servings **PREP** 20 minutes **ROAST** at 425° for 20 minutes **GRILL OR BROIL** 6 minutes

- 3 **tablespoons white or regular balsamic vinegar**
- 3 **tablespoons olive oil**
- 1 **teaspoon Dijon mustard**
- ½ **teaspoon salt**
- ¼ **teaspoon ground black pepper**
- 2 **packages (10.5 ounces each) cherry tomatoes**
- 1 **package (10.5 ounces) yellow cherry tomatoes**
- 2 **cloves garlic, sliced**
- 1 **loaf (¾ to 1 pound) sourdough oval**
- 1 **package (8 ounces) mozzarella pearls (such as BelGioioso) or quartered small fresh mozzarella balls**
- 1 **cup packed basil leaves, torn**

■ Heat oven to 425°. In a small bowl, whisk vinegar, oil, mustard, salt and pepper. Toss tomatoes and garlic with 2 tablespoons of the dressing. Spread onto 2 rimmed baking sheets. Roast at 425° for 20 minutes, shaking pans halfway through to turn tomatoes. Cool slightly.

■ Heat grill or grill pan to medium-high; if broiling, increase oven temperature to broil. Slice bread lengthwise into 1-inch planks. Spritz with nonstick cooking spray. Grill or broil bread 2 to 3 minutes. Turn over and grill or broil 2 to 3 minutes more, until toasted. Cut into 1-inch cubes.

■ In a very large bowl, combine bread cubes, tomatoes and sliced garlic, mozzarella and basil. Drizzle with remaining dressing and gently toss. If making ahead, keep all salad components (including dressing) separate until just before serving.

PER SERVING 263 **CAL**; 15 g **FAT** (5 g **SAT**); 7 g **PRO**; 24 g **CARB**; 2 g **FIBER**; 349 mg **SODIUM**; 54 mg **CHOL**

SHRIMP SALAD SLIDERS

CHOCOLATE-COCONUT BARS

Chocolate-Coconut Bars

MAKES 24 servings **PREP** 25 minutes **BAKE** at 350° for 45 minutes **MICROWAVE** 1½ minutes

CRUST

- 1 box (9 ounces) Nabisco Famous chocolate wafer cookies
- 6 tablespoons unsalted butter, melted
- 1 teaspoon vanilla extract

BAR BATTER

- 2 cups all-purpose flour
- 1 teaspoon baking soda
- 1 teaspoon salt
- 1 stick (½ cup) unsalted butter, softened
- 1 can (15 ounces) cream of coconut
- 2 large eggs
- 2 cups (one 11-ounce bag) semisweet chocolate chips
- 1¾ cups sweetened flake coconut
- 1 cup walnuts, chopped

■ Heat oven to 350°.

■ **Crust.** Place wafer cookies in a food processor and pulse on and off until finely crushed. Drizzle with melted butter and vanilla and process until crumbs begin to stick together. Pour into a 15 x 10 x 1-inch jellyroll pan and press evenly into bottom. Refrigerate while making bar batter.

■ **Bar Batter.** In a medium bowl, whisk flour, baking soda and salt. In a large bowl, with an electric mixer, beat softened butter and cream of coconut until smooth. Beat in eggs on medium speed. On low, beat in flour mixture. Fold in 1½ cups of the chocolate chips, 1 cup of the coconut and the walnuts. Pour over crust in pan, spreading to edges. Bake at 350° for 35 minutes, until puffed, golden and set. Cool in pan on a wire rack.

■ Chop remaining ¾ cup coconut and bake at 350° for 10 minutes, until golden.

■ Place remaining ½ cup chocolate chips in a glass bowl. Microwave 45 seconds and stir. Microwave an additional 45 seconds and stir until smooth. Transfer to a piping bag or small resealable plastic bag. Snip off a small corner and drizzle over cooled cake. Sprinkle with toasted coconut. Let set, then cut into 24 bars.

PER BAR 386 **CAL**; 22 g **FAT** (13 g **SAT**); 5 g **PRO**; 45 g **CARB**; 3 g **FIBER**; 258 mg **SODIUM**; 38 mg **CHOL**

Kale and Jicama Slaw

MAKES 8 servings **PREP** 30 minutes

- ⅓ cup lime juice (from 2 large limes)
- 1 tablespoon honey
- 1 teaspoon grainy mustard
- ¾ teaspoon salt
- ¼ teaspoon ground black pepper
- ½ cup olive oil
- 1 bunch kale, tough stems discarded, shredded
- ½ medium jicama, peeled and cut into matchsticks (3½ cups)
- 1 medium sweet orange pepper, cored, seeded and cut into thin strips
- ½ cup sweetened dried cranberries
- 2 small shallots, thinly sliced (¼ cup)
- ¼ cup sunflower seeds (optional)

■ In a medium bowl, combine lime juice, honey, mustard, ½ teaspoon of the salt and the pepper. While whisking, gradually add oil.

■ Combine kale, jicama, sweet pepper, cranberries and shallots in a very large bowl or on a large platter. Drizzle with ⅔ cup of the dressing and season with remaining ¼ teaspoon salt. Toss to combine, adding sunflower seeds, if using. Serve with remaining dressing alongside.

PER SERVING 220 **CAL**; 14 g **FAT** (2 g **SAT**); 3 g **PRO**; 24 g **CARB**; 5 g **FIBER**; 268 mg **SODIUM**; 0 mg **CHOL**

KALE AND JICAMA SLAW

TURKISH LAMB BURGERS,
PAGE 162

JUNE

151

152

166

RACK 'EM UP

Cook. Baste. Eat. Repeat. Finger-lickin'-good ribs.

PEPPER-STUDDED
CORNBREAD, PAGE 156

COFFEE-MOLASSES
ST. LOUIS–STYLE RIBS,
PAGE 156

BROWN SUGAR-
BOURBON-GLAZED
BABY BACK RIBS,
PAGE 155

GRILLED SPARE RIBS
WITH TEXAS RIB SAUCE

No matter how they're sauced and slathered, a big pile of smoky, sticky ribs and all the fixings is a sure sign that summer is here. Serve with lots of napkins.

Grilled Spare Ribs with Texas Rib Sauce

MAKES 8 servings **PREP** 10 minutes
COOK 60 minutes **GRILL** 10 minutes

- **4 pounds pork spare ribs, cut into individual ribs**
- **1 recipe Texas Rib Sauce (recipe at right)**

■ Bring a large pot of lightly salted water to a boil. Add ribs; gently simmer 60 minutes. Drain and remove ribs to a large cutting board.

■ Heat a gas grill to medium-high or the coals in a charcoal grill to medium-hot.

■ Generously brush ribs with Texas Rib Sauce. Grill about 5 minutes per side, brushing with more sauce as needed, until ribs are nicely browned.

■ Serve with remaining sauce on the side.

PER SERVING 529 **CAL**; 39 g **FAT** (12 g **SAT**); 25 g **PRO**; 17 g **CARB**; 1 g **FIBER**; 684 mg **SODIUM**; 127 mg **CHOL**

Texas Rib Sauce

MAKES 1½ cups (8 servings) **PREP** 10 minutes
COOK 16 minutes

- **1 tablespoon canola oil**
- **2 cloves garlic, chopped**
- **6 tablespoons tomato paste**
- **½ cup beef broth**
- **½ cup packed light brown sugar**
- **¼ cup Worcestershire sauce**
- **¼ cup lemon juice**
- **1 chipotle pepper in adobo, seeded and chopped**
- **1 tablespoon adobo sauce**

■ In a medium saucepan, heat oil over medium heat. Add garlic and cook 1 minute. Add tomato paste, broth, brown sugar, Worcestershire sauce, lemon juice, chipotle and adobo sauce. Whisk until smooth.

■ Bring to a boil. Reduce heat to medium-low and simmer 15 minutes, stirring occasionally. Sauce will reduce to about 1½ cups.

PER SERVING 89 **CAL**; 2 g **FAT** (0 g **SAT**); 1 g **PRO**; 17 g **CARB**; 1 g **FIBER**; 555 mg **SODIUM**; 0 mg **CHOL**

Broccoli and Red Cabbage Slaw

MAKES 8 servings **PREP** 15 minutes
REFRIGERATE 4 hours

- 2 bags (12 ounces each) broccoli slaw (12 cups)
- ½ cup sliced red cabbage
- ½ red onion, thinly sliced
- ½ green bell pepper, seeded and thinly sliced
- ¾ cup reduced-fat mayonnaise
- ¼ cup sour cream
- ¼ cup white distilled vinegar
- 1 tablespoon olive oil
- 1 tablespoon sugar
- 2 teaspoons celery seeds
- 1 teaspoon seasoned salt
- ½ teaspoon black pepper
- ½ teaspoon dry mustard

■ In a large bowl, combine broccoli slaw, red cabbage, onion and green pepper.

■ In a medium bowl, whisk mayonnaise, sour cream, vinegar, olive oil, sugar, celery seeds, seasoned salt, black pepper and mustard. Fold into broccoli slaw mixture and stir to evenly coat all ingredients. Cover and refrigerate 4 hours.

PER SERVING 149 **CAL**; 11 g **FAT** (2 g **SAT**); 2 g **PRO**; 11 g **CARB**; 4 g **FIBER**; 461 mg **SODIUM**; 13 mg **CHOL**

Grilled Potato and Onion Salad with Maytag Blue Cheese

MAKES 8 servings **PREP** 20 minutes
GRILL 45 minutes **REFRIGERATE** 2 hours

- 2½ pounds small red potatoes or fingerling potatoes cut into 1-inch pieces
- 1 large sweet onion, thinly sliced
- 2 tablespoons canola oil
- 1 teaspoon salt
- ½ teaspoon black pepper
- ⅔ cup reduced-fat mayonnaise
- ¼ cup white wine vinegar
- 2 teaspoons spicy brown mustard
- 1 teaspoon sugar
- 1 teaspoon garlic powder
- 3 ribs celery, thinly sliced
- 3 tablespoons chopped parsley
- 4 ounces Maytag blue cheese

■ Heat a gas grill to medium-high or the coals in a charcoal grill to medium-hot.

■ Make a foil packet with potatoes and onion, drizzling with oil and seasoning with ½ teaspoon of the salt and ¼ teaspoon of the black pepper before sealing. Grill, covered, 15 minutes. Turn packet over and grill an additional 15 minutes. Turn again and grill 15 minutes more or until potatoes are tender. Allow to cool.

■ In a large bowl, whisk mayonnaise, vinegar, mustard, sugar, garlic powder and remaining ½ teaspoon salt and ¼ teaspoon pepper. Add potatoes, onion and celery. Toss to coat; stir in parsley and blue cheese.

■ Cover with plastic wrap and refrigerate 2 hours.

PER SERVING 212 **CAL**; 10 g **FAT** (1 g **SAT**); 3 g **PRO**; 27 g **CARB**; 3 g **FIBER**; 467 mg **SODIUM**; 7 mg **CHOL**

Root Beer Baked Beans

MAKES 8 servings **PREP** 15 minutes
COOK 12 minutes **BAKE** at 375° for 45 minutes

- 6 slices smoked bacon
- 2 onions, chopped
- 2 cans (15 ounces) pinto beans, drained and rinsed
- 1 can (15 ounces) pink beans, drained and rinsed
- 1 can (15 ounces) cannellini beans, drained and rinsed
- 1 cup root beer (not diet)
- ½ cup ketchup
- ¼ cup cider vinegar
- ¼ cup packed dark brown sugar
- 2 tablespoons grainy mustard
- 2 tablespoons Frank's hot sauce
- 1 teaspoon salt

■ Heat oven to 375°.

■ Cook bacon in a large flame-proof baking dish over medium-high heat until crisp, about 7 minutes. Remove bacon to a cutting board and coarsely chop. Add onions to baking dish, reduce heat to medium and cook 5 minutes, until golden brown.

■ Stir in beans, root beer, ketchup, vinegar, brown sugar, mustard, hot sauce and salt. Add chopped bacon. Bring to a simmer and transfer dish to oven.

■ Bake, uncovered, at 375° for 45 minutes. Serve warm.

PER SERVING 477 **CAL**; 9 g **FAT** (3 g **SAT**); 22 g **PRO**; 76 g **CARB**; 15 g **FIBER**; 1,119 mg **SODIUM**; 14 mg **CHOL**

BROCCOLI AND
RED CABBAGE SLAW

ROOT BEER
BAKED BEANS

GRILLED POTATO AND
ONION SALAD WITH
MAYTAG BLUE CHEESE

**DOUBLE SMOKY
COUNTRY RIBS**

Double Smoky Country Ribs

MAKES 8 servings **PREP** 10 minutes
BAKE at 450° for 30 minutes; at 300°
for 60 minutes **BROIL** 10 minutes

- 2 tablespoons smoked paprika
- 1 teaspoon salt
- ½ teaspoon dried thyme
- ½ teaspoon garlic powder
- ½ teaspoon onion powder
- ¼ teaspoon cayenne pepper
- 8 bone-in country-style pork ribs, 4 to 5 pounds
- 1 tablespoon canola oil
- 1 recipe Texas Rib Sauce (page 151)

■ Heat oven to 450°.

■ In a small bowl, combine smoked paprika, salt, thyme, garlic powder, onion powder and cayenne. Brush ribs with oil and season with smoked paprika mixture.

■ Place ribs in a large roasting dish and add ½ cup water. Cover very tightly with aluminum foil. Bake at 450° for 30 minutes. Reduce oven temperature to 300° and bake an additional 60 minutes.

■ Heat broiler. Set rack 6 inches from heat source. Brush ribs generously with some of the Texas Rib Sauce. Broil 4 to 5 minutes per side, turning once.

■ Serve with remaining rib sauce on the side.

PER SERVING 374 **CAL**; 17 g **FAT** (5 g **SAT**); 35 g **PRO**; 18 g **CARB**; 1 g **FIBER**; 958 mg **SODIUM**; 115 mg **CHOL**

BROWN SUGAR-BOURBON-GLAZED BABY BACK RIBS

Brown Sugar-Bourbon-Glazed Baby Back Ribs

MAKES 8 servings **PREP** 15 minutes **COOK** 15 minutes **MARINATE** overnight **GRILL** 60 minutes

- 1 cup bourbon
- 2 tablespoons canola oil
- 1 cup red onion, chopped
- 4 cloves garlic, chopped
- 1 cup ketchup
- ½ cup dark brown sugar
- ¼ cup cider vinegar
- ½ teaspoon red pepper flakes
- ½ teaspoon salt
- ¼ teaspoon black pepper
- 1 rack baby back ribs, about 3½ pounds, cut into 2 equal pieces

■ Place bourbon in a medium saucepan and set over medium heat. Gently simmer until reduced to ⅔ cup, about 5 minutes.

■ In another medium saucepan, heat oil over medium-high heat. Add onion and garlic; cook 5 minutes, stirring occasionally. Carefully stir in ketchup, reduced bourbon, brown sugar, vinegar, red pepper flakes, salt and pepper.

■ Place ribs in a large baking dish and add bourbon-ketchup sauce. Turn to coat evenly. Cover with plastic wrap and refrigerate overnight.

■ Heat a gas grill to medium-high or the coals in a charcoal grill to medium-hot. Lightly grease grates of grill. Add ribs meaty side up and grill, covered, 20 minutes, until lightly charred. Baste with sauce, turn and grill 20 minutes more. Baste ribs again and turn. Grill an additional 20 minutes.

■ Place remaining sauce in a small pot. Simmer 5 minutes.

■ Place racks on a cutting board and slice into individual ribs. Serve with remaining sauce on the side.

PER SERVING 484 **CAL**; 24 g **FAT** (8 g **SAT**); 24 g **PRO**; 23 g **CARB**; 0 g **FIBER**; 639 mg **SODIUM**; 86 mg **CHOL**

COFFEE-MOLASSES
ST. LOUIS–STYLE RIBS

Coffee-Molasses St. Louis–Style Ribs

MAKES 8 servings **PREP** 10 minutes **MARINATE** overnight **GRILL** over indirect heat 2 hours, then over direct heat 6 minutes **COOK** 3 minutes

- 1 **cup very strong brewed black coffee**
- 1 **cup sweet onion, chopped**
- ⅓ **cup molasses**
- ¼ **cup ketchup**
- ¼ **cup cider vinegar**
- ¼ **cup reduced-sodium soy sauce**
- 2 **tablespoons Frank's hot sauce**
- 2 **racks St. Louis–style ribs (about 5 pounds total)**

■ In a medium bowl, combine coffee, onion, molasses, ketchup, vinegar, soy sauce and hot sauce.

■ Place ribs in a large baking dish and pour marinade over the top. Evenly coat ribs with marinade. Cover with plastic wrap and refrigerate overnight.

■ Set a gas or charcoal grill for indirect heat. Wrap ribs tightly in a single layer in heavy-duty aluminum foil. Grill ribs in foil over indirect heat for 2 hours, turning after 1 hour.

■ Remove ribs to a cutting board and cut into 3 portions. Set grill to high. Brush ribs with marinade and grill about 3 minutes per side. Place marinade in a saucepan, bring to a rolling boil and cook 3 minutes. Cool.

■ Serve ribs with cooled marinade as a dipping sauce.

PER SERVING 460 **CAL**; 29 g **FAT** (10 g **SAT**); 35 g **PRO**; 14 g **CARB**; 0 g **FIBER**; 670 mg **SODIUM**; 123 mg **CHOL**

Pepper-Studded Cornbread

MAKES 8 servings **PREP** 15 minutes
MICROWAVE 1 minute
BAKE at 350° for 35 minutes **COOL** 15 minutes

- 1 **cup finely chopped red and yellow sweet peppers**
- 1 **jalapeño, seeded and finely chopped**
- ¾ **cup all-purpose flour**
- ¾ **cup coarse cornmeal**
- 3 **tablespoons sugar**
- 2 **teaspoons baking powder**
- ½ **teaspoon baking soda**
- ½ **teaspoon salt**
- 1 **cup buttermilk**
- 1 **egg, lightly beaten**
- 4 **tablespoons butter, melted**
- ¾ **cup frozen corn, thawed**

■ Heat oven to 350°. Coat a 10-inch cast-iron skillet with nonstick cooking spray.

■ Place sweet peppers and jalapeño in a microwave-safe dish and microwave 1 minute.

■ In a large bowl, whisk flour, cornmeal, sugar, baking powder, baking soda and salt. Stir in buttermilk, egg and butter until dry ingredients are just moistened. Fold in peppers and corn.

■ Spoon batter evenly into prepared skillet. Bake at 350° for 35 minutes. Cool on a wire rack 15 minutes.

■ Cut into 8 wedges and serve warm or at room temperature.

PER SERVING 197 **CAL**; 6 g **FAT** (4 g **SAT**); 5 g **PRO**; 21 g **CARB**; 1 g **FIBER**; 370 mg **SODIUM**; 39 mg **CHOL**

PEPPER-STUDDED
CORNBREAD

HEALTHY FAMILY DINNERS

Fire up for these globe-trotting grilled suppers.

MOROCCAN-SPICED
SALMON AND
ZUCCHINI, PAGE 165

TANDOORI CHICKEN
AND LENTIL SALAD,
PAGE 162

'Churrasco' is a Spanish, Portuguese and Latin American term that refers to grilled meats—usually beef. In a churrascaria, a restaurant that specializes in grilled meats, waiters walk among the patrons with crisp-crusted meat on a skewer, serving up slices tableside. Tostones are simply crisp-fried plantains.

Churrasco and Tostones

MAKES 4 servings **PREP** 10 minutes **GRILL** 23 minutes **BAKE** at 400° for 20 minutes

SALSA

- 1 **package (10.5 ounces) cherry tomatoes**
- 2 **ears corn, husks and silk discarded**
- 2 **tablespoons lime juice**
- 1½ **teaspoons olive oil**
- ¼ **teaspoon salt**
- 1 **to 2 tablespoons chopped cilantro (optional)**

TOSTONES

- 1½ **pounds green plantains**
- 3 **tablespoons vegetable oil**
- ½ **teaspoon salt**

CHURRASCO

- 1 **pound flank steak**
- ½ **teaspoon ancho chile powder**
- ½ **teaspoon salt**
- ½ **teaspoon ground black pepper**
- 4 **bunches scallions, cleaned and trimmed**

■ Heat grill to medium-high; heat oven to 400°.

■ **Salsa.** Thread tomatoes onto skewers and spritz with nonstick cooking spray. Grill corn 12 minutes, turning frequently, and grill tomatoes 8 minutes, turning once. Transfer to a cutting board and remove tomatoes from skewers into a bowl. Cut kernels from corn cobs and add to bowl along with lime juice, oil, salt and, if using, cilantro. Set aside.

■ **Tostones.** Peel plantains and cut into ½- to ¾-inch slices. Toss in a bowl with 1½ tablespoons of the oil and ¼ teaspoon of the salt. Place on a nonstick baking sheet and bake at 400° for 15 minutes.

■ **Churrasco.** Meanwhile, carefully split flank steak in half horizontally as if opening a book, cutting into 2 thin pieces. Slice each piece in half (for a total of 4 pieces). Season with ancho chile powder, salt and pepper. Grill steak to taste, about 5 minutes, turning once, for medium-rare. Transfer to a platter to rest. Add scallions to grill; grill 6 minutes, turning once, until charred.

■ Remove plantains from oven, smash with the bottom of a glass to flatten, and flip over. Brush with remaining 1½ tablespoons oil, sprinkle with remaining ¼ teaspoon salt and bake at 400° for an additional 5 minutes. Serve steak and scallions with salsa and tostones alongside.

PER SERVING 523 **CAL**; 22 g **FAT** (4 g **SAT**); 30 g **PRO**; 59 g **CARB**; 8 g **FIBER**; 804 mg **SODIUM**; 68 mg **CHOL**

TANDOORI CHICKEN AND LENTIL SALAD

Tandoori Chicken and Lentil Salad

MAKES 6 servings **PREP** 20 minutes **MARINATE** 8 hours or overnight **GRILL** 12 minutes

- 6 **boneless, skinless chicken breast halves (about 6 ounces each)**
- ¾ **teaspoon salt**
- 1 **cup plain low-fat yogurt**
- 6 **tablespoons fresh lemon juice**
- 1 **tablespoon grated ginger**
- 2 **cloves garlic, grated**
- 2 **teaspoons turmeric**
- 2 **teaspoons paprika**
- 1 **teaspoon ground cumin**
- 1 **teaspoon ground coriander**
- ¼ **teaspoon cayenne pepper**
- 2 **packages (9 ounces each) Melissa's steamed lentils**
- 1 **medium tomato, seeded and diced**
- 2 **ribs celery, finely diced**
- 2 **medium carrots, peeled and grated**
- ¼ **cup extra-virgin olive oil**
- 3 **tablespoons chopped parsley**
- ¼ **teaspoon ground black pepper**

■ Make marinade: Season chicken with ½ teaspoon of the salt. In a medium bowl, whisk yogurt, 3 tablespoons of the lemon juice, the ginger, garlic, turmeric, paprika, cumin, coriander and cayenne. Transfer to a glass dish or resealable plastic bag and add chicken, turning to coat. Cover and refrigerate 8 hours or overnight.

■ When ready to eat, heat grill to medium-high. Brush grill grate with oil. Remove chicken from marinade; let excess drip off. Add chicken and grill 10 to 12 minutes, depending on thickness, turning once. Meanwhile, make lentil salad. Open packages and gently break lentils apart. Stir in tomato, celery, carrots, olive oil, parsley and remaining 3 tablespoons lemon juice. Season with remaining ¼ teaspoon salt and the black pepper. Serve with chicken.

PER SERVING 437 **CAL**; 14 g **FAT** (2 g **SAT**); 50 g **PRO**; 27 g **CARB**; 6 g **FIBER**; 618 mg **SODIUM**; 126 mg **CHOL**

Turkish Lamb Burgers

MAKES 6 servings **PREP** 20 minutes **GRILL** 14 minutes

- 8 **medium mushrooms (about 4 ounces)**
- 1 **small red onion, halved**
- 1 **pound ground lamb**
- ¾ **pound ground chicken**
- 1 **teaspoon chopped fresh oregano**
- ¾ **teaspoon ground cumin**
- ¾ **teaspoon ground cinnamon**
- ¾ **teaspoon salt**
- ½ **teaspoon ground black pepper**
- ¼ **teaspoon ground allspice**
- ½ **cup 2% plain Greek yogurt**
- ¼ **cup white wine vinegar**
- ¼ **cup crumbled feta cheese**
- ¼ **cup fresh mint leaves, chopped**
- 2 **tablespoons olive oil**
- 2 **teaspoons sugar**
- 1 **package (5 ounces) baby kale**
- 1 **package (5 ounces) baby spinach**
- 1 **medium cucumber, trimmed and thinly sliced**
- 1 **cup cherry tomatoes, halved**
- 6 **whole wheat pitas, warmed**

■ Heat grill to medium-high. Grate mushrooms and half the onion into a large bowl. Add lamb, chicken, oregano, cumin, cinnamon, ½ teaspoon of the salt, ¼ teaspoon of the pepper and the allspice. Mix together well. With wet hands, shape into 6 patties.

■ Prepare dressing: In a medium bowl, whisk yogurt, vinegar, feta, mint, oil, sugar and remaining ¼ teaspoon each salt and pepper. Slice remaining onion into half-moons.

■ Grill burger patties 12 to 14 minutes, turning halfway through. Toss kale, spinach, sliced onion, cucumber and tomatoes. Place 3 cups salad on each plate and top with a burger patty. Serve with dressing and warm pita on the side.

PER SERVING 476 **CAL**; 22 g **FAT** (7 g **SAT**); 34 g **PRO**; 37 g **CARB**; 7 g **FIBER**; 724 mg **SODIUM**; 105 mg **CHOL**

TURKISH LAMB BURGERS

THAI GREEN CURRY SHRIMP

Thai Green Curry Shrimp

MAKES 4 servings **PREP** 15 minutes
COOK 23 minutes **MARINATE** 15 minutes
GRILL 16 minutes

- **1 cup jasmine rice**
- **1 can (13.5 ounces) light coconut milk**
- **2 tablespoons plus 1 teaspoon green curry paste**
- **3 tablespoons fresh lime juice**
- **2 teaspoons grated ginger**
- **1¼ pounds cleaned and deveined raw shrimp**
- **1 tablespoon olive oil**
- **3 sweet red peppers, seeded and cut lengthwise into 4 sections**
- **½ teaspoon salt**
- **¼ teaspoon ground black pepper**
- **½ cup basil leaves, sliced**

- Cook rice per package directions, about 20 minutes. Set aside and keep warm.

- In a bowl, whisk coconut milk, 2 tablespoons of the curry paste, 2 tablespoons of the lime juice and the ginger. Place shrimp in a resealable plastic bag, add coconut milk mixture and marinate 15 minutes. Heat grill to medium-high.

- In a large bowl, whisk remaining 1 teaspoon curry paste, remaining 1 tablespoon lime juice and the oil. Toss pepper pieces in bowl to coat. Season with ¼ teaspoon of the salt. Grill pepper pieces 10 minutes, turning frequently. Remove to a cutting board.

- Thread shrimp onto skewers, reserving marinade. Grill shrimp skewers 6 minutes, turning once, until cooked through. Season with remaining ¼ teaspoon salt and the pepper. Meanwhile, bring 1 cup of the reserved marinade to a boil (discard remaining marinade). Boil 3 minutes. Slice peppers into thin strips.

- Spoon rice onto a platter. Top with pepper strips, shrimp and basil. Drizzle a little sauce over platter and serve remaining sauce alongside.

PER SERVING 425 **CAL**; 10 g **FAT** (5 g **SAT**); 33 g **PRO**; 50 g **CARB**; 4 g **FIBER**; 657 mg **SODIUM**; 228 mg **CHOL**

MOROCCAN-SPICED SALMON AND ZUCCHINI

Moroccan-Spiced Salmon and Zucchini

MAKES 6 servings **PREP** 10 minutes **LET STAND** 5 minutes **GRILL** 16 minutes

- **1 cup vegetable broth**
- **1 box (7.6 ounces) wheat couscous**
- **30 small pitted Mediterranean green olives, halved**
- **8 pitted dates (Medjool or Deglet Noor), chopped**
- **1½ teaspoons ras el hanout Moroccan seasoning (see Note)**
- **1 teaspoon salt**
- **1¾ pounds zucchini, trimmed and cut on the bias into ½- to ¾-inch slices**
- **1 tablespoon olive oil**
- **½ teaspoon ground black pepper**
- **6 salmon fillets (about 5 ounces each)**

- Heat grill to medium-high. Bring vegetable broth and ½ cup water to a boil in a medium lidded pot. Stir in couscous, olives, dates, ½ teaspoon of the ras el hanout and ¼ teaspoon of the salt. Cover, remove from heat and let stand 5 minutes.

- Place zucchini slices in a large bowl and toss with oil. Thread onto skewers and sprinkle on both sides with ½ teaspoon of the ras el hanout and ¼ teaspoon each of the salt and pepper. Grill zucchini 5 minutes; turn over and grill an additional 5 minutes. Transfer to a platter and remove skewers.

- Season salmon with remaining ½ teaspoon ras el hanout, ½ teaspoon salt and ¼ teaspoon pepper. Spritz with nonstick cooking spray. Grill salmon skin sides up 3 minutes. Flip salmon and continue to grill 2 to 3 minutes. Remove to platter with zucchini, leaving salmon skin on the grill.

- Fluff couscous and transfer to a bowl. Serve alongside salmon and zucchini.

Note: The Moroccan spice blend ras el hanout is available from McCormick's, Williams-Sonoma and Whole Foods or at teenytinyspice.com.

PER SERVING 512 **CAL**; 16 g **FAT** (3 g **SAT**); 40 g **PRO**; 53 g **CARB**; 5 g **FIBER**; 760 mg **SODIUM**; 90 mg **CHOL**

The beautiful bright colors of this grilled vegetable platter are enough on their own to entice hungry eaters to indulge. The herb-infused vinaigrette in which they're bathed is a flavor bonus. Serve with a side of Beans and Orzo for a complete vegetarian meal.

Tuscan Grilled Veggie Platter

MAKES 6 servings **PREP** 30 minutes **GRILL** 10 minutes

- 2 **tablespoons chianti vinegar or other red wine vinegar**
- 2 **teaspoons sugar**
- 1 **teaspoon spicy brown mustard**
- ½ **teaspoon salt**
- ¼ **teaspoon black pepper**
- 5 **tablespoons extra-virgin olive oil**
- 1 **tablespoon chopped fresh sage**
- 1 **tablespoon chopped fresh parsley**
- 2 **tablespoons chopped fresh basil**
- 1 **pound asparagus, trimmed**
- 1 **medium eggplant (about 1 pound), cut into ½-inch slices**
- 1 **large summer squash (about 8 ounces), cut into ½-inch slices**
- 1 **sweet red pepper, seeded and cut into ½-inch strips**
- 8 **ounces small carrots, halved lengthwise**
- 2 **large shallots (about 6 ounces total), peeled and cut into 8 pieces**
- **Beans and Orzo (recipe follows)**

■ In a small bowl, whisk vinegar, sugar, mustard, ¼ teaspoon of the salt and the black pepper. Gradually whisk in oil; add sage, parsley and basil. Set aside.

■ Heat a gas grill to medium-high or the coals in a charcoal grill to medium-hot. Lightly grease grates.

■ Brush vegetables with dressing. Grill about 5 minutes per side, until crisp-tender. Brush with additional dressing and turn as needed to prevent burning. Cook in batches if necessary. (You may want to use a grilling grid for thinner vegetables.)

■ Arrange grilled vegetables on a platter. Season with remaining ¼ teaspoon salt. Serve with Beans and Orzo.

PER SERVING 502 **CAL**; 19 g **FAT** (3 g **SAT**); 16 g **PRO**; 74 g **CARB**; 14 g **FIBER**; 770 mg **SODIUM**; 0 mg **CHOL**

Beans and Orzo

Cook 6 ounces (1⅓ cups) orzo as per package directions. Toss with 1 can (14.5 ounces) butter beans, drained and rinsed, 1 tablespoon of the dressing, 1 teaspoon olive oil and 1 teaspoon grated lemon peel.

**TUSCAN GRILLED
VEGGIE PLATTER**

STRAWBERRY
KEY LIME PIE,
PAGE 183

173

177

195

ALL IN THE FAMILY

Join New York's news and restaurant superstars, the Scottos, for an al fresco Italian feast.

GRILLED SALMON WITH WHITE BEAN, SUN-DRIED TOMATO AND SPINACH SALAD, PAGE 174

BLUEBERRY-STRAWBERRY
SHORTCAKE, PAGE 178

GRILLED PIZZA
MARGHERITA

Cooking pizza on the grill gives it a crisp crust and smoky flavor similar to that of pizza cooked in a wood-fired oven.

Grilled Pizza Margherita

MAKES 12 pizzas **PREP** 30 minutes **LET STAND** 45 minutes **GRILL** 6 minutes

4	cups lukewarm water
1	teaspoon fresh yeast
1	tablespoon molasses
3	tablespoons kosher salt
2	cups extra-virgin olive oil
4½	cups all-purpose flour
4½	cups high-gluten flour (such as bread flour)
1	cup whole wheat flour
1½	cups grated Pecorino Romano cheese
1½	cups grated Bel Paese cheese
1	cup canned tomato sauce
6	tablespoons chopped fresh parsley
½	cup chopped fresh basil

■ In a large mixing bowl, combine water, yeast and molasses. Mix gently until all yeast dissolves. Set mixture aside 5 to 10 minutes, until yeast bubbles and floats to the surface. Stir in salt and 1 cup of the olive oil.

■ With mixer on low speed, add all-purpose, high-gluten and whole wheat flour. Mix until flour is absorbed and dough pulls away from side of bowl. Roll dough into a large ball and let stand 5 minutes.

■ Cut dough into 12 pieces. Roll pieces into balls and place on an oiled baking sheet. Brush balls lightly with olive oil and cover with plastic wrap.

■ If you are using dough right away, let it sit 30 minutes before grilling. If not, it can be stored for up to one day in the refrigerator but it must sit at room temperature for an hour before stretching.

■ When dough is ready, prepare a grill to medium-hot (preferably charcoal, but gas works nicely too). Make sure rack is set at least 4 inches from fire.

■ On an oiled piece of parchment paper, stretch out a piece of dough using the (lightly oiled) palms of your hands. If dough is sticking to the surface, lift it and drizzle a little more oil on surface. The dough should be a 12-inch circle and paper-thin. The shape of the dough is not as important as its thickness.

■ Lift dough with parchment, invert it onto hot spot of grill and peel off paper. Dough will start to rise immediately. After about 2 minutes, carefully lift edge of dough to check color of the underside, which should be an even golden brown.

■ Flip dough over and place it on edge of grate or on a cooler spot of grill. Brush cooked side of dough with olive oil. Combine cheeses in a medium bowl. Evenly spread a scant ¼ cup of the combined cheese to very edge of dough. Next, with a tablespoon, dollop tomato sauce on pizza (8 to 10 small spoonfuls)—don't spread sauce over entire surface. Drizzle pizza with 1 tablespoon of the olive oil and sprinkle with ½ tablespoon of the parsley.

■ Carefully slide pizza back to edge of hot section of grill, and rotate until bottom is evenly golden brown. It should take 3 to 4 minutes. Do not put pizza directly over fire, or the bottom may burn before the cheese melts.

■ Garnish with chopped basil and serve.

GRILLED SALMON WITH WHITE BEAN,
SUN-DRIED TOMATO AND SPINACH SALAD

Panzanella is an Italian bread salad that was created to use up day-old bread—and to showcase sweet and juicy summer tomatoes. This version is served on a stick.

Grilled Salmon with White Bean, Sun-Dried Tomato and Spinach Salad

MAKES 6 servings **PREP** 20 minutes **MARINATE** 2 hours **GRILL** 8 minutes

MARINADE AND SALMON

- ⅓ cup extra-virgin olive oil
- Salt and freshly ground black pepper
- Juice of 1 lemon
- Juice of 1 orange
- 2 tablespoons chopped fresh basil
- 6 1-inch-thick boneless, skinless salmon fillets (about 8 ounces each)

BALSAMIC VINAIGRETTE

- ½ cup balsamic vinegar
- 1 teaspoon Dijon mustard
- 2 cups extra-virgin olive oil
- Salt and freshly ground black pepper
- 2 minced shallots
- 3 tablespoons chopped fresh parsley
- 3 tablespoons chopped fresh basil

SALAD

- 2 pounds baby spinach, cleaned
- 2 cups cooked cannellini beans
- 1 roasted red bell pepper, cut into thin strips
- ½ cup thinly sliced sun-dried tomatoes

■ **Marinade and Salmon.** In a small bowl, combine olive oil, salt and pepper to taste, lemon juice, orange juice and basil.

■ Season salmon with salt and pepper to taste. Brush salmon with marinade 1 to 2 hours before grilling, cover in plastic and refrigerate. Pat salmon dry before grilling to avoid flare-ups.

■ Lightly oil the hot grill and grill salmon over very high heat 3 to 4 minutes per side, until browned but inside is medium-rare.

■ **Balsamic Vinaigrette.** In a medium bowl, combine balsamic vinegar and mustard. Gradually whisk in olive oil, then stir in salt and pepper to taste, shallots and fresh herbs.

■ **Salad.** In a large bowl, toss spinach with beans, roasted pepper and sun-dried tomatoes. Dress salad with desired amount of balsamic vinaigrette. (You can also serve vinaigrette as a sauce to accompany grilled salmon.)

■ Place salmon, hot off the grill, on top of salad and serve.

Panzanella Skewers with Mozzarella, Tomato and Focaccia Bread

MAKES 6 to 8 servings **PREP** 15 minutes
GRILL 4 minutes

- 1 loaf focaccia bread
- 4 vine-ripened tomatoes, or 1 pint vine-ripened cherry tomatoes
- 1 pound fresh mozzarella, cut into twelve ½-inch-thick slices
- 1 cup whole basil leaves
- 6-inch metal skewers
- Extra-virgin olive oil

■ Using a sharp knife, cut focaccia into 2 x 2¾ x ¾-inch rectangles. Cut tomatoes into slices about ¼ inch thick, then cut them in half again. If using cherry tomatoes, leave them whole.

■ To assemble skewers, stack a slice of bread, a slice of mozzarella, a basil leaf and a slice of tomato. Secure stack with 2 of the skewers. Repeat with remaining ingredients.

■ Preheat a grill to high heat. Brush and clean grill grid with a cloth, and lightly oil grill so that skewers will get a good sear but still release from grate. Grill for 1½ to 2 minutes per side, or until bread is light brown and cheese is melted.

■ Remove Panzanella Skewers from grill, place on a platter and remove skewers. Drizzle with olive oil and serve.

PANZANELLA SKEWERS WITH MOZZARELLA, TOMATO AND FOCACCIA BREAD

ITALIAN GRILLED BURGERS

Italian Grilled Burgers

MAKES 6 to 8 servings **PREP** 15 minutes
GRILL 8 minutes

- 2¾ **pounds ground round, chuck or sirloin**
- 1 **tablespoon chopped fresh flat-leaf parsley**
- 1 **small garlic clove, crushed and finely chopped**
- **Dash Worcestershire sauce**
- **Dash Tabasco sauce**
- **Pinch dried Greek oregano**
- **Salt and freshly ground black pepper**
- **Olive oil**
- 2 **cups mild Gorgonzola cheese, cut into ½-inch-thick slices or crumbled, or mild blue cheese**
- 6 **to 8 ciabatta or other bread rolls**
- 12 **slices cooked pancetta or bacon**

■ In a bowl, combine meat, parsley, garlic, Worcestershire, Tabasco and oregano. Season with salt and pepper to taste. Form patties 4 to 5 inches across and 1 inch thick.

■ Heat a grill to its highest setting. Brush, clean and rub grill grate with an oiled towel before starting; this will prevent meat from sticking.

■ Brush burgers with a tiny bit of olive oil and place on hottest part of grill. Grill until burgers are nicely browned, about 4 minutes per side for medium. When burgers are almost done on second side, top with Gorgonzola. Split rolls and place on grill to be toasted. Close lid and cook burgers until cheese is melted (check often so buns do not burn; they should only take about 30 seconds).

■ Remove buns, place on a platter, add a burger to each and top with crispy pancetta.

Eggplant and Zucchini Pie

MAKES 6 to 12 servings **PREP** 1 hour
SOAK 2 hours **COOK** 12 minutes per batch
BAKE at 450° for 35 minutes

CHEESE MIXTURE
- 1 **pound fresh ricotta**
- 1 **pound fresh mozzarella, diced**
- ½ **cup grated Parmesan**
- 2 **tablespoons chopped fresh parsley**
- 2 **eggs**
- **Salt and freshly ground black pepper**

EGGPLANT AND ZUCCHINI PIE
- 1 **medium eggplant, peeled**
- 2 **medium zucchini**
- **Salt**
- 2 **cups all-purpose flour**
- 5 **eggs**
- 2 **cups packaged bread crumbs**
- 1 **cup grated Parmesan**
- 2 **tablespoons chopped fresh flat-leaf parsley**
- **Freshly ground black pepper**
- 1 **quart olive oil or vegetable cooking oil**
- 2½ **cups tomato sauce**

■ **Cheese Mixture.** In a large bowl, combine ricotta, mozzarella, Parmesan, parsley and eggs. Mix well and season with salt and pepper to taste. Refrigerate briefly so mixture becomes slightly firm.

■ **Eggplant and Zucchini Pie.** Cut eggplant and zucchini into ¼-inch-thick round slices. Set zucchini aside. Fill a bowl with lightly salted water, add eggplant and soak for 1½ to 2 hours to remove bitterness. Drain.

■ Place flour in a shallow bowl. In a second bowl, beat eggs with a fork until blended. In a third bowl, mix bread crumbs, ¾ cup of the Parmesan, the parsley, and salt and pepper to taste. Line up bowls on a work surface.

EGGPLANT AND ZUCCHINI PIE

■ One at a time, carefully dip eggplant and zucchini slices into flour—making sure both sides are covered—then into egg mixture and finally into bread crumb mixture. Coat both sides very well and gently tap off any excess coating. Transfer eggplant and zucchini slices to a large plate and season with salt and pepper to taste.

■ In a large, heavy skillet, heat olive oil over medium heat. Add eggplant slices in a single layer (try not to crowd the pan) and sauté on both sides until golden brown, about 3 minutes per side, making sure slices are soft and cooked all the way through. Remove eggplant to a paper-towel-lined plate to soak up excess oil. Add zucchini to skillet and sauté on both sides until golden brown, about 3 minutes per side. Remove to a paper-towel-lined plate.

■ Heat oven to 450°. In a 13 x 9-inch baking pan, spread 1 cup of the tomato sauce, then a layer of half the eggplant and zucchini, and top with a layer of half the cheese mixture. Repeat. Top with remaining ½ cup tomato sauce and sprinkle with remaining ¼ cup Parmesan.

■ Bake at 450° for 35 minutes or until golden brown.

As beautiful as it is delicious, this triple-layer shortcake filled with fresh berries and whipped cream is the essence of summer.

Blueberry-Strawberry Shortcake

MAKES 10 servings **PREP** 20 minutes **REFRIGERATE** 3 hours **BAKE** at 325° for 30 minutes

- **4 cups all-purpose flour**
- **¼ cup sugar, plus extra for sprinkling and to sweeten cream**
- **¾ teaspoon salt**
- **1 cup (2 sticks) unsalted butter, very cold**
- **1 cup solid vegetable shortening, very cold**
- **½ cup buttermilk**
- **1 quart strawberries, hulled and sliced**
- **1 quart blueberries**
- **3 cups heavy cream, whipped**

■ In a large mixing bowl, combine flour, ¼ cup sugar and salt. Cut in butter and shortening until mixture resembles coarse sand. Add buttermilk and mix just until dough comes together in a ball. Divide dough evenly into thirds; wrap in plastic and refrigerate 2 to 3 hours.

■ Heat oven to 325°. Roll each piece of dough on lightly floured parchment to a 10-inch circle. Prick with a fork and sprinkle liberally with sugar. Bake at 325° for 30 minutes.

■ To assemble: Set aside a few strawberries and blueberries to top finished dessert. Place one pastry disk on a serving plate and cover with a third of the remaining berries, followed by a third of the whipped cream. Repeat layering two more times and finish with reserved berries.

BERRY BERRY GOOD

Try a fresh-picked dessert inspired by farms from across the country.

BLUEBERRY-PISTACHIO
ICE CREAM, PAGE 184

**MINI BERRY GOAT
CHEESE CAKES,
PAGE 183**

STRAWBERRY
KEY LIME PIE

Strawberry Key Lime Pie

MAKES 12 servings **PREP** 25 minutes
COOK 10 minutes **BAKE** at 375° for 15 minutes;
at 350° for 17 minutes
REFRIGERATE 3 hours or overnight

- ½ **pound strawberries, hulled and finely diced, plus 6 strawberries, hulled and sliced**
- ½ **cup plus 2 tablespoons sugar**
- 3 **tablespoons unsalted butter, cold**
- 2 **whole eggs, beaten**
- 18 **graham cracker boards**
- 1 **stick (½ cup) unsalted butter, melted**
- 5 **egg yolks**
- ½ **cup Key lime juice (such as Nellie & Joe's)**
- 1 **can (14 ounces) sweetened condensed milk**
- ¾ **cup heavy cream**

■ Combine ½ pound diced strawberries, ½ cup of the sugar, the cold butter and whole eggs in a pot over medium heat. Stir constantly until thickened, being careful not to scramble, 8 to 10 minutes. Pour through a fine-mesh strainer and cool. Refrigerate strawberry curd at least 1 hour.

■ Heat oven to 375°. Add graham crackers and 1 tablespoon of the sugar to a food processor and process until finely ground. Pour in melted butter and process until well combined. Transfer to a 9-inch pie plate and press into bottom and sides of dish with the bottom of a measuring cup. Bake at 375° for 15 minutes. Cool slightly.

■ Reduce heat to 350°. In a bowl, beat egg yolks, lime juice, condensed milk and strawberry curd until smooth. Pour into pie shell and bake at 350° for 15 to 17 minutes, until set. Cool, then refrigerate at least 2 hours or overnight.

■ Whip heavy cream and remaining 1 tablespoon sugar until stiff peaks form. Transfer to a piping bag fitted with a star tip. Pipe a circle around the pie and a few circles in the center. Garnish with sliced strawberries.

PER SERVING 390 **CAL**; 23 g **FAT** (13 g **SAT**); 7 g **PRO**; 43 g **CARB**; 1 g **FIBER**; 105 mg **SODIUM**; 170 mg **CHOL**

MINI BERRY GOAT CHEESE CAKES

Mini Berry Goat Cheese Cakes

MAKES 12 servings **PREP** 20 minutes **BAKE** at 350° for 15 minutes

- 8 **ounces gingersnaps**
- 4 **tablespoons unsalted butter, melted**
- 8 **ounces goat cheese, at room temperature**
- 8 **ounces cream cheese, at room temperature**
- ⅔ **cup plus 1 tbsp sugar**
- ⅛ **teaspoon salt**
- 2 **eggs**
- 1 **teaspoon vanilla extract**
- 1 **cup blackberries**
- 1 **cup raspberries**
- 1 **cup blueberries**
  Mint leaves, for garnish (optional)

■ Heat oven to 350°. Add gingersnaps to a food processor; process until finely ground (yields about 1 cup). Pour in melted butter; process until well combined. Insert 12 liners in a standard-size square or round muffin pan. Press 2 tbsp of the ground gingersnaps firmly into each liner.

■ Beat goat cheese and cream cheese with a hand mixer on low until smooth. Add ⅔ cup of the sugar and the salt; beat until combined. Incorporate eggs one at a time, then add vanilla. Beat on high until smooth, about 2 minutes.

■ Pour evenly into muffin liners. Bake at 350° for 15 minutes, until set. Cool to room temperature, then refrigerate until cold.

■ Meanwhile, combine blackberries, raspberries, blueberries, remaining 1 tablespoon sugar and 1 tablespoon water in a pot. Cook over medium heat until berries burst, about 5 minutes. Cool. Refrigerate until using.

■ Remove cakes from pan and peel off liners. Spoon berries on top of each cake and garnish with mint leaves, if using.

PER SERVING 310 **CAL**; 20 g **FAT** (11 g **SAT**); 8 g **PRO**; 28 g **CARB**; 2 g **FIBER**; 290 mg **SODIUM**; 75 mg **CHOL**

BLUEBERRY-PISTACHIO ICE CREAM

Blueberry-Pistachio Ice Cream

MAKES 12 servings **PREP** 10 minutes **COOK** 15 minutes **PROCESS** according to manufacturer's instructions **FREEZE** at least 2 hours

- 2   **cups blueberries**
- 1   **tablespoon lemon juice**
- ½   **cup plus 1 tablespoon sugar**
- 4   **egg yolks**
- 2   **cups whole milk**
- 1   **cup heavy cream**
- ¼   **teaspoon salt**
- ½   **teaspoon vanilla extract**
- 1   **cup unsalted chopped pistachios**

■ Combine blueberries, lemon juice and 1 tablespoon of the sugar in a saucepan over medium heat. Cook 5 to 7 minutes or until berries burst and become a bit syrupy. Cool.

■ In a bowl, whisk egg yolks and ¼ cup of the sugar. Heat milk, cream, salt and remaining ¼ cup sugar in a pot until barely simmering. Remove from heat and slowly whisk into yolk-sugar mixture to temper. Pour back into pot and cook over medium heat. Stir constantly until mixture coats the back of a wooden spoon (170° to 180°), 4 to 8 minutes. Pour through fine mesh strainer into a new bowl; cool over an ice bath or in refrigerator.

■ Whisk vanilla and blueberries into cooled liquid. Process in an ice cream maker according to manufacturer's directions. Add pistachios during last 5 minutes. Transfer to a lidded container and freeze at least 2 hours.

PER SERVING 210 **CAL**; 15 g **FAT** (6 g **SAT**); 5 g **PRO**; 16 g **CARB**; 2 g **FIBER**; 45 mg **SODIUM**; 95 mg **CHOL**

Blackberry Corn Cake with Honey Whipped Cream

MAKES 9 servings **PREP** 15 minutes
BAKE at 350° for 45 minutes **COOL** 20 minutes

- 1   **cup plus 1 tablespoon all-purpose flour**
- ¾   **cup fine yellow cornmeal**
- 2   **teaspoon baking powder**
- ½   **teaspoon salt**
- ¾   **cup granulated sugar**
- ⅔   **cup milk**
- 6   **tablespoons unsalted butter, melted**
- 2   **eggs**
- 12   **ounces blackberries**
- 1   **tablespoon turbinado or demerera sugar (optional)**
- 1   **cup heavy cream**
- 2   **tablespoons honey**

■ Heat oven to 350°. Butter and flour a 9 x 9-inch baking pan. In a bowl, mix 1 cup of the flour, the cornmeal, baking powder and salt. In a separate bowl, whisk sugar, milk, butter and eggs. Fold dry mixture into wet mixture until just combined.

■ Toss blackberries with remaining 1 tablespoon flour. Gently fold into batter. Transfer to baking pan, using a spatula to smooth the top. Sprinkle with turbinado sugar, if using.

■ Bake at 350° for 40 to 45 minutes, until a toothpick inserted in center of cake comes out clean. Place on a wire rack and immediately run a paring knife around edge of cake. Cool 20 minutes.

■ Whisk heavy cream and honey in a bowl until stiff peaks form. Serve cake warm or at room temperature with whipped cream.

PER SERVING 350 **CAL**; 20 g **FAT** (12 g **SAT**); 5 g **PRO**; 4 g **CARB**; 3 g **FIBER**; 260 mg **SODIUM**; 100 mg **CHOL**

BLACKBERRY CORN
CAKE WITH HONEY
WHIPPED CREAM

RASPBERRY-ALMOND TART

The center of this raspberry-studded tart is essentially frangipane [FRAN-juh-payn], a French pastry filling made with ground almonds. This simplified version is based on almond flour.

Raspberry-Almond Tart

MAKES 12 servings **PREP** 25 minutes **REFRIGERATE** 1 hour **BAKE** at 375° for 45 minutes

CRUST

- 1¼ **cups all-purpose flour**
- 1 **stick (½ cup) unsalted butter, cold, cut into cubes**
- 1 **tablespoon sugar**
- ¼ **teaspoon salt**

FILLING

- 5 **tablespoons unsalted butter, softened**
- ½ **cup plus 1 tablespoon sugar**
- ⅛ **teaspoon salt**
- ¾ **cup almond flour (such as Bob's Red Mill)**
- 1 **whole egg plus 1 egg white**
- 1 **tablespoon all-purpose flour**
- ½ **teaspoon almond extract**
- 12 **ounces raspberries**
- 1 **teaspoon lemon zest**

■ **Crust.** Combine flour, butter, sugar and salt in a food processor; pulse until mixture resembles coarse crumbs (butter will be the size of peas). Add 3 tablespoons ice water and process until just combined. Pour onto a clean counter and form into a disk. Wrap in plastic and refrigerate 1 hour.

■ Heat oven to 375°. Roll dough into a 10½-inch circle on a floured surface. Fit into a 9-inch tart pan with a removable bottom, trimming edge. Refrigerate while making filling.

■ **Filling.** In a food processor, combine butter, ½ cup of the sugar and salt. Process until smooth. Add almond flour, eggs, all-purpose flour and almond extract. Process until smooth.

■ Toss raspberries with remaining 1 tablespoon sugar and the lemon zest. Scatter half the berries in bottom of tart shell. Spread almond mixture (frangipane) evenly over top. Scatter remaining berries over frangipane. Bake at 375° for 45 minutes, until lightly browned. Cool on a wire rack.

PER SERVING 250 **CAL**; 17 g **FAT** (8 g **SAT**); 4 g **PRO**; 23 g **CARB**; 3 g **FIBER**; 90 mg **SODIUM**; 50 mg **CHOL**

HEALTHY FAMILY DINNERS

Don't be a square. Dinner is better in bowls!

FARRO STEAK SALAD,
PAGE 192

BLACK RICE, SHRIMP
AND CHARRED CORN,
PAGE 195

GRILLED QUINOA BOWL

COCONUT CHICKEN
SOBA NOODLES

Grilled Quinoa Bowl

MAKES 4 servings **PREP** 15 minutes
COOK 15 minutes **LET STAND** 5 minutes
GRILL 18 minutes

1½	**cups red quinoa**
6	**slices bacon (6 ounces), diced**
2	**peaches, halved and pitted**
8	**ounces red chard**
2	**tablespoons white balsamic vinegar**
1	**tablespoon extra-virgin olive oil**
1	**tablespoon honey**
1	**teaspoon Dijon mustard**
¾	**teaspoon salt**
¼	**teaspoon freshly cracked black pepper**

■ In a medium pot, combine quinoa and 3 cups water. Cover and bring to a boil. Reduce to a low simmer and cook 15 minutes. Let stand 5 minutes.

■ Meanwhile, heat a skillet to medium heat. Add bacon and sauté 6 minutes, until crisp. Remove to a paper-towel-lined plate with a slotted spoon. Pour 1 tablespoon of the bacon fat into a large bowl; discard any remaining fat.

■ Heat a grill or grill pan to medium-high. Toss peaches and chard in bowl with bacon fat. Grill peaches 3 minutes per side and chard 2 minutes per side (in 3 batches). Slice peach halves; chop chard. Return to bowl and toss gently with quinoa and bacon.

■ Whisk vinegar, oil, honey, mustard, salt and pepper. Gently stir into quinoa mixture.

PER SERVING 400 **CAL**; 14 g **FAT** (3 g **SAT**); 13 g **PRO**; 60 g **CARB**; 8 g **FIBER**; 700 mg **SODIUM**; 10 mg **CHOL**

Coconut Chicken Soba Noodles

MAKES 6 servings **PREP** 15 minutes **GRILL** 22 minutes **COOK** 11 minutes

2	**tablespoons packed light brown sugar**
½	**teaspoon salt**
¼	**teaspoon cayenne**
1½	**pounds boneless, skinless chicken breasts**
1	**pound mini sweet peppers**
4	**scallions**
2	**teaspoons vegetable oil**
1	**box (12 ounces) soba noodles (such as Annie Chun's)**
¼	**cup unsweetened flaked coconut**
3	**cloves garlic, minced**
1	**tablespoon grated ginger**
1	**can (13.5 ounces) light coconut milk**
2	**tablespoons lime juice**
1	**tablespoon fish sauce**
1	**teaspoon cornstarch**
	Cilantro, for garnish

■ Heat a grill or grill pan to medium-high and brush grate with oil. In a small bowl, combine 1 tablespoon of the brown sugar, ¼ teaspoon of the salt and ⅛ teaspoon of the cayenne. Rub onto chicken breasts. Grill chicken over medium-high heat 5 to 6 minutes per side, until cooked through.

■ Toss peppers and scallions in 1 teaspoon of the vegetable oil.

Skewer peppers and grill 4 minutes; flip and grill another 4 minutes. Grill scallions 2 minutes per side. Thinly slice chicken on the bias. Cut peppers into rings, discarding stems, and chop scallions.

■ Bring a pot of lightly salted water to a boil. Add soba and cook 4 to 5 minutes, until tender. Drain and rinse immediately under cold water.

■ Heat a skillet over medium heat. Toast coconut 2 to 3 minutes, stirring frequently. Remove to a plate. Add remaining 1 teaspoon oil to skillet. Add garlic and ginger to skillet; sauté 1 minute. Pour in coconut milk, lime juice, fish sauce, remaining 1 tablespoon brown sugar, remaining ¼ teaspoon salt and remaining ⅛ teaspoon cayenne. Bring to a simmer. Mix cornstarch with 1 teaspoon cold water. Add to mixture and simmer 2 minutes, until thickened.

■ In a large bowl, toss sauce with chicken, peppers, scallions and soba. Divide among 6 bowls and garnish with coconut and cilantro.

PER SERVING 440 **CAL**; 10 g **FAT** (4.5 g **SAT**); 35 g **PRO**; 52 g **CARB**; 5 g **FIBER**; 880 mg **SODIUM**; 85 mg **CHOL**

FARRO STEAK SALAD

Streamlining suppertime is never more appreciated than in summer, when there is so much to do outside. These meals-in-a-bowl are simple and satisfying.

Couscous with Summer Pesto

MAKES 6 servings **PREP** 20 minutes **COOK** 10 minutes

- 1¾ **cups pearl couscous**
- 2 **cups packed basil leaves**
- 2 **tablespoons pine nuts, toasted**
- 1 **clove garlic, halved**
- 1 **tablespoon lemon juice**
- ⅓ **cup extra-virgin olive oil**
- 2 **tablespoons grated Parmesan**
- ¾ **teaspoon salt**
- 4 **cups shredded chicken breast**
- 1 **package (10.5 ounces) cherry tomatoes, halved**
- 4 **ounces smoked mozzarella, cubed**

■ In a medium pot, bring 2½ cups water to a boil. Add couscous, cover and cook 10 minutes. Drain and rinse under cold water.

■ Meanwhile, make pesto. In a blender or food processor, combine basil, pine nuts, garlic and lemon juice. Process, slowly streaming in oil until smooth. Remove to a large bowl and stir in Parmesan and ¼ teaspoon of the salt.

■ Mix couscous, chicken, tomatoes, mozzarella and remaining ½ teaspoon salt into pesto. Stir well to combine.

PER SERVING 500 **CAL**; 22 g **FAT** (5 g **SAT**); 39 g **PRO**; 36 g **CARB**; 3 g **FIBER**; 520 mg **SODIUM**; 95 mg **CHOL**

Farro Steak Salad

MAKES 4 servings **PREP** 10 minutes **COOK** 15 minutes **GRILL** 10 minutes **REST** 5 minutes

- 1 **cup quick-cook farro**
- 1 **pound flatiron steak**
- ¾ **teaspoon salt**
- ⅜ **teaspoon freshly cracked black pepper**
- 3 **tablespoons balsamic vinegar**
- 1 **tablespoon extra-virgin olive oil**
- 1 **teaspoon Dijon mustard**
- 1 **package (5 ounces) baby spinach**
- 4 **medium heirloom tomatoes (combination of red, yellow, orange and green), cut into wedges**
- ⅓ **cup thinly sliced shallots**
- 2 **ounces blue cheese, crumbled**

■ Heat grill or grill pan to medium-high. In a medium pot, combine farro and 3 cups water. Cover and bring to a boil. Reduce to a simmer and cook 15 minutes. Drain.

■ Season steak on both sides with ¼ teaspoon of the salt and ⅛ teaspoon of the pepper. Grill over medium-high heat 5 minutes per side. Let rest 5 minutes. Meanwhile, in a large bowl, whisk vinegar, oil, mustard, ¼ teaspoon of the salt and ⅛ teaspoon of the pepper.

■ Thinly slice steak against the grain. Toss in bowl with cooked farro, spinach, tomatoes, shallots, blue cheese and remaining ¼ teaspoon salt and ⅛ teaspoon pepper.

PER SERVING 480 **CAL**; 16 g **FAT** (6 g **SAT**); 36 g **PRO**; 51 g **CARB**; 10 g **FIBER**; 760 mg **SODIUM**; 90 mg **CHOL**

**COUSCOUS WITH
SUMMER PESTO**

VEGGIE BIBIMBAP

Veggie Bibimbap

MAKES 4 servings **PREP** 15 minutes
COOK 45 minutes **LET STAND** 10 minutes

- 1½ **cups brown rice**
- 1 **bag (8 ounces) shredded carrots**
- 1 **teaspoon sesame oil**
- 1 **tablespoon vegetable oil**
- 1 **package (11 ounces) fresh spinach**
- ⅛ **teaspoon salt**
- 4 **eggs**
- 1 **can (14 ounces) drained bean sprouts (such as La Choy)**
- **Kimchi (optional)**
- 4 **teaspoon sesame seeds**
- 8 **teaspoon gochujang (Korean hot chile paste) or sriracha**

■ In a medium pot, combine rice and 3 cups water. Cover pot and bring to a boil. Reduce heat and cook 45 minutes. Remove from heat and let stand 10 minutes.

■ Meanwhile, bring a separate pot of lightly salted water to a boil. Add carrots and cook 2 minutes, until just tender. Drain and toss in ½ teaspoon of the sesame oil.

■ Add 1 teaspoon of the vegetable oil and remaining ½ teaspoon sesame oil to a large skillet over medium-high heat. Stir in spinach and cook until just wilted, 1 to 2 minutes. Season with salt. Remove to a bowl.

■ Add remaining 2 teaspoons vegetable oil to skillet. Crack in eggs and fry 2 to 3 minutes each, until whites are set.

■ Divide rice among 4 bowls. Top each with one-fourth of the spinach, carrots and sprouts. Add kimchi, if using. Place 1 egg on top, sprinkle with 1 teaspoon sesame seeds and dollop with 2 teaspoons gochujang.

PER SERVING 460 **CAL**; 13 g **FAT** (2.5 g **SAT**); 17 g **PRO**; 71 g **CARB**; 9 g **FIBER**; 550 mg **SODIUM**; 185 mg **CHOL**

BLACK RICE, SHRIMP AND CHARRED CORN

Black Rice, Shrimp and Charred Corn

MAKES 6 servings **PREP** 20 minutes **COOK** 40 minutes **GRILL** 20 minutes

- 1½ **cups uncooked black rice (such as Lundberg)**
- 1½ **pounds shrimp, peeled, deveined and tails removed**
- 2 **tablespoons extra-virgin olive oil**
- 1 **teaspoon salt**
- ¼ **teaspoon cayenne pepper**
- 2 **ears corn, husked**
- ½ **small red onion**
- 1 **avocado, peeled, seeded and halved**
- 3 **tablespoons lime juice**
- 6 **tablespoons Cotija cheese or queso fresco**

■ Combine rice with 3 cups water, cover and bring to a boil. Reduce to a low simmer and cook 40 minutes. Remove from heat and let stand 10 minutes. Fluff with a fork and transfer to a large bowl.

■ Meanwhile, heat grill or grill pan to medium-high. Toss shrimp with 1 tablespoon of the oil, ¼ teaspoon of the salt and ⅛ teaspoon of the cayenne.

■ Thread shrimp onto skewers. Grill corn 3 to 5 minutes per side, turning 3 times (12 to 20 minutes total). Grill red onion 3 minutes per side, and avocado and shrimp 2 minutes per side.

■ Cut kernels from corn cobs, dice onion and avocado, and remove shrimp from skewers. Toss in bowl with cooked rice. Gently toss with lime juice and remaining 1 tablespoon oil, ¾ teaspoon salt and ⅛ teaspoon cayenne. Garnish each serving with 1 tablespoon cheese.

PER SERVING 420 **CAL**; 14 g **FAT** (3 g **SAT**); 31 g **PRO**; 47 g **CARB**; 6 g **FIBER**; 630 mg **SODIUM**; 190 mg **CHOL**

HEIRLOOM TOMATO
SALAD, PAGE 206

AUGUST

201

205

212

JUICY FRUIT

The time is ripe to make these sweet and savory recipes.

**COCONUT-MANGO
TAPIOCA PUDDING,
PAGE 205**

GRILLED MAHI MAHI
WITH PLUM SALSA,
PAGE 202

GRAPE PIE

Grape Pie

MAKES 12 servings **PREP** 25 minutes
REFRIGERATE 2 hours, 15 minutes
BAKE at 375° for 1 hour

- 2½   cups all-purpose flour
- 1   cup (2 sticks) unsalted butter, cut into pieces and chilled
- 1   teaspoon salt
- ½   cup ice water
- 1¾   pounds red table grapes (about 5 cups)
- ⅓   cup granulated sugar
- 2   tablespoons instant tapioca
- 1   tablespoon lemon juice
- 1   egg, beaten
- 2   tablespoons coarse or granulated sugar

■ Combine flour, butter and salt in a food processor. Pulse until butter is the size of peas. Slowly stream in ¼ to ½ cup ice water, until dough just comes together (squeeze between your hands). Form into 2 equal rounds, wrap in plastic wrap and refrigerate 2 hours.

■ Heat oven to 375°. On a lightly floured surface, roll one round of dough to fit inside a 9-inch pie dish. Refrigerate 15 minutes.

■ Combine grapes, granulated sugar, tapioca and lemon juice. Transfer to piecrust. Roll out second crust and cut out about 18 three-quarter-inch circles with a pastry cutter. Place crust on top of pie and pinch edges of both crusts together, then crimp. Brush top and edges with egg, then sprinkle on coarse sugar.

■ Bake pie at 375° for 30 minutes. Carefully wrap foil around edges of crust to prevent burning, then bake another 30 minutes, until golden brown. Allow pie to cool completely on a wire rack before slicing.

PER SERVING 320 **CAL**; 16 g **FAT** (10 g **SAT**); 4 g **PRO**; 41 g **CARB**; 1 g **FIBER**; 200 mg **SODIUM**; 55 mg **CHOL**

WATERMELON MARGARITAS

Watermelon Margaritas

MAKES 8 servings **PREP** 10 minutes

- 5   cups cubed watermelon
- 3   cups ice
- 12   ounces (1½ cups) silver (blanco) tequila
- ⅓   cup fresh lime juice
- 2   tablespoons agave syrup
- ½   teaspoon kosher salt

  Salt and lime wedges, for garnish (optional)

■ In a blender, combine watermelon, ice, tequila, lime juice, agave and kosher salt. Blend until smooth. Serve over ice in, if desired, salt-rimmed glasses with lime wedges.

PER SERVING 140 **CAL**; 0 g **FAT** (0 g **SAT**); 1 g **PRO**; 12 g **CARB**; 0 g **FIBER**; 120 mg **SODIUM**; 0 mg **CHOL**

GRILLED MAHI MAHI
WITH PLUM SALSA

Stone fruits such as peaches and plums are at their peak in mid- to late-summer. Enjoy in both sweet and savory dishes—the season is fleeting!

Grilled Mahi Mahi with Plum Salsa

MAKES 4 servings **PREP** 15 minutes **GRILL** 9 minutes

- 4 red and yellow plums, pitted and finely diced
- 2 teaspoons sugar
- 1 teaspoon lemon juice
- ½ teaspoon plus ⅛ teaspoon salt
- 1¼ pounds mahi mahi or sea bass (four 5-ounce fillets)
- 1 tablespoon olive oil
- ⅛ teaspoon black pepper
- ½ cup fresh basil, chopped

■ Heat grill or grill pan to medium-high. In a bowl, combine plums, sugar, lemon juice and ⅛ teaspoon of the salt.

■ Rub mahi mahi with olive oil and season with remaining ½ teaspoon salt and the black pepper. Grill on medium-high for 5 minutes. Flip and grill another 3 to 4 minutes, until fish is cooked through.

■ Stir basil into salsa; spoon salsa over fish before serving.

PER SERVING 280 **CAL**; 4.5 g **FAT** (1 g **SAT**); 27 g **PRO**; 34 g **CARB**; 6 g **FIBER**; 490 mg **SODIUM**; 105 mg **CHOL**

Grilled Chicken and Peaches on Ciabatta

MAKES 4 servings **PREP** 15 minutes **GRILL** 10 minutes

- 4 boneless, skinless chicken breasts (about 5 ounces each)
- 1 tablespoon olive oil
- ¼ teaspoon salt
- ⅛ teaspoon black pepper
- 4 ounces Brie, cut into 8 slices
- 2 peaches, halved and pitted
- 4 mini ciabattas (about 3 ounces each), sliced horizontally
- 4 teaspoons Dijon mustard
- 1 cup arugula

■ Heat grill or grill pan to medium-high. Rub chicken on both sides with oil and season with salt and pepper. Grill on medium-high for 5 minutes. Flip chicken and place 2 Brie slices on each breast. Grill another 5 minutes, or until chicken is cooked.

■ Meanwhile, grill peaches 3 minutes per side. Slice. Grill rolls 1 to 2 minutes on cut sides.

■ Spread 1 teaspoon mustard on the bottom of each ciabatta. Follow with chicken breast, some peach slices, ¼ cup arugula and top half of ciabatta.

PER SERVING 500 **CAL**; 15 g **FAT** (7 g **SAT**); 46 g **PRO**; 46 g **CARB**; 3 g **FIBER**; 910 mg **SODIUM**; 125 mg **CHOL**

**GRILLED CHICKEN AND
PEACHES ON CIABATTA**

WILD RICE, CANTALOUPE AND CUCUMBER SALAD

COCONUT-MANGO
TAPIOCA PUDDING

Orange-fleshed fruits such as cantaloupe and mango are rich in beta-carotene, an antioxidant that can help prevent cancer.

Wild Rice, Cantaloupe and Cucumber Salad

MAKES 8 servings **PREP** 20 minutes
COOK 40 minutes **LET STAND** 20 minutes

- 1½ **cups wild rice blend (such as Lundberg)**
- 1 **container (5.3 ounces) 0% plain Greek yogurt**
- ½ **cup light mayonnaise**
- ¼ **cup white balsamic vinegar**
- ½ **teaspoon salt**
- ¼ **teaspoon black pepper**
- 3 **cups diced cantaloupe**
- 2 **cups diced cucumber**
- 1 **cup finely diced celery**
- 1 **cup raisins**
- ½ **cup roasted sunflower seeds**
- ¼ **cup finely diced shallots**

■ In a lidded pot, combine rice and 3 cups water. Bring to a boil. Reduce to a simmer, cover and cook 40 minutes or per package directions. Let stand 20 minutes.

■ Meanwhile, in a large bowl, whisk yogurt, mayonnaise, vinegar, salt and pepper. When rice is slightly cooled, stir into dressing with cantaloupe, cucumber, celery, raisins, sunflower seeds and shallots. Serve at room temperature or chilled.

PER SERVING 320 CAL; 10 g **FAT** (1 g **SAT**); 7 g **PRO**; 54 g **CARB**; 5 g **FIBER**; 300 mg **SODIUM**; 5 mg **CHOL**

Coconut-Mango Tapioca Pudding

MAKES 6 servings **PREP** 15 minutes **SOAK** overnight **COOK** 50 minutes **COOL** 10 minutes
REFRIGERATE at least 2 hours

- ½ **cup large pearl tapioca**
- 2 **cups coconut water**
- 1 **can (13.5 ounces) coconut milk**
- 1 **teaspoon vanilla extract**
- ⅛ **teaspoon salt**
- 1 **egg yolk**
- ⅓ **cup sugar**
- 2 **ripe mangoes, peeled, pitted and diced (2 cups)**
- 1 **cup unsweetened large flake coconut (such as Bob's Red Mill), toasted**

■ Soak tapioca in coconut water overnight in a bowl covered with plastic wrap.

■ In a medium lidded pot, combine tapioca–coconut water mixture, coconut milk, vanilla and salt. Cover, bring to a boil, then reduce to a low simmer. Cook, covered, for 40 minutes.

■ In a bowl, whisk egg yolk and sugar. Slowly whisk in half the tapioca; pour contents from bowl into pot. Cook another 10 minutes over low heat, until thickened. Remove from heat and cool 10 minutes.

■ Meanwhile, puree 1 cup of the mango in a blender or food processor. Mix into remaining 1 cup mango.

■ In each of 6 cups, layer ¼ cup mango, followed by 1 heaping tablespoon coconut, ½ cup tapioca, another ¼ cup mango and another 1 heaping tablespoon coconut. Cover and refrigerate until cool, at least 2 hours.

PER SERVING 390 CAL; 23 g **FAT** (20 g **SAT**); 4 g **PRO**; 48 g **CARB**; 4 g **FIBER**; 80 mg **SODIUM**; 30 mg **CHOL**

OFF THE VINE

Salad doesn't get much simpler than summer tomatoes drizzled with vinaigrette.

Heirloom Tomato Salad

MAKES 6 servings **PREP** 15 minutes

3	tablespoons fresh lemon juice
2	teaspoons snipped chives
1	teaspoon grated lemon zest
1	teaspoon Dijon mustard
1	teaspoon honey
¼	teaspoon sea salt
¼	teaspoon cracked black pepper
¼	cup olive oil
5	to 6 heirloom tomatoes

■ Whisk the fresh lemon juice, snipped chives, grated lemon zest, Dijon mustard, honey, sea salt and cracked black pepper. While whisking, add the olive oil in a thin stream until blended.

■ Slice 5 or 6 heirloom tomatoes and fan slices onto a board or large platter. Season with additional chives, sea salt and cracked pepper. Serve with dressing.

Juicy and sweet vine-ripened tomatoes require little but slicing and a splash of dressing to achieve perfection. Heirloom tomatoes—passed down the generations because of their fabulous flavor and texture qualities—can be found at farmer's markets this time of year.

HEIRLOOM
TOMATO SALAD

HEALTHY FAMILY DINNERS

Eat your greens! Salads aren't just a lunch thing—here are six dinner-worthy ideas.

PANKO HONEY-FRIED CHICKEN AND NAPA SLAW, PAGE 212

Seven-Layer Thai Salad

MAKES 8 servings **PREP** 25 minutes **COOK** 7 minutes

- 1 tablespoon canola oil
- 1½ pounds lean ground beef
- 2 tablespoons chopped ginger
- 4 tablespoons reduced-sodium or gluten-free soy sauce
- 6 cups shredded iceberg lettuce
- 2 sweet red peppers, seeded and thinly sliced
- 1 cup packed cilantro leaves, plus more for garnish
- 2 cups shelled edamame
- 1 large seedless cucumber, peeled and thinly sliced
- 1 large bunch scallions, trimmed and sliced
- ½ cup smooth peanut butter
- 1 teaspoon chopped garlic
- ⅔ cup light mayonnaise
- Chopped peanuts, for garnish

■ In a large nonstick skillet, heat oil over medium-high heat. Crumble in beef and add ginger; cook 7 minutes, stirring occasionally. Stir in 2 tablespoons of the soy sauce and allow to cool.

■ In the bottom of a 14-cup trifle dish, place lettuce and pack down slightly. Top with a layer of red peppers followed by layers of cilantro (packing down each), cooled beef mixture, edamame, cucumber and scallions.

■ In a small bowl, whisk peanut butter with 2 tablespoons warm water and remaining 2 tablespoons soy sauce until smooth. Stir in garlic and mayonnaise.

■ Spread peanut butter dressing over top of salad. Garnish with chopped peanuts and, if using, cilantro. If desired, toss salad before serving.

PER SERVING 341 **CAL**; 22 g **FAT** (4 g **SAT**); 25 g **PRO**; 14 g **CARB**; 4 g **FIBER**; 619 mg **SODIUM**; 52 mg **CHOL**

SCALLOP FRISÉE
SALAD

Scallop Frisée Salad

MAKES 4 servings **PREP** 20 minutes
COOK 7 minutes

DRESSING

- ½ **cup buttermilk**
- ¼ **cup reduced-fat sour cream**
- ¼ **cup reduced-fat mayonnaise**
- ¼ **cup snipped chives**
- 1 **teaspoon lemon juice**
- ¼ **teaspoon salt**
- ¼ **teaspoon black pepper**
- ½ **cup finely chopped peeled seedless cucumber**

SCALLOPS AND SALAD

- 3 **tablespoons canola oil**
- 1¼ **pounds large sea scallops, halved horizontally**
- ⅓ **cup all-purpose flour**
- ¼ **teaspoon salt**
- ¼ **teaspoon black pepper**
- **Kernels from 3 ears of corn**
- 8 **cups spring salad greens**
- ½ **large bunch frisée**
- ½ **fennel bulb, trimmed and thinly sliced**
- **Lemon wedges (optional)**

■ **Dressing.** In a medium bowl, whisk buttermilk, sour cream, mayonnaise, chives, lemon juice, salt and pepper. Stir in cucumber. Refrigerate.

■ **Scallops and Salad.** Heat 2 tablespoons of the oil in a large nonstick skillet over medium-high heat. Coat scallops in flour and add half to skillet; cook 2 minutes per side. Season with ⅛ teaspoon each of the salt and pepper. Remove to a plate. Add remaining 1 tablespoon oil to skillet and cook remaining scallops. Season with remaining ⅛ teaspoon each salt and pepper. Remove to plate.

■ In the same skillet, add corn and cook until charred, about 3 minutes. Stir occasionally.

■ In a large bowl, toss greens, frisée and fennel with half the dressing. Add scallops and corn. Serve with remaining dressing and, if desired, lemon wedges.

PER SERVING 496 **CAL**; 22 g **FAT** (3 g **SAT**); 44 g **PRO**; 36 g **CARB**; 4 g **FIBER**; 800 mg **SODIUM**; 103 mg **CHOL**

WILD SALMON CAESAR

Wild Salmon Caesar

MAKES 4 servings **PREP** 25 minutes **ROAST** 14 minutes at 450°

- 1 **wild-caught salmon fillet (1 pound), cut into 4 pieces**
- 1 **bunch thin asparagus, trimmed**
- 2 **tablespoons olive oil**
- ¾ **teaspoon salt**
- ½ **teaspoon black pepper**
- ½ **cup reduced-fat sour cream**
- 2 **tablespoons lemon juice**
- 2 **cloves garlic, finely chopped**
- 1 **teaspoon spicy brown mustard**
- 1 **teaspoon Worcestershire sauce**
- 1 **teaspoon anchovy paste (optional)**
- 5 **tablespoons grated Parmesan**
- 8 **cups sliced romaine**
- ½ **small red onion, sliced**
- 1 **cup grape tomatoes**

■ Heat oven to 450°. Place salmon and asparagus on separate baking pans. Drizzle 1 tablespoon of the olive oil over asparagus; season salmon and asparagus with ½ teaspoon of the salt and ¼ teaspoon of the pepper. Roast at 450° for 12 to 14 minutes, until salmon flakes and asparagus is tender. Cut asparagus into 1-inch pieces.

■ Meanwhile, whisk sour cream, remaining 1 tablespoon olive oil, the lemon juice, garlic, mustard, Worcestershire, anchovy paste (if using), remaining ¼ teaspoon each salt and pepper and 3 tablespoons of the Parmesan. Set aside.

■ In a large bowl, toss romaine, onion, tomatoes and asparagus. Add half the dressing and remaining 2 tablespoons Parmesan; toss to coat.

■ Serve salad with salmon and remaining dressing on the side.

PER SERVING 387 **CAL**; 21 g **FAT** (6 g **SAT**); 34 g **PRO**; 17 g **CARB**; 7 g **FIBER**; 661 mg **SODIUM**; 87 mg **CHOL**

PANKO HONEY-FRIED
CHICKEN AND NAPA SLAW

Panko Honey-Fried Chicken and Napa Slaw

MAKES 4 servings   PREP 25 minutes   REFRIGERATE 1 hour   COOK 8 minutes

NAPA SLAW

- 6 cups shredded napa cabbage
- 2 cups sliced snow peas
- 2 thinly sliced carrots
- 1 cup shredded red cabbage
- 1 container (7 ounces) Greek 2% plain yogurt
- 2 tablespoons milk
- 1 tablespoon honey
- 1 tablespoon lemon juice
- 1 teaspoon spicy brown mustard
- ½ teaspoon salt
- ⅛ teaspoon black pepper
- 2 tablespoons chopped parsley

FRIED CHICKEN

- 1 pound uncooked chicken tenders (fillets)
- ¼ cup honey combined with 2 tablespoons warm water
- 1½ cups panko bread crumbs
- 5 tablespoons canola oil

- ½ teaspoon salt
- ⅛ teaspoon black pepper

■ **Slaw.** In a large bowl, combine napa cabbage, snow peas, carrots and red cabbage. Whisk yogurt, milk, honey, lemon juice, mustard, salt and pepper. Stir in parsley. Fold mixture into slaw. Cover and refrigerate 1 hour.

■ **Chicken.** Dip chicken in honey mixture. Coat with panko.

■ In a large skillet, heat 3 tablespoons of the oil over medium-high heat. Season chicken with ¼ teaspoon of the salt and the pepper. Add half to pan; cook 1 to 2 minutes per side or until internal temperature reaches 160°. Add remaining 2 tablespoons oil; cook second batch. Remove to a plate and season with remaining ¼ teaspoon salt. Serve chicken topped with slaw.

PER SERVING 523 CAL; 21 g FAT (2 g SAT); 29 g PRO; 57 g CARB; 6 g FIBER; 746 mg SODIUM; 66 mg CHOL

Escarole, Bean and Pork Salad

MAKES 4 servings   PREP 15 minutes
GRILL 12 minutes

- 1 pork tenderloin (about 1¼ pounds)
- 1 teaspoon dried Italian seasoning
- ½ teaspoon plus ⅛ teaspoon salt
- ½ teaspoon black pepper
- 1 large bunch escarole, washed and cut into bite-size pieces (about 10 cups)
- 1 can (15 ounces) cannellini beans, drained and rinsed
- 1 sweet yellow pepper, seeded and diced
- 2 ribs celery, thinly sliced
- ¼ cup pitted Kalamata olives, sliced
- 1 shallot, sliced
- 3 tablespoons Champagne vinegar
- 2 tablespoons olive oil

■ Heat grill to medium-high. Season pork tenderloin with Italian seasoning and ¼ teaspoon each of the salt and pepper. Grill about 6 minutes per side, turning as needed to avoid burning, or until internal temperature reaches 140°. Place on a platter and loosely cover with foil.

■ In a large bowl, combine escarole, beans, yellow pepper, celery, olives and shallot. Combine vinegar, olive oil and ⅛ teaspoon each of the salt and pepper. Toss dressing with escarole and bean mixture.

■ Thinly slice pork tenderloin. Serve with salad. Season pork and salad with remaining ¼ teaspoon salt and ⅛ teaspoon pepper.

PER SERVING 327 CAL; 11 g FAT (2 g SAT); 31 g PRO; 25 g CARB; 10 g FIBER; 668 mg SODIUM; 70 mg CHOL

ESCAROLE, BEAN
AND PORK SALAD

BUFFALO TURKEY
CHOPPED SALAD

The tangy, vinegary, spicy flavors of America's favorite football-watching snack are brought to bear in this healthful main-dish salad made with lean turkey and packed with veggies.

Buffalo Turkey Chopped Salad

MAKES 4 servings **PREP** 30 minutes **COOK** 2 minutes

- 1 **pound fresh turkey cutlets**
- 3 **tablespoons Frank's Original Hot Sauce**
- 2 **tablespoons red wine vinegar**
- ⅛ **teaspoon salt**
- ⅛ **teaspoon black pepper**
- 1 **teaspoon Dijon mustard**
- 3 **tablespoons olive oil**
- 1 **head red leafy lettuce, torn into bite-size pieces**
- 2 **large carrots, diced**
- 1 **large zucchini, diced**
- 1 **cup diced radishes**
- ½ **English cucumber, diced**
- 2 **ribs celery, diced**
- 1 **avocado, peeled, pitted and sliced into 16 thin wedges**
- ¼ **cup blue cheese crumbles**

■ Place turkey cutlets in a lidded skillet and add water to cover by at least 1 inch. Cover and bring to a simmer. Gently simmer 2 minutes, or until cooked through. Remove to a cutting board and slice or dice into pieces. Place turkey pieces in a medium bowl and toss with hot sauce. Set aside.

■ In a large bowl, whisk vinegar, salt, pepper and mustard. Gradually whisk in olive oil. Add red leafy lettuce, carrots, zucchini, radishes, cucumber and celery. Toss to combine and coat all ingredients with dressing.

■ Divide salad among 4 plates. Top each with 4 avocado slices, turkey and blue cheese crumbles.

PER SERVING 383 **CAL**; 22 g **FAT** (4 g **SAT**); 33 g **PRO**; 16 g **CARB**; 7 g **FIBER**; 703 mg **SODIUM**; 71 mg **CHOL**

**HOISIN SHRIMP WITH BOK CHOY,
SHIITAKES AND PEPPERS, PAGE 227**

SEPTEMBER

221

233

242

WEEKNIGHT DINNERS

Eat well—and on budget—with these quick-to-fix dinners for $20 and under.

HERB-CRUSTED PORK TENDERLOIN, PAGE 221

**SIRLOIN KABOBS,
PAGE 225**

BEEF RAGÙ

Beef Ragù

MAKES 4 servings **PREP** 10 minutes
SLOW COOK 6 hours on HIGH

- 2 teaspoons olive oil
- 1 thinly sliced large sweet onion
- 1 grated carrot
- 4 minced garlic cloves
- 2 teaspoons Italian seasoning
- 2 pounds trimmed boneless beef chuck roast
- ½ teaspoon kosher salt
- ½ teaspoon black pepper
- 1 28-ounce can whole plum tomatoes in puree
- ¾ cup reduced-sodium beef broth
- 1 tablespoon red-wine vinegar
- 1 12-ounce package gluten-free or regular pasta
- 1 dollop part-skim ricotta
  Chopped basil

■ Heat olive oil in a large saucepan. Add sweet onion, carrot, garlic cloves and Italian seasoning. Cook, stirring frequently until vegetables soften, 5 minutes.

■ Transfer mixture to a 5- to 6-quart slow cooker. Add trimmed boneless beef chuck roast. Sprinkle with kosher salt and black pepper. Add whole plum tomatoes in puree and reduced-sodium beef broth.

■ Cover and slow cook on HIGH until beef is fork-tender, 6 hours.

■ Transfer beef to a cutting board and shred using 2 forks. Mash tomato mixture and stir beef back into slow cooker. Stir in red-wine vinegar. Spoon half the beef mixture into a freezer container and reserve for a second meal.

■ Cook gluten-free or regular pasta according to package directions. Divide pasta and ragú among serving bowls. Top each with 1 dollop part-skim ricotta and chopped basil.

HERB-CRUSTED PORK TENDERLOIN

Herb-Crusted Pork Tenderloin

MAKES 4 servings **PREP** 12 minutes **ROAST** 25 minutes at 400°

- ¼ cup fresh bread crumbs
- 2 teaspoons chopped thyme
- 1 teaspoon garlic powder
- 1 teaspoon smoked paprika
- ¼ teaspoon plus another ¼ teaspoon kosher salt
- 1¼ pounds pork tenderloin
- 1 tablespoon Dijon mustard
- 1 pound small red new potatoes
- 1 thinly sliced shallot
- 1 tablespoon plus 2 teaspoons olive oil
- ¼ teaspoon black pepper
- 1 pound trimmed asparagus

■ Heat oven to 400°. In a small bowl, combine fresh bread crumbs, chopped thyme, garlic powder, smoked paprika and ¼ teaspoon kosher salt. Brush pork tenderloin with Dijon mustard. Pat bread crumb mixture evenly on tenderloin. Place tenderloin on a baking sheet.

■ In a bowl, toss small red new potatoes and shallot with olive oil, ¼ teaspoon kosher salt and black pepper. Place on a separate baking sheet. In a bowl, toss trimmed asparagus with olive oil and a pinch of salt.

■ Roast pork and potatoes at 400° for 25 minutes or until pork registers 145°. After 15 minutes of roasting, move potatoes to one side of baking sheet. Add asparagus and continue roasting until potatoes are fork-tender. Let pork rest 5 minutes. Slice and serve with potatoes and asparagus.

LEMON-TARRAGON SCALLOPS

Chicken Saltimbocca

MAKES 4 servings PREP 5 minutes
COOK 20 minutes

- 1½ **pounds large russet potatoes**
- ½ **cup 2% milk**
- 2 **tablespoons plus 1 tablespoon butter**
- ½ **teaspoon salt**
- ¼ **teaspoon black pepper**
- 4 **boneless, skinless chicken breasts (about 5 ounces each)**
- 8 **sage leaves**
- 4 **slices of prosciutto**
- 1 **tablespoon olive oil**
- ½ **cup sweet vermouth**
- ½ **cup chicken broth**
- 1 **teaspoon cornstarch**

■ Peel and cube large russet potatoes. In a medium pot, combine potatoes with enough cool salted water to cover by an inch. Bring to a boil over high heat. Cook until potatoes are tender, about 12 minutes. Drain well. Mash potatoes with 2% milk, 2 tablespoons butter and salt. Set aside; keep warm.

■ Sprinkle black pepper on 4 boneless, skinless chicken breasts (about 5 ounces each), slightly pounded. Top each breast with 2 sage leaves. Wrap 1 slice prosciutto over each breast.

■ Heat 1 tablespoon olive oil in a large nonstick skillet. Place chicken, prosciutto side down, in skillet; cook until prosciutto is nicely seared, 2 minutes. Turn chicken over; cook until internal temperature registers 170° on an instant-read thermometer, about 3 minutes. Remove to a warm plate.

■ Add sweet vermouth to skillet. Scrape any browned bits from bottom of skillet; cook 1 minute. In a small bowl, stir chicken broth and cornstarch. Add to skillet. Simmer, stirring until thickened, 1 to 2 minutes. Remove from heat and stir in 1 tablespoon butter. Pour over chicken and serve with mashed potatoes and steamed green beans.

Lemon-Tarragon Scallops

MAKES 4 servings PREP 10 minutes COOK 13 minutes

- 1 **tablespoon plus 2 teaspoons olive oil**
- 1 **shallot**
- 2 **minced garlic cloves**
- 1 **bag (13.25 ounces) baby kale and spinach blend**
- ¼ **teaspoon kosher salt**
- ½ **cup white wine**
- 2 **tablespoons fresh lemon juice**
- 1 **tablespoon flour**
- 2 **teaspoons chopped tarragon**
- 1 **pound frozen baby scallops**
- 1 **tablespoon unsalted butter**
- 2 **cups cooked whole wheat couscous**

■ In a large skillet, heat 1 tablespoon olive oil over medium heat. Finely chop shallot and add half; cook, stirring constantly, until translucent, 2 minutes. Add 1 minced garlic clove and baby kale and spinach blend. Cook, stirring frequently until greens soften, 4 minutes. Transfer to a bowl, sprinkle with kosher salt and keep warm.

■ Combine white wine, fresh lemon juice, flour and chopped tarragon. In the same skillet, heat 2 teaspoons olive oil over medium heat. Add remaining ½ shallot and 1 minced garlic clove. Cook, stirring, 2 minutes. Add frozen bay scallops, defrosted. Cook 2 minutes. Turn scallops over and cook 1 minute. Stir wine mixture into pan; cook, stirring constantly, until sauce thickens, about 2 minutes. Stir in unsalted butter and a pinch of kosher salt. Serve scallops with greens and cooked whole wheat couscous.

CHICKEN
SALTIMBOCCA

**LEMON-FENNEL
ROASTED CHICKEN
AND VEGETABLES**

SIRLOIN KABOBS

Lemon-Fennel Roasted Chicken and Vegetables

MAKES 4 servings **PREP** 25 minutes
ROAST 1 hour at 450°F **STAND** 10 minutes

1	whole chicken (3½ to 4 pounds)
½	teaspoon plus another ½ teaspoon kosher salt
½	teaspoon plus another ½ teaspoon black pepper
2	sliced cloves of garlic
1	fennel bupound
½	sliced lemon
1	cup chicken broth
2	carrots
2	sweet potatoes
1	small red onion
1	red bell pepper
2	tablespoons olive oil
1	tablespoon chopped thyme

■ Heat oven to 450°. Remove giblets from cavity of a chicken. Gently lift skin from breast and legs; season with ½ teaspoon each of the kosher salt and black pepper. Place garlic and frond leaves from fennel bupound (reserve bupound for later) under the skin. Place trimmed ends of fennel and lemon in cavity of chicken. Place chicken on a rack in a large roasting pan. Tie legs. Pour chicken broth into bottom of pan. Roast at 450° for 50 to 60 minutes or until internal temperature reaches 170° on an instant-read thermometer. Let rest 10 minutes.

■ Meanwhile, toss carrots, cut diagonally into slices; sweet potatoes, peeled and cut into chunks; red onion, cut into wedges; bell pepper, seeded and cut into thick pieces; and fennel bupound, halved and sliced, in a large bowl with olive oil, thyme leaves and ½ teaspoon each kosher salt and black pepper. Place on a baking sheet and roast with chicken for 35 minutes, until browned and fork-tender.

Sirloin Kabobs

MAKES 4 servings **PREP** 10 minutes **CHILL** 30 minutes **GRILL** 6 minutes

8	10-inch bamboo skewers
1	pound sirloin, cut into 16 pieces
¼	cup bottled balsamic vinaigrette
1	tablespoon reduced-sodium soy sauce
	Baby bella mushrooms
	Red onions, cut into wedges
	Grape tomatoes
	Corn on the cob
	Rice

■ Soak skewers in warm water. Combine sirloin, balsamic vinaigrette and soy sauce in a resealable plastic bag. Refrigerate 30 minutes.

■ Heat gas grill to medium-high or coals in charcoal grill to medium hot. On a skewer, thread 1 baby bella mushroom, 1 beef cube, 1 wedge red onion and 1 grape tomato, and repeat to fill skewer. Continue threading to fill 8 skewers. Grill kabobs 3 to 4 minutes per side, until cooked through. Serve with corn on the cob and rice.

A PAN THAT CAN!

These one-dish dinners offer great taste—and easy cleanup.

HOISIN SHRIMP WITH BOK CHOY, SHIITAKES AND PEPPERS

Hoisin Shrimp with Bok Choy, Shiitakes and Peppers

MAKES 4 servings **PREP** 20 minutes
ROAST 20 minutes at 400°

- ¼ cup hoisin sauce
- 2 tablespoons reduced-sodium soy sauce, plus more for serving (optional)
- 1 tablespoon rice wine vinegar
- 2 teaspoons sesame oil
- 1 teaspoon sriracha
- 1 large bok choy, cut into 3-inch pieces
- 2 sweet red peppers, seeded and cut into ½-inch strips
- 1 pound small shiitake mushrooms, stems removed
- 2 tablespoons canola oil
- 1½ pounds jumbo shrimp, peeled and deveined
- 2 teaspoons toasted sesame seeds
- **Chopped scallions (optional)**

■ Line a 13 x 9-inch rimmed sheet pan with nonstick foil.

■ In a small bowl, combine hoisin, soy sauce, vinegar, sesame oil and sriracha. Set aside.

■ Place bok choy, peppers and shiitakes on prepared sheet pan. Combine 3 tablespoons of the hoisin mixture with canola oil. Pour over vegetables and toss to coat.

■ Toss shrimp with remaining hoisin mixture. Place shrimp over vegetables.

■ Roast at 450° for 20 minutes. Garnish with sesame seeds and, if using, scallions. Serve with additional soy sauce if desired.

Garam Masala Pork and Apples

MAKES 4 servings **PREP** 20 minutes
ROAST 18 minutes at 450° **BROIL** 2 minutes

- 3 tablespoons canola oil
- ¾ teaspoon salt
- ¾ teaspoon pepper
- ¼ teaspoon ground ginger
- ¼ teaspoon cumin
- 2 sliced Honeycrisp apples
- 1 sliced red onion
- 1 can (15 ounces) garbanzo beans, drained and rinsed
- 2 teaspoons garam masala
- 4 bone-in pork chops (8 ounces each)

■ Combine canola oil, salt, pepper, ground ginger and cumin. In prepared sheet pan, combine apples, onion and garbanzo beans. Toss with 2 tablespoons of the oil mixture. Combine garam masala with remaining oil mixture and brush over pork chops. Arrange chops over vegetables and roast at 450° for 18 minutes. Broil 2 minutes.

Maple-Mustard Chicken with Fingerlings and Brussels Sprouts

MAKES 4 servings **PREP** 20 minutes
ROAST 35 minutes at 450°

- 3 tablespoons canola oil
- 1 teaspoon salt
- 1 teaspoon dried thyme
- ¼ teaspoon black pepper
- 1½ pounds fingerling potatoes
- 1 pound Brussels sprouts
- 3 tablespoons maple syrup
- 1 tablespoon coarse-grain mustard
- 8 small chicken thighs (5 ounces each)

■ Line a 13 x 9-inch rimmed sheet pan with nonstick foil. Combine canola oil, salt, thyme and black pepper. In prepared sheet pan, combine fingerling potatoes and Brussels sprouts with 2 tablespoons of the oil mixture. Combine remaining oil mixture, maple syrup and coarse-grain mustard; spoon over chicken thighs. Place on sheet pan and roast at 450° for 35 minutes.

Lamb Meatballs, Greek Potatoes and Broccoli Rabe

MAKES 4 servings **PREP** 25 minutes
ROAST 30 minutes at 450° **BROIL** 1 minute

- 1¼ pounds ground lamb
- ⅓ cup plain bread crumbs
- 1 lightly beaten egg
- 2 tablespoons chopped fresh mint
- 1 teaspoon garlic salt
- 1 teaspoon onion powder
- 1 teaspoon dried oregano
- ¼ teaspoon cinnamon
- ¼ teaspoon black pepper
- 1½ pounds potato wedges
- 2 teaspoons olive oil
- ½ teaspoon plus ⅛ teaspoon salt
- ½ teaspoon plus ⅛ teaspoon pepper
- ½ pound trimmed broccoli rabe
- 2 containers (5.3 ounces each) plain Greek yogurt
- ½ peeled and diced cucumber
- ½ teaspoon lemon juice

■ Line a 13 x 9-inch rimmed sheet pan with nonstick foil. Combine lamb, bread crumbs, egg, mint, garlic salt, onion powder, dried oregano, cinnamon, and black pepper. Form into 28 meatballs.

■ In prepared sheet pan, toss potato wedges (½ inch thick) with olive oil and ½ teaspoon each salt and pepper. Scatter broccoli rabe over potatoes. Arrange meatballs on top.

■ Roast at 450° for 30 minutes. Broil 1 minute. Serve with yogurt sauce: Combine plain Greek yogurt, cucumber, ⅛ teaspoon each salt and pepper, and lemon juice.

TAKE FIVE

You can count on these easy meals—all you need is a handful of ingredients.

SAUSAGE AND SPINACH QUESADILLAS

Sausage and Spinach Quesadillas

MAKES 6 servings **PREP** 10 minutes
COOK 5 minutes **BROIL** 2 minutes

- 1 tablespoon vegetable oil
- 4 mild fresh chicken or turkey sausages
- 1 bag (8 ounces) baby spinach
- 8 fajita-size flour tortillas
- 8 ounces pepper Jack cheese
  Jarred salsa

■ Heat 1 tablespoon vegetable oil in a large nonstick skillet over medium-high heat. Crumble in chicken or turkey sausages and cook, breaking apart with a silicone spatula, 3 minutes. Add baby spinach and cook 2 minutes, until wilted.

■ Place 4 fajita-size flour tortillas on a large baking sheet. Shred pepper Jack cheese and top each tortilla with ¼ cup of the shredded cheese. Divide sausage mixture among tortillas and top each with another ¼ cup cheese. Stack with 4 more tortillas and spritz with nonstick cooking spray.

■ Broil 3 inches from heat for 1 minute. Flip over and spray tortillas again. Broil 1 additional minute. Serve with salsa on the side.

Chunky Beef Chili

MAKES 6 servings **PREP** 5 minutes
COOK 4 minutes **SLOW COOK** on HIGH for 5 hours or LOW for 7 hours

- 2¼ pounds beef chuck for stew
- 1 package (1¼-ounces) McCormick chili seasoning mix
- ¼ teaspoon salt
- ¼ teaspoon pepper
- 2 tablespoons vegetable oil
- 1 can (10 ounces) red enchilada sauce
- 2 cans (14.5 ounces each) low-sodium kidney beans
- 1 diced avocado

■ Season beef chuck with 1 tablespoon McCormick chili seasoning mix, salt and pepper. Sear in 2 tablespoons vegetable oil 4 minutes over medium-high heat.

■ Transfer beef to a slow cooker and add enchilada sauce and remaining seasoning mix.

■ Cover and slow cook on HIGH for 5 hours or LOW for 7 hours.

■ Drain and rinse cans of kidney beans. Stir into chili. Serve with diced avocado on top.

Rigatoni with Chicken

MAKES 6 servings **PREP** 10 minutes
COOK 15 minutes

- ½ pound trimmed green beans
- 1 thinly sliced sweet red pepper
- 1 pound rigatoni pasta
- 2 tablespoons vegetable oil
- 1 pound thinly sliced boneless chicken breasts
- ½ teaspoon salt
- ¼ teaspoon pepper
- ¾ cup Alouette garlic and herb cheese

■ Bring a large pot of lightly salted water to a boil. Add green beans and red pepper and cook 3 minutes. Remove to a bowl with a slotted spoon. Return water to a boil and add rigatoni. Boil 12 minutes.

■ While rigatoni cooks, heat 2 tablespoons oil in a large skillet over medium-high heat. Add chicken breasts and sauté 3 minutes. Stir green beans and sweet red pepper into skillet; cook 2 minutes. Season with salt and pepper. Crumble in Alouette garlic and herb cheese.

■ Drain rigatoni, reserving ½ cup pasta water. Toss rigatoni in a large bowl with chicken mixture, adding a little pasta water to thin sauce, if desired.

Pulled Turkey Sandwiches

MAKES 6 servings **PREP** 10 minutes
SLOW COOK on HIGH for 3 hours or LOW for 6 hours

- 2½ pounds boneless, skinless turkey breast
- 1 cup bottled barbecue sauce
- 2 Gala apples
- 6 kaiser rolls
  Deli coleslaw

■ Place a turkey breast in a slow cooker. In a medium bowl, whisk barbecue sauce and 1 cored and grated Gala apple. Pour over turkey in slow cooker; cover and slow cook on HIGH for 3 hours or LOW for 6 hours.

■ Remove turkey breast to a cutting board and shred with 2 forks. Return to sauce and stir to coat.

■ Toast kaiser rolls and spread each with a little barbecue sauce. Core another Gala apple and slice into ⅛-inch-thick slices. Place ¾ cup of the turkey mixture and a few apple slices on each roll. Serve with deli coleslaw on the side.

Grilled Steak Caesar

MAKES 4 servings **PREP** 10 minutes
GRILL 10 minutes

- 1¼ pounds skirt steak
- ½ teaspoon salt
- ¼ teaspoon ground pepper
- 2 romaine hearts
- 1 cup red and yellow cherry tomatoes, halved
- ½ cup croutons
  Brianna's Asiago Caesar salad dressing

■ Season steak with salt and ground pepper. Heat a grill or grill pan to medium-high heat. Grill steak 8 minutes, turning once. Let rest 5 minutes.

■ Meanwhile, split romaine hearts in half lengthwise and rinse. Grill romaine, cut sides down, 2 minutes. Place romaine hearts, cut sides up, on a platter. Add cherry tomatoes.

■ Slice steak across the grain and scatter over lettuce and tomatoes. Top with croutons and drizzle with Brianna's Asiago Caesar salad dressing.

CRACKING THE CODE

A staple for breakfast, eggs double as a go-to dinner.

Southwestern Burritos

MAKES 4 servings START TO FINISH 30 minutes

- 1 **tablespoon vegetable oil**
- 1 **package (5 ounces) baby spinach**
- 6 **eggs**
- 2 **sliced scallions**
- ⅓ **cup chopped cilantro**
- ½ **teaspoon chili powder**
- ¼ **teaspoon salt**
- ¼ **teaspoon pepper**
- 1 **can (15 ounces) black beans**
- 1 **cup shredded Monterey Jack**
- ¼ **cup salsa**
- 4 **large whole wheat tortillas**

■ In a large nonstick skillet, heat 1 tablespoon olive oil over medium heat. Stir in baby spinach and cook 2 minutes, until wilted.

■ Whisk eggs in a bowl with scallions, cilantro, chili powder, salt and pepper. Pour into skillet with spinach and stir 2 minutes, until cooked.

■ Distribute eggs, beans, Monterey Jack and salsa among warmed tortillas. Roll burrito-style and serve immediately.

SOUTHWESTERN BURRITOS

Bacon, Potato and Onion Frittata

MAKES 4 servings **START TO FINISH** 30 minutes

- **4 slices diced bacon**
- **1 pound thinly sliced red potatoes**
- **1 small diced red onion**
- **1 tablespoon chopped rosemary**
- **6 eggs**
- **¼ cup milk**
- **½ teaspoon salt**
- **¼ teaspoon black pepper**

■ In an ovenproof nonstick skillet, cook bacon over medium heat 5 minutes. Transfer to a paper towel with a slotted spoon.

■ Reduce heat to medium-low, add red potatoes, red onion and rosemary. Cover and cook 10 minutes, until potatoes are tender.

■ Whisk eggs, milk, salt and black pepper in a bowl. Pour over potatoes and stir in bacon. Bake uncovered at 350° for 10 minutes, until set.

■ Slice and serve with an arugula salad.

BACON, POTATO AND ONION FRITTATA

ITALIAN BAKED EGGS

Eggs poached in tomato sauce is a popular dish in Italy, France, Israel (where it's called 'shakshuka'), and Tunisia. Some versions call for crushed red pepper to be stirred into the tomatoes for a bit of spiciness. Serve with crusty bread to mop up the yolks and savory sauce.

Italian Baked Eggs

MAKES 4 servings **PREP** 10 minutes **COOK** 11 minutes **BAKE** 8 minutes at 400°

- 1 **tablespoon olive oil**
- 1 **small onion, diced**
- 3 **garlic cloves, chopped**
- 1 **28-ounce can crushed tomatoes**
- ½ **cup chopped fresh basil**
- ¼ **teaspoon salt**
- ⅛ **teaspoon pepper**
- 4 **eggs**
- 4 **ounces smoked or regular fresh mozzarella, sliced**
  Crusty bread

■ Heat oven to 400°. In a large oven-safe skillet (not nonstick), heat olive oil over medium heat. Stir in onion; cook 3 to 5 minutes until softened. Stir in garlic; cook 1 minute until softened. Pour in tomatoes, ¼ cup of the basil, the salt and pepper. Reduce heat to medium-low and simmer 5 minutes.

■ Remove skillet from heat. Crack eggs into sauce, spacing evenly apart. Distribute cheese around skillet. Bake at 400° on top rack until egg whites are set, about 8 minutes.

■ Carefully remove skillet from oven. Scatter remaining ¼ cup basil on top and serve immediately with crusty bread.

MIX IT UP: Swap 1 cup tomatoes with 1 cup diced roasted red peppers; basil with mint. Add ½ teaspoon cumin and ¼ teaspoon cayenne.

PER SERVING 267 **CAL**; 16 g **FAT** (7 g **SAT**); 232 mg **CHOL**; 679 mg **SODIUM**; 19 g **CARB**; 4 g **FIBER**; 16 g **PRO**

GET HOOKED!

These kid-friendly fish dishes will help you get your twice-weekly catch.

OLIVE OIL-POACHED SALMON WITH WHITE BEANS

Olive Oil-Poached Salmon with White Beans

MAKES 4 servings **START TO FINISH** 30 minutes

- 1 **large lemon**
- 4 **cups olive oil**
- 2 **cloves smashed garlic**
- 1 **sprig plus ½ teaspoon chopped rosemary**
- 4 **skinless salmon fillets (5 ounces each)**
- ½ **teaspoon plus ⅛ teaspoon salt**
- ¼ **teaspoon plus ⅛ teaspoon black pepper**
- 2 **cans (15 ounces each) cannellini beans, rinsed and drained**
- 2 **tablespoons lemon juice**
- 1 **teaspoon lemon zest**

■ Remove peel from lemon in several large strips with a vegetable peeler. In a large, deep sauté pan, heat olive oil, garlic, 1 sprig rosemary and lemon peel until temperature reaches 180°.

■ Season salmon fillets with ½ teaspoon of the salt and ¼ teaspoon of the black pepper; add to oil and cook 12 minutes or until fish reaches desired temperature.

■ Meanwhile, in a pot over medium heat, combine cannellini beans, 2 tablespoons of the hot oil, lemon juice, lemon zest, the ½ teaspoon chopped rosemary, the remaining ⅛ teaspoon salt and pepper. Stir until heated through. Serve salmon on top of beans.

Variation: Poach shrimp in olive oil, and serve over black beans with a cilantro-lime sauce.

**CURRIED FLOUNDER
WITH COCONUT SWEET
POTATOES**

Curried Flounder with Coconut Sweet Potatoes

MAKES 4 servings **START TO FINISH** 30 minutes

2	**pounds sweet potatoes**
½	**cup coconut milk**
¼	**teaspoon plus ⅛ teaspoon salt**
1	**tablespoon Madras curry powder**
⅛	**teaspoon cayenne**
1¼	**pounds flounder**
	Cilantro

■ Pierce potatoes several times with a fork and place in a microwave-safe baking dish. Microwave 8 to 10 minutes (depending on size), until flesh is soft.

■ Cool slightly, then scoop flesh into a pot with coconut milk and ¼ teaspoon of the salt. Mix well over medium-low heat; cover to keep warm.

■ Combine curry powder, remaining ⅛ teaspoon salt, and cayenne. Rub on flounder.

■ Place fish on a foil-lined nonstick baking sheet and bake at 375° for 7 to 9 minutes, until cooked. Serve over sweet potatoes and garnish with cilantro.

Note: For a flavor variation, rub sole fillets with a mixture of lemon zest, chopped parsley, chopped garlic and salt. Bake, then serve with herb mashed potatoes.

The American Heart Association recommends eating fish—especially fatty fish like salmon and tuna—at least two times a week. It even tastes great with just fresh herbs, lemon and spices.

Grilled Tuna Salad

MAKES 4 servings **START TO FINISH** 30 minutes

- ⅓ **cup light mayonnaise**
- 3 **tablespoons red wine vinegar**
- 2 **tablespoons capers**
- ½ **teaspoon grated garlic**
- ½ **teaspoon Dijon mustard**
- ½ **teaspoon anchovy paste (optional)**
- ¼ **teaspoon black pepper**
- 1 **package (5 ounces) baby spinach**
- 1 **pint cherry tomatoes**
- ⅓ **cup sliced shallots**
- 4 **tuna fillets (5 ounces each)**
- ¼ **teaspoon salt**
- ¼ **teaspoon pepper**

■ Whisk mayonnaise, vinegar, capers, garlic, mustard, anchovy paste (if desired), and pepper in a small bowl.

■ In a large bowl combine spinach, tomatoes and shallots. Toss ½ cup of the dressing with the spinach mixture. Divide among 4 dinner plates.

■ Season tuna fillets with salt and pepper. Grill on medium-high heat for 4 minutes, turning once, until medium.

■ Slice tuna on the diagonal. Serve tuna over salad with remaining dressing on the side.

Variation: Swap in swordfish, adding grilled red peppers. Toss with mixed greens, Kalamata olives, red onion, and a white wine vinaigrette.

GRILLED TUNA SALAD

SIDE SHOW

These veggie-centric dishes are hearty and healthy ways to round out a meal. Follow the "Make It a Meal" suggestions to complete the menu.

Buffalo Broccoli and Cauliflower

MAKES 4 servings **START TO FINISH** 15 minutes

- 4 **cups cauliflower florets**
- 4 **cups broccoli florets**
- ⅓ **cup Frank's Buffalo Wing Sauce**
- 2 **tablespoons melted butter**
- 1 **tablespoon lemon juice**
- ½ **cup chunky blue cheese dressing**
- ¼ **cup sour cream**
- 2 **tablespoons milk**

■ Add cauliflower florets to a large pot of boiling water; cook 4 minutes. After 2 minutes add broccoli florets. Drain. Combine Frank's Buffalo Wing Sauce, melted butter and lemon juice; toss with vegetables. Stir chunky blue cheese dressing, sour cream and milk. Serve veggies with dressing.

Make it a Meal Grill 1½ pounds boneless, skinless chicken breasts. Brush with balsamic vinegar and slice. Stir into broccoli and cauliflower.

Nutty Roasted Asparagus

MAKES 4 servings **START TO FINISH** 20 minutes

- 1 **pound asparagus, trimmed**
- ¼ **cup sliced shallots**
- 1 **tablespoon olive oil**
- ¼ **teaspoon salt**
- ⅛ **teaspoon black pepper**
- ½ **cup skinless toasted hazelnuts**

■ On a large rimmed baking sheet, toss asparagus and sliced shallots with olive oil; season with salt and black pepper. Roast at 400° for 15 minutes. Sprinkle skinless, toasted hazelnuts over the top.

Make it a Meal: Toss 8 cups baby lettuces with 2 tablespoons olive oil, 1 tablespoon red wine vinegar and ⅛ teaspoon each salt and pepper. Serve asparagus on top and sprinkle with 1 cup each drained and rinsed butter beans and crumbled feta.

Carrot-Zucchini Cheese "Fries"

MAKES 4 servings **START TO FINISH** 30 minutes

- 1 **pound peeled carrots**
- 1 **pound zucchini**
- 2 **teaspoons vegetable oil**
- ¼ **teaspoon salt**
- ⅛ **teaspoon black pepper**
- ⅛ **teaspoon Old Bay Seasoning**
- ¼ **cup shredded mozzarella**
- ¼ **cup American cheese**

■ Cut peeled carrots and zucchini into 3½ x ½-inch sticks. Place on 2 rimmed baking pans. Toss each with vegetable oil, salt, black pepper and Old Bay Seasoning. Roast at 425° for 20 minutes, turning after 10 minutes. Combine shredded mozzarella and American cheese and sprinkle over vegetables. Broil 2 minutes. Serve immediately.

Make it a Meal: Season 1½ pounds London broil with salt and pepper. Broil until medium-rare, 12 minutes, turning once. Season with 2 teaspoons Worcestershire sauce and slice thin. Place steak on a large platter. With large spatula, slide "fries" on top.

Wild Rice with Mango and Cucumber

MAKES 4 servings **START TO FINISH** 30 minutes

- 2 cups wild and brown rice blend
- 1 diced mango
- 1 peeled and diced cucumber
- 4 sliced scallions
- ¼ cup chopped cilantro
- ¼ cup orange juice
- 2 teaspoons orange zest
- 3 tablespoons olive oil
- 1 teaspoon salt
- ⅛ teaspoon cayenne

■ Prepare wild and brown rice blend as per package instructions and cool to room temperature. Stir in mango, peeled and diced cucumber, sliced scallions and chopped cilantro. Combine orange juice, orange zest, olive oil, salt and cayenne. Fold into rice mixture.

Make it a Meal: Grill 4 mango and jalapeño chicken sausages and slice. Stir into rice mixture.

Teriyaki Green Beans and Cashews

MAKES 4 servings **START TO FINISH** 15 minutes

- 2 tablespoons canola oil
- 1¼ pounds green beans, trimmed
- 1 bunch scallions, cut into 1-inch pieces
- ⅓ cup cashews
- 2 tablespoons reduced-sodium teriyaki sauce
- 2 teaspoons sesame oil
- 2 teaspoons toasted sesame seeds

■ Heat canola oil in a large nonstick skillet. Add green beans and sauté 6 minutes. Add scallions, cut into 1-inch pieces; cook 6 more minutes. Stir in cashews, reduced-sodium teriyaki sauce and sesame oil. Garnish with toasted sesame seeds.

Make it a Meal: Toss ½ pound ½-inch firm tofu cubes with 2 tablespoons teriyaki sauce. Sauté in 2 tablespoons vegetable oil 2 minutes per side. Toss with green beans.

A NEW LEAF

Get a dose of super-healthy dark, leafy greens in one of these fun ways.

Creamed Collard Greens

MAKES 6 servings **START TO FINISH** 20 minutes

- 1¾ **pounds stemmed and chopped collard greens**
- 2 **tablespoons butter**
- ⅓ **cup chopped shallots**
- 3 **cloves chopped garlic**
- 2 **tablespoons flour**
- 1½ **cups whole milk**
- ½ **teaspoon salt**
- ¼ **teaspoon ground nutmeg**
- ¼ **teaspoon black pepper**

■ In a pot of salted boiling water, cook collard greens 3 minutes. Drain and press out most of the liquid. In a large skillet, melt butter; add shallots and garlic. Stir in flour; cook 1 minute.

■ Whisk in milk, salt, ground nutmeg and black pepper. Bring to a simmer and cook 2 minutes, until thickened. Stir in collards.

Sesame Mustard Greens and Shiitake Mushrooms

MAKES 4 servings **PREP** 20 minutes

- 2 **tablespoons plus 1 tablespoon olive oil**
- ½ **pound stemmed and sliced shiitake mushrooms**
- 1 **pound roughly chopped mustard greens (or 2 bunches), roughly chopped**
- 1 **tablespoon toasted sesame seeds**
- 2 **teaspoons rice wine vinegar**
- 1 **teaspoon sesame oil**
- ¼ **teaspoon salt**
- ⅛ **teaspoon black pepper**

■ In a skillet, heat 2 tablespoons olive oil over medium-high heat. Add mushrooms; sauté 7 minutes.

■ Add mustard greens, ¼ cup water and another 1 tablespoon oil; sauté 3 more minutes.

■ Stir in sesame seeds, rice wine vinegar, sesame oil, salt and black pepper.

Rainbow Chard and Bacon Flatbread

MAKES 2 servings **START TO FINISH** 30 minutes

- 1¼ **pounds rainbow chard (1 bunch)**
- 1 **tablespoon olive oil**
- 2 **cloves sliced garlic**
- ¼ **teaspoon salt**
- 1 **Stonefire garlic naan**
- 2 **pieces chopped, cooked bacon**
- ¼ **cup Fontina cheese**

■ Remove stems from rainbow chard and slice into ½-inch pieces; roughly chop leaves.

■ In a sauté pan, heat oil over medium-high heat; add stems and sauté 4 minutes. Stir in leaves and garlic; cook another 4 minutes, until tender. Season with salt.

■ Scatter on a Stonefire garlic naan, along with bacon and Fontina cheese. Bake at 400° for 10 minutes, until Fontina is melted.

Wilted Kale Pasta

MAKES 4 servings **START TO FINISH** 20 minutes

- ½ **pound whole wheat spaghetti**
- ¾ **pound dinosaur kale (1 bunch), stemmed and roughly chopped**
- ⅓ **cup chopped walnuts**
- 2 **tablespoons extra-virgin olive oil**
- 1 **tablespoon lemon juice**
- ½ **teaspoon lemon zest**
- ¼ **teaspoon salt**
- ¼ **teaspoon freshly cracked black pepper**
- **Pecorino-Romano cheese**

■ In a pot of salted boiling water, cook spaghetti per package directions. During the last 2 minutes of cooking, add dinosaur kale.

■ Drain, saving ¼ cup of the pasta water, and return to pot with walnuts, oil, lemon juice, lemon zest, salt and black pepper. Garnish with grated Pecorino-Romano cheese.

Spinach and Avocado Salad

MAKES 6 servings **START TO FINISH** 10 minutes

- 3 **tablespoons white wine vinegar**
- 2 **tablespoons extra-virgin olive oil**
- 1 **tablespoon honey**
- ¼ **teaspoon salt**
- ¼ **teaspoon black pepper**
- 1 **package (5 ounces) baby spinach**
- 1 **diced avocado**
- ½ **cup golden raisins**
- ½ **cup crumbled feta cheese**
- ¼ **cup sunflower seeds**

■ In a large bowl, whisk white wine vinegar, extra-virgin olive oil, honey, salt and black pepper.

■ Gently toss in baby spinach with avocado, raisins, feta cheese and sunflower seeds.

THREE FAST DESSERTS

Sweeten the dinner deal with one of these speedy treats.

GRILLED PIÑA COLADA

PEACH-AND-BLUEBERRY FOOLS

Peach-and-Blueberry Fools

MAKES 4 servings PREP 7 minutes

½ **cup heavy cream**

1 **container (6 ounces) plain, nonfat Greek yogurt**

1 **tablespoon confectioners' sugar**

3 **ripe peaches, peeled, pitted and sliced**

1½ **cups blueberries**

2 **teaspoons apricot preserves**

■ In a bowl, whip heavy cream until stiff peaks form. Fold in Greek yogurt and confectioners' sugar. In a large bowl, combine peaches, blueberries and apricot preserves. In four 6-ounce glasses, alternate layers of fruit and yogurt mixture.

Grilled Piña Colada

MAKES 4 servings PREP 4 minutes
GRILL 3 minutes

4 **¾-inch-thick slices pineapple**

Coconut sorbet

Caramel sauce

■ Place pineapple on a hot grill; sear 1 to 1½ minutes on each side. Transfer to plates and top each with a scoop of coconut sorbet and 1 teaspoon caramel sauce.

Variation: For an adult option add 1 tablespoon dark rum to caramel sauce before drizzling over sorbet.

Dirty Snowballs

MAKES 12 servings PREP 15 minutes

1 **cup toasted sweetened flaked coconut**

1 **cup crushed chocolate wafers**

1 **pint frozen vanilla yogurt**

■ Place toasted sweetened flaked coconut on a sheet of wax paper. Place crushed chocolate wafers on second sheet of wax paper. Line a baking sheet with foil; place in freezer.

■ From 1 pint frozen vanilla yogurt, roll a scoop of yogurt (about 1¾ inches) in either coconut or wafer coating and place on chilled baking sheet. Repeat to make 12 balls; freeze on sheet for at least 2 hours. Store in airtight container in freezer for up to 2 weeks.

DIRTY SNOWBALLS

PROTEIN POWER

These healthful snacks help stave off hunger till supper.

Twisted Trail Mix

MAKES 6 servings **PREP** 5 minutes
BAKE 15 minutes at 325°

- 4 **ounces soft beef or turkey jerky**
- ¾ **cup dried cherries**
- ⅔ **cup whole almonds**
- 2 **teaspoons olive oil**
- 1 **tablespoon packed dark brown sugar**
- ½ **teaspoon ground cinnamon**
- ⅛ **teaspoon cayenne**

■ Heat oven to 325°. Line a sheet pan with foil. Chop soft beef or turkey jerky (such as Boar's Head or Krave). Toss in a bowl with dried cherries and whole almonds. Drizzle with olive oil and season with packed dark brown sugar, ground cinnamon and cayenne. Combine mixture with your hands to evenly distribute brown sugar. Spread onto prepared pan and bake at 325° for 15 minutes. Let cool, then divide into ⅓-cup servings.

Bacon Deviled Eggs

MAKES 12 servings **PREP** 5 minutes
COOK 10 minutes

- 12 **large eggs**
- ⅓ **cup light mayo**
- 1 **tablespoon Dijon mustard**
- ¼ **teaspoon salt**
- ¼ **teaspoon pepper**
- 1 **tablespoon cooked bacon crumbles, plus more for garnish**

■ Hard cook eggs. Drain and rinse in cold water until cool to the touch. Peel eggs.

■ Line a mini muffin pan with paper liners. Cut a thin piece from tapered end of egg. Slice the top third off the bottom to expose yolk. Pop yolk out into a bowl and place white in muffin pan. Repeat with all eggs.

■ Mash yolks with mayo, Dijon mustard, 1 tablespoon water or milk, salt and pepper. Stir in 1 tablespoon bacon crumbles.

■ Spoon mixture into egg whites. Garnish with additional bacon crumbles.

TWISTED TRAIL MIX

BACON DEVILED EGGS

Mini Turkey Sliders

MAKES 12 servings **PREP** 15 minutes
COOK 12 minutes

- 1 **medium zucchini**
- 1 **pound ground chicken or turkey**
- ½ **cup shredded cheddar cheese**
- ½ **teaspoon salt**
- ¼ **teaspoon pepper**
- 12 **dinner rolls**
- **Plum tomato slices**

■ Peel and shred zucchini. Mix with chicken or turkey, cheese, salt and pepper. Shape into 12 mini patties, a scant ¼ cup mixture for each.

■ Heat 1 tablespoon oil in a large nonstick skillet over medium-high heat. Pan-fry 6 patties for 6 minutes, flipping halfway through. Repeat with remaining patties.

■ Split dinner rolls and place a patty on each. Top patties with slices of plum tomato.

■ Kids can microwave slider patties for 30 seconds on 70% power to reheat.

Banana Cashew Smoothie

MAKES 2 servings **PREP** 5 minutes

- 1 **frozen banana, cut up**
- ½ **cup ice**
- 1 **tablespoon caramel sauce or maple syrup**
- 1 **cup vanilla almond milk**
- 2 **tablespoons cashew butter**
- **Pinch of ground cinnamon**

■ In a blender, combine frozen banana, ice, caramel sauce or maple syrup, almond milk, cashew butter and a pinch of cinnamon. Blend until ice is crushed, banana is smooth and all ingredients are well blended.

■ Divide between 2 glasses. For an added protein hit, swap in milk for the almond milk and add 2 tablespoons Greek yogurt.

BANANA CASHEW SMOOTHIE

MINI TURKEY SLIDERS

CANDY CORN CAKE,
PAGE 273

OCTOBER

255

265

277

OH, THE PASTABILITIES!

Think beyond the tried-and-true with seven new twists on a family favorite.

SLOW-COOKED PEPPERY BEEF AND FUSILLI, PAGE 255

LASAGNA ROLL-UP
CASSEROLE, PAGE 251

**STRAW-AND-HAY LINGUINE
WITH ARRABIATA SAUCE AND
BAY SCALLOPS**

Straw-and-Hay Linguine with Arrabbiata Sauce and Bay Scallops

MAKES 6 servings **PREP** 15 minutes **COOK** 16 minutes

- 2 **tablespoons olive oil**
- 4 **cloves garlic, sliced**
- 1 **can (28 ounces) San Marzano tomatoes, drained and broken up**
- 1 **teaspoon red pepper flakes**
- 1 **teaspoon sugar**
- ½ **teaspoon salt**
- 1½ **pounds frozen bay scallops, thawed**
- ½ **pound spinach linguine**
- ½ **pound traditional linguine**
- ⅓ **cup shredded ricotta salata**
- ½ **cup sliced basil**

■ In a medium saucepan, heat oil over medium-high heat; add garlic and cook 2 minutes. Add tomatoes, red pepper flakes, sugar and salt. Simmer, covered, 10 minutes, stirring occasionally.

■ Stir in scallops and simmer an additional 3 to 4 minutes or until cooked through.

■ Meanwhile, cook pasta following package directions, about 8 minutes. Drain, reserving ¼ cup pasta cooking water.

■ In a large serving bowl, toss pasta with tomato sauce and scallops. Add pasta water as needed to loosen sauce.

■ Top with ricotta salata and basil. Serve immediately.

PER SERVING 470 **CAL**; 9 g **FAT** (2 g **SAT**); 25 g **PRO**; 72 g **CARB**; 5 g **FIBER**; 855 mg **SODIUM**; 30 mg **CHOL**

LASAGNA ROLL-UP CASSEROLE

Lasagna Roll-Up Casserole

MAKES 6 servings **PREP** 20 minutes **BAKE** at 375° for 45 minutes

- 2½ **cups beef mixture, from Slow-Cooked Peppery Beef and Fusilli (see page 255), gently heated**
- 2 **cups shredded mozzarella**
- 1 **cup ricotta**
- 2 **cups jarred marinara sauce, heated**
- 12 **lasagna noodles (from a 16-ounce package), cooked per package directions**
- 2 **tablespoons grated Parmesan**

■ Heat oven to 375°. Coat a 13 x 9 x 2-inch baking dish with nonstick cooking spray.

■ In a large bowl, gently fold together beef mixture, ½ cup of the mozzarella and the ricotta. Spread 1 cup of the marinara in bottom of prepared dish.

■ Place a cooked noodle on a flat work surface and spread about ¼ cup of the beef and cheese mixture over the top. Roll up from a short end and place, seam side down, in baking dish. Repeat with remaining noodles and beef mixture.

■ Spoon remaining marinara over roll-ups. Scatter remaining 1½ cups mozzarella over sauce and sprinkle with Parmesan.

■ Cover dish with foil and bake at 375° for 30 minutes. Remove foil and bake 15 minutes more. Cool slightly and serve.

PER SERVING 653 **CAL**; 28 g **FAT** (12 g **SAT**); 44 g **PRO**; 54 g **CARB**; 5 g **FIBER**; 985 mg **SODIUM**; 117 mg **CHOL**

GLUTEN-FREE PENNE
WITH GORGONZOLA
AND PROSCIUTTO

Pasta makes the perfect one-dish meal. Just add vegetables and meat (a little for flavor or more for heartiness) and a delicious dinner is done.

Gluten-Free Penne with Gorgonzola and Prosciutto

MAKES 6 servings **PREP** 5 minutes **COOK** 16 minutes

- 2 **tablespoons olive oil**
- 3 **cloves garlic, sliced**
- 2 **bunches broccolini, trimmed and cut into 1-inch pieces**
- ¼ **teaspoon salt**
- ⅛ **teaspoon black pepper**
- 1 **package (12 ounces) gluten-free penne (such as Ronzoni)**
- ¾ **cup half-and-half**
- ¾ **cup crumbled Gorgonzola cheese**
- ⅛ **teaspoon ground nutmeg**
  Pinch cayenne pepper
- 3 **ounces prosciutto, cut into ribbons**
- ⅓ **cup toasted walnuts, coarsely chopped**

■ In a large skillet, heat oil over medium-high heat; add garlic and cook 1 minute, until lightly browned. Add broccolini and cook 5 to 7 minutes, stirring, until crisp-tender. Season with salt and pepper and keep warm.

■ Cook pasta following package directions, about 8 minutes. Drain and keep warm.

■ Meanwhile, in a medium saucepan, heat half-and-half until barely simmering. Remove from heat and stir in Gorgonzola, nutmeg and cayenne. Stir until smooth.

■ In a large serving bowl, toss cooked pasta with cheese sauce. Stir in prosciutto, walnuts and broccolini. Serve immediately.

PER SERVING 447 **CAL**; 19 g **FAT** (7 g **SAT**); 16 g **PRO**; 60 g **CARB**; 8 g **FIBER**; 635 mg **SODIUM**; 37 mg **CHOL**

Bow Ties and Cheesy Brats

MAKES 8 servings **PREP** 15 minutes
COOK 13 minutes **BAKE** at 350° for 17 minutes

- 1 **tablespoon canola oil**
- 2 **red onions, chopped**
- 4 **fully cooked bratwurst (about 12 ounces total), chopped into large dice**
- 1 **sweet red pepper, seeded and sliced**
- 4 **cloves garlic, chopped**
- ½ **cup apple cider**
- 1 **pound bow tie pasta**
- 2 **cups shredded triple cheddar cheese (such as Kraft)**

■ Heat oven to 350°.

■ In a large nonstick skillet, heat oil over medium-high heat; add onions and cook 4 minutes, stirring occasionally; add bratwurst and cook 4 minutes. Add red pepper and garlic; cook 2 minutes. Stir in apple cider and simmer 3 minutes.

■ Meanwhile, cook pasta following package directions, about 10 minutes. Drain, reserving ½ cup pasta cooking water.

■ Toss pasta with bratwurst mixture, pasta water and 1½ cups of the cheddar. Spoon into a 3-quart baking dish. Bake at 350° for 12 minutes. Sprinkle remaining ½ cup cheddar over top and bake for an additional 5 minutes. Serve warm.

PER SERVING 536 **CAL**; 27 g **FAT** (12 g **SAT**); 20 g **PRO**; 51 g **CARB**; 3 g **FIBER**; 543 mg **SODIUM**; 64 mg **CHOL**

**BOW TIES AND
CHEESY BRATS**

**BUCATINI WITH
BRUSSELS SPROUTS
AND BACON**

SLOW-COOKED PEPPERY BEEF AND FUSILLI

Bucatini with Brussels Sprouts and Bacon

MAKES 6 servings **PREP** 15 minutes
COOK 11 minutes

- 1 tablespoon olive oil
- 5 slices thick-cut smoked bacon, cut into ½-inch strips
- 1 pound Brussels sprouts, trimmed and quartered
- 4 cloves garlic, chopped
- ½ teaspoons red pepper flakes
- ½ teaspoon salt
- 1 pound bucatini pasta
- 2 tablespoons unsalted butter
- ½ cup shaved Parmesan
- ¼ cup parsley, chopped
  Asian chili oil (optional)

■ In a large skillet, heat oil over medium-high heat. Add bacon and cook until crisp, about 5 minutes. Remove bacon and reserve. Add Brussels sprouts to drippings in skillet; cook, covered, over medium heat about 5 minutes, stirring occasionally, until tender. Add garlic, red pepper flakes and salt; cook 1 minute.

■ Meanwhile, cook pasta following package directions, about 10 minutes. Drain and reserve ½ cup pasta cooking water.

■ In a large serving bowl, toss pasta with butter. Add Brussels sprouts and drippings from skillet. Stir in Parmesan, parsley, reserved bacon and reserved pasta water as needed to create a sauce.

■ Serve immediately. If using, drizzle chili oil over each portion.

PER SERVING 533 **CAL**; 23g **FAT** (8 g **SAT**); 18 g **PRO**; 64 g **CARB**; 4 g **FIBER**; 698 mg **SODIUM**; 35 mg **CHOL**

Slow-Cooked Peppery Beef and Fusilli

MAKES 6 servings, plus 2½ cups beef mixture for Lasagna Roll-Up Casserole (page 251)
PREP 10 minutes **COOK** 10 minutes **SLOW COOK** on HIGH for 6 hours

- 2¼ pounds beef chuck roast
- 1¼ teaspoons salt
- ½ teaspoon finely ground black pepper
- 1 tablespoon canola oil
- 2 cups grape tomatoes
- 1½ teaspoons coarsely ground black pepper
- 1 bag (5 ounces) baby spinach
- 1 pound fusilli pasta
- 2 tablespoons olive oil
- 2 tablespoons balsamic vinegar

■ Season beef with 1 teaspoon of the salt and the finely ground black pepper. In a large skillet, heat canola oil over medium-high heat. Add beef; sear on all sides, about 10 minutes.

■ Coat slow cooker bowl with nonstick cooking spray. Add beef and distribute tomatoes around the sides. Sprinkle ½ teaspoon of the coarsely ground pepper over beef. Cover and slow cook on HIGH for 6 hours.

■ Remove beef to a cutting board and shred with 2 forks. Return to slow cooker and stir in spinach until wilted. Add ½ teaspoon of the coarsely ground black pepper. Reserve 2½ cups of the mixture for Lasagna Roll-Up Casserole (see page 251).

■ Meanwhile, cook pasta following package directions, about 11 minutes. Drain and reserve ½ cup pasta cooking water. Toss pasta with remaining 2½ cups beef mixture and pasta water.

■ Spoon pasta into a serving bowl and stir in olive oil, vinegar and remaining ¼ teaspoon salt. Sprinkle remaining ½ teaspoon coarsely ground pepper over the top. Serve immediately.

PER SERVING 550 **CAL**; 20 g **FAT** (6 g **SAT**); 29 g **PRO**; 61 g **CARB**; 4 g **FIBER**; 341 mg **SODIUM**; 81 mg **CHOL**

Burrata is an Italian cheese similar to fresh mozzarella, but it has an even softer texture. Cheesemakers form the curd into a bag shape—the center of which is full of cream. When the burrata is cut in half, the cream drips into the pasta.

Tagliatelle with Heirloom Tomatoes, Mushrooms and Chicken

MAKES 6 servings **PREP** 15 minutes **COOK** 8 minutes

- 2 **tablespoons olive oil**
- ½ **pound mixed mushrooms**
- 1 **pound boneless, skinless chicken breasts, cut into 1-inch pieces**
- 3 **cloves garlic, chopped**
- 1 **teaspoon salt**
- ¼ **teaspoon black pepper**
- 1½ **pounds heirloom tomatoes, cut into 1-inch pieces**
- 1 **pound tagliatelle pasta**
- 1 **8-ounce burrata cheese**
  Freshly cracked black pepper
  Basil, for garnish

■ In a large nonstick skillet, heat oil over medium-high heat. Add mushrooms and cook 1 minute, stirring frequently. Add chicken, garlic, ½ teaspoon of the salt and the black pepper; cook 5 minutes, stirring occasionally. Add tomatoes and cook 1 minute to heat through.

■ Meanwhile, cook pasta following package directions, about 8 minutes. Drain and reserve ½ cup pasta cooking water.

■ In a large serving bowl, toss cooked pasta with chicken and tomato mixture. Add pasta water if needed to create a sauce. Season with remaining ½ teaspoon salt.

■ Place burrata on top of pasta and cut into large pieces with 2 knives. Toss, season with freshly cracked black pepper and garnish with basil. Serve immediately.

PER SERVING 544 **CAL**; 16 g **FAT** (7 g **SAT**); 35 g **PRO**; 65 g **CARB**; 2 g **FIBER**; 473 mg **SODIUM**; 81 mg **CHOL**

**TAGLIATELLE
WITH HEIRLOOM
TOMATOES,
MUSHROOMS
AND CHICKEN**

EAT THIS, BEAT THAT

Knock out the risk factors for three diseases with these healthful, tailor-made meals.

**LENTIL BOWL,
PAGE 261**

Osteopenia Potassium-rich lentils, butternut squash and collard greens help maintain bone strength.

Prehypertension Mineral-rich cauliflower is loaded with vitamin C, calcium and magnesium (also found in the heart-healthy cod).

BAKED COD WITH CAULIFLOWER, PAGE 265

__Prediabetes__ Quinoa and brown rice pack 7 grams of dietary fiber, while garbanzo beans and chicken are good sources of lean protein.

CHICKEN AND SPINACH SOUP

LENTIL BOWL

Chicken and Spinach Soup

MAKES Five 2-cup servings
PREP 15 minutes **COOK** 26 minutes

- 2 **tablespoons olive oil**
- 2 **cups diced carrots**
- 1 **medium onion, diced**
- 2 **cloves garlic, minced**
- 2 **cans (14.5 ounces each) reduced-sodium chicken broth**
- 1 **package (5 ounces) Hodgson Mill garlic and herb quinoa and brown rice blend**
- 2 **cups yellow and red cherry or grape tomatoes**
- ½ **rotisserie chicken**
- 1 **bunch spinach, trimmed and rinsed well**
- 1 **can (15 ounces) garbanzo beans, drained and rinsed**
- ½ **cup fresh basil, chopped**
- ¼ **teaspoon salt**
- ¼ **teaspoon black pepper**
- 5 **tablespoons shredded Parmesan**

  Whole-grain crackers (optional)

■ Heat oil in a large lidded stockpot over medium heat. Add carrots and onion and cook 5 minutes. Stir in garlic and cook 1 additional minute. Add chicken broth and 3 cups water. Bring to a boil over high heat.

■ Stir in quinoa-rice blend. Cover and reduce heat to medium-low. Simmer 15 minutes.

■ Meanwhile, quarter tomatoes and remove meat from chicken bones; discard skin and bones. Cut into bite-size pieces (you should have about 2 cups). Stir into soup along with spinach, garbanzo beans, basil, salt and pepper. Cook 5 minutes.

■ Ladle soup into bowls and top each serving with 1 tablespoon shredded Parmesan. Serve with crackers, if using.

PER SERVING 391 **CAL**; 13 g **FAT** (3 g **SAT**); 27 g **PRO**; 46 g **CARB**; 9 g **FIBER**; 797 mg **SODIUM**; 52 mg **CHOL**

Lentil Bowl

MAKES 6 servings **PREP** 25 minutes **COOK** 50 minutes **ROAST** at 425° for 25 minutes

- 1¼ **cups French green lentils**
- 1½ **pounds butternut squash, peeled and cut into ½-inch cubes (about 4½ cups)**
- 5 **tablespoons olive oil**
- ½ **teaspoons salt**
- ¼ **teaspoon plus ⅛ teaspoon black pepper**
- 1 **medium onion, diced**
- 1 **bunch collard greens, trimmed, tough stems discarded, chopped**
- 3 **tablespoons white wine vinegar**
- 1 **teaspoon Dijon mustard**
- 1 **teaspoon sugar**
- ¼ **cup sliced almonds**
- ¼ **cup (2 ounces) crumbled feta cheese**
- 6 **large eggs**

■ Heat oven to 425°. Cook lentils in boiling salted water 35 to 40 minutes.

■ Meanwhile, on a large baking sheet, toss squash with 1 tablespoon of the oil, ¼ teaspoon of the salt and ⅛ teaspoon of the pepper. Roast at 425° for 25 minutes, stirring once.

■ Add 2 tablespoons of the oil to a large nonstick skillet and heat over medium to medium-high heat. Add onion; cook 2 minutes. Stir in collard greens, remaining ¼ teaspoon salt and ⅛ teaspoon of the pepper. Cook 8 minutes. Transfer to a large bowl and coat skillet with nonstick cooking spray. Drain lentils.

■ Add lentils and squash to collard green mixture in bowl. In a small bowl, whisk remaining 2 tablespoons oil, the vinegar, mustard, sugar and remaining ⅛ teaspoon pepper. Toss lentil mixture with dressing, almonds and feta and set aside.

■ Fry eggs in nonstick skillet coated with nonstick cooking spray to desired doneness (this can be done in multiple batches). Divide lentil salad among 6 plates or shallow bowls and top each serving with a fried egg.

PER SERVING 427 **CAL**; 23 g **FAT** (5 g **SAT**); 20 g **PRO**; 39 g **CARB**; 12 g **FIBER**; 626 mg **SODIUM**; 193 mg **CHOL**

Prehypertension *Eating whole grains such as barley may help reduce your risk of high blood pressure by aiding in weight control by helping you feel full. Whole grains also increase your intake of potassium, which has been linked to lower blood pressure.*

Roast Chicken with Barley Pilaf

MAKES 4 servings **PREP** 20 minutes **ROAST** at 425° for 30 minutes **COOK** 19 minutes **LET STAND** 5 minutes

1 teaspoon lemon zest

1 teaspoon fresh rosemary, chopped

1 teaspoon fresh thyme, chopped

½ teaspoon plus a pinch kosher salt

⅛ teaspoon plus a pinch black pepper

1 cut-up chicken (about 3 pounds)

1 tablespoon olive oil

¾ cup shredded carrot, coarsely chopped

1 large rib celery, diced (¾ cup)

2 medium shallots, peeled and diced

2 cups unsalted chicken broth

1 cup quick-cook barley

1 seedless cucumber, peeled and cut into 1-inch wedges

1 package (8 ounces) Melissa's ready-to-eat beets, quartered

⅓ cup plain Greek yogurt

2 tablespoons lemon juice

½ teaspoon sugar

■ Heat oven to 425°. In a small bowl, combine lemon zest, rosemary, thyme, ¼ teaspoon of the salt and ⅛ teaspoon of the pepper. Tuck under skin of chicken and spread pieces on a baking sheet. Roast at 425° for 30 minutes.

■ Meanwhile, heat oil in a medium lidded saucepan over medium heat. Add carrot, celery and shallots and cook 5 minutes. Add broth, increase heat to high and bring to a boil. Stir in barley and ¼ teaspoon of the salt. Cover, reduce heat to medium-low and simmer 12 to 14 minutes. Let stand 5 minutes; drain if needed.

■ Assemble salad and make dressing: Combine cucumber and beets in a bowl. Whisk yogurt, lemon juice, sugar and remaining pinch of salt and pepper in a medium bowl. Serve chicken with barley pilaf and beet salad. Drizzle salad with dressing just before serving.

PER SERVING 493 **CAL**; 14 g **FAT** (5 g **SAT**); 49 g **PRO**; 41 g **CARB**; 7 g **FIBER**; 515 mg **SODIUM**; 193 mg **CHOL**

**ROAST CHICKEN
WITH BARLEY PILAF**

Prediabetes *This salmon boasts 3 grams of omega-3s while black beans and wheat berries offer a whopping 13 grams of dietary fiber.*

SOUTHWESTERN SALMON

BAKED COD WITH CAULIFLOWER

Southwestern Salmon

MAKES 4 servings **PREP** 10 minutes
COOK 22 minutes **BROIL** 6 minutes

- 3   teaspoons olive oil
- ½   medium onion, diced
- 1   cup quick-cook wheat berries (such as Nature's Earthly Choice)
- 1¼ pounds salmon fillets (4 pieces), thawed, if frozen
- 1   teaspoon ancho chile powder
- ½   teaspoon ground cumin
- ½   teaspoon salt
- 1   can (13.5 ounces) low-sodium black beans, drained and rinsed
- ⅓   cup cilantro leaves, chopped
- 2   limes

■ Heat broiler to high. Heat 2 teaspoon of the oil in a medium lidded pot over medium heat. Add onion and cook 5 minutes, until softened.

■ Stir in 2½ cups water and the wheat berries and bring to a boil over high heat. Cover, reduce heat to medium-low and simmer 15 to 17 minutes.

■ Meanwhile, brush salmon with remaining 1 teaspoon oil. In a small bowl, combine ancho chile powder, cumin and ¼ teaspoon of the salt. Sprinkle over salmon and transfer to a baking sheet or broiler pan. Broil 6 minutes, until cooked through.

■ Drain wheat berries and place in a large bowl. Stir in remaining ¼ teaspoon salt, the black beans and cilantro. Grate zest from one of the limes; juice same lime. Cut remaining lime into wedges. Add 1 teaspoon of the lime zest and 2 tablespoons of the lime juice to wheat berry mixture. Spoon onto plates and top each with a piece of salmon. Serve with lime wedges on the side.

PER SERVING 503 **CAL**; 15 g **FAT** (2 g **SAT**); 44 g **PRO**; 49 g **CARB**; 13 g **FIBER**; 500 mg **SODIUM**; 90 mg **CHOL**

Baked Cod with Cauliflower

MAKES 4 servings **PREP** 15 minutes **BAKE** at 450° for 25 minutes **LET STAND** 5 minutes

- 1   small head purple, green or white cauliflower (about 2½ pounds), cut into florets
- 6   cloves garlic, halved
- 2   tablespoons olive oil
- 1   teaspoon fresh thyme, chopped
- ¾   teaspoon salt
- ¼   teaspoon black pepper
- 1¼ pounds cod fillets (4 pieces), thawed, if frozen
- ½   cup panko bread crumbs
- 2   tablespoons grated Parmesan
- 4   tablespoons chopped parsley
- 1   egg white, lightly beaten
- ⅓   cup golden raisins
- ⅓   cup chopped walnuts
- 1   cup vegetable broth
- ¾   cup whole wheat couscous

■ Combine cauliflower, garlic, olive oil, thyme, ¼ teaspoon of the salt and the pepper on a large rimmed baking sheet. Bake at 450° for 15 minutes.

■ Meanwhile, place cod on a cutting board. In a small bowl, combine panko, Parmesan and 2 tablespoons of the parsley. Dip top of each fillet in egg white, then in panko mixture, and place on a baking sheet. Once cauliflower has cooked for 15 minutes, add cod to oven. Stir raisins and walnuts into cauliflower, and bake cod and cauliflower at 450° for 10 minutes or until desired doneness.

■ Bring broth and remaining ½ teaspoon salt to a boil. Stir in couscous, cover and remove from heat. Let stand 5 minutes. Fluff with a fork.

■ Stir remaining 2 tablespoons parsley into cauliflower. Serve cod with couscous and cauliflower.

PER SERVING 489 **CAL**; 16 g **FAT** (2 g **SAT**); 36 g **PRO**; 56 g **CARB**; 11 g **FIBER**; 666 mg **SODIUM**; 56 mg **CHOL**

Osteopenia *Get a hearty helping of potassium from the pork and sweet potatoes, plus calcium for strong bones from the sautéed kale.*

Pork Tenderloin with Apple Compote

MAKES 6 servings **PREP** 30 minutes **COOK** 21 minutes **BAKE** at 375° for 20 minutes **LET REST** 5 minutes

- 2¼ **pounds sweet potatoes, peeled and diced**
- 4 **tablespoons packed dark brown sugar**
- ¾ **teaspoon plus ⅛ teaspoon salt**
- ¾ **teaspoon plus a pinch ground cinnamon**
- ½ **teaspoons ground cumin**
- 2 **small pork tenderloins (about 2 pounds total)**
- 2 **tablespoons canola or olive oil (not extra-virgin)**
- 1 **Golden Delicious apple, peeled, cored and diced**
- ⅓ **cup dried dates, chopped**
- ⅓ **cup dried apricots, chopped**
- 1 **medium onion, chopped**
- 2 **bunches kale, tough stems trimmed, chopped and cleaned**
- ¼ **teaspoon black pepper**

■ Heat oven to 375°. Place sweet potatoes in a large pot and add enough water to cover by 1 inch. Bring to a boil; boil 8 minutes and drain. Mash with 2 tablespoons of the brown sugar and ¼ teaspoon of the salt. Keep warm.

■ Meanwhile, combine ¼ teaspoon of the salt, ¾ teaspoon of the cinnamon and the cumin in a small bowl. Rub all over pork tenderloins. Heat oil in a large lidded stainless-steel skillet over medium-high heat. Add pork and brown on all sides, 5 minutes. Transfer pork to a baking sheet (keep skillet handy) and bake at 375° for 20 minutes, until pork registers 145° on an instant-read thermometer. Let rest 5 minutes before slicing.

■ While pork is in oven, combine apple, ½ cup water, dates, apricots, remaining 2 tablespoons brown sugar and remaining ⅛ teaspoon salt and pinch of cinnamon in a small saucepan. Simmer over medium heat 5 minutes.

■ Add onion to the skillet used for pork and cook over medium heat 3 minutes. Gradually add kale, covering skillet to help wilt greens, and cook 5 minutes. Season with remaining ¼ teaspoon salt and the pepper.

■ Slice pork, spoon apple mixture over top and serve with mashed sweet potatoes and sautéed kale.

PER SERVING 504 **CAL**; 8 g **FAT** (1 g **SAT**); 37 g **PRO**; 74 g **CARB**; 9 g **FIBER**; 525 mg **SODIUM**; 93 mg **CHOL**

**PORK TENDERLOIN
WITH APPLE COMPOTE**

CREATURE FEATURE

No tricks here! These easy cakes are a treat to make—and eat.

FRANKENSTEIN
CAKE

Turn your kitchen into a mad doctor's laboratory to create this cute monster cake. No special decorating skills needed—just a few smartly arranged candies create his smiling face.

Frankenstein Cake

MAKES 16 servings **PREP** 45 minutes **BAKE** at 350° for 38 minutes **COOL** 45 minutes

- 1 box (15.25 ounces) Pillsbury Moist Supreme Devil's Food cake mix
- 1 cup buttermilk
- ½ cup vegetable oil
- 3 eggs
- 2 sticks unsalted butter, softened
- 1 box (1 pound) confectioners' sugar
- 3 tablespoons milk or heavy cream
- Green gel food coloring
- 1 cup heavy cream
- 8 ounces semisweet chocolate, chopped
- 2 Junior Mints candies
- 2 white candy melt disks
- 1 large green gumdrop
- 2 mini Twix bars

■ Cut parchment to fit in the bottom of two 8-inch round baking pans. Coat with nonstick cooking spray. Prepare cake mix according to package directions for two 8-inch cakes, replacing water with buttermilk and using vegetable oil and eggs. Pour evenly into pans and bake at 350° for 34 to 38 minutes, until a toothpick inserted in the center comes out clean. Cool in pans on baking racks 15 minutes. Remove from pans, remove parchment and cool cake layers completely.

■ Meanwhile, prepare frosting. Using a stand mixer or hand mixer, combine butter, confectioners' sugar and milk. Beat on low until just combined, then on high 3 to 5 minutes, until fluffy. Mix green food coloring into frosting.

■ Heat heavy cream in a small pot until simmering. Place chopped chocolate in bowl of a stand mixer. Pour cream over chocolate and stir until smooth. Beat with whisk attachment on medium-high 5 to 7 minutes, until fluffy. Let ganache stand 10 minutes. Set aside ¼ cup, and transfer remaining ganache to a piping bag fitted with a flat tip.

■ Trim cake layers to make each flat. Place one layer on a stand. Spread ¾ cup of the green frosting evenly over top. Place second layer on top, then spread remaining frosting on sides of cake.

■ Pipe ganache in strips on top of cake to resemble strands of hair. Fill another piping bag, fitted with a small circular tip, with the remaining ganache. Pipe a mouth and stitches on face. Use a bit of ganache to secure Junior Mints on candy melts for eyeballs. Press eyeballs and gumdrop (for the nose) on the cake. Press Twix bars into the bottom sides of cake to resemble bolts.

All eyes are on you! This googly-eyed cake made with Oreo sandwich cookies and M&M's will elicit giggles, oohs and ahhs—and not a single boo!

Ghost Cake

MAKES 16 servings **PREP** 35 minutes **BAKE** at 350° for 38 minutes **COOL** 45 minutes

- 1 **box (15.25 ounces) Pillsbury Moist Supreme Devil's Food cake mix**
- 1 **cup buttermilk**
- ½ **cup vegetable oil**
- 3 **eggs**
- 2 **sticks unsalted butter, softened**
- 1 **box (1 pound) confectioners' sugar**
- 3 **tablespoons milk or heavy cream**
- 10 **mini Oreo cookies**
- 10 **Oreo cookies**
- 20 **brown M&M's (mixed mini, regular and mega sizes)**

■ Cut parchment to fit in the bottom of two 8-inch round baking pans. Coat with nonstick cooking spray. Prepare cake mix according to package directions for two 8-inch cakes, substituting buttermilk for water and using vegetable oil and eggs. Pour into pans and bake at 350° for 34 to 38 minutes, until a toothpick inserted in the center comes out clean. Cool in pans on baking racks 15 minutes. Remove from pans, remove parchment and cool completely.

■ Meanwhile, prepare frosting. Using a stand mixer or hand mixer, combine butter, confectioners' sugar and milk. Beat on low until just combined, then on high 3 to 5 minutes, until fluffy. Set aside 1 tablespoon of the frosting.

■ Carefully take apart mini and regular Oreo cookies, making sure frosting sticks completely to one of the halves. Place nonfrosted halves in a resealable plastic bag and smash into pieces.

■ Trim layers to make each flat. Place one cake layer on a stand. Spread ¾ cup of the frosting evenly over top and sprinkle with smashed cookies, pressing slightly into frosting. Place second cake layer on top, then spread remaining frosting over top and sides of cake. With a bit of the reserved frosting, secure one of the M&M's to each of the 20 Oreo halves. Arrange on cake so they look like pairs of eyeballs.

GHOST CAKE

CANDY CORN CAKE

A devil's food cake mix and candy corn make an eye-catching cake that's suitable for any kind of Halloween event, from a kid's pre-trick-or-treat party to a grown-up gathering.

Candy Corn Cake

MAKES 16 servings **PREP** 45 minutes **BAKE** at 350° for 38 minutes **COOL** 45 minutes

- 1 **box (15.25 ounces) Pillsbury Moist Supreme Devil's Food cake mix**
- 1 **cup buttermilk**
- ½ **cup vegetable oil**
- 3 **eggs**
- 2 **sticks unsalted butter, softened**
- 1 **box (1 pound) confectioners' sugar**
- 3 **tablespoons milk or heavy cream**
  Orange and yellow gel food coloring
- 1 **cup heavy cream**
- 8 **ounce semisweet chocolate, chopped**
  Candy corns (about 55)

■ Cut parchment to fit in the bottom of two 8-inch round baking pans. Coat with nonstick cooking spray. Prepare cake mix according to package directions for two 8-inch cakes, replacing water with buttermilk and using vegetable oil and eggs. Pour evenly into pans and bake at 350° for 34 to 38 minutes, until a toothpick inserted in the center comes out clean. Cool in pans on baking racks 15 minutes. Remove from pans, remove parchment and cool completely.

■ Meanwhile, prepare frosting. Using a stand mixer or hand mixer, combine butter, confectioners' sugar and milk. Beat on low until just combined, then on high 3 to 5 minutes, until fluffy. Mix orange food coloring into 1½ cups of the frosting and yellow food coloring into ⅔ cup of the frosting. Keep remaining ⅓ cup of the frosting white. Transfer ¾ cup of the orange and all the yellow and white frosting to individual piping bags fitted with a star tip.

■ Heat heavy cream in a small pot until simmering. Place chopped chocolate in bowl of a stand mixer. Pour cream over chocolate and stir until smooth. Let cool 5 minutes. Beat with whisk attachment on high 10 minutes, until fluffy. Let ganache stand 10 minutes.

■ Trim layers to make each flat. Place one cake layer on a stand. Spread reserved orange frosting evenly over top. Place second cake layer on top, then spread ganache evenly around the sides. Pipe white frosting in a circle, starting from center of cake, followed by remaining orange frosting and finally the yellow frosting until it reaches the edges. Press candy corns into base of cake, alternating direction with each one. Slice into wedges. (Each wedge will resemble a piece of candy corn from the top.)

GLOBAL WARMERS

Come home to these slow-cooker soups and stews from around the world.

AFRICAN CHICKEN AND PEANUT STEW

African Chicken and Peanut Stew

MAKES 8 servings **PREP** 15 minutes
SLOW COOK on HIGH for 4 hours or LOW for 6 hours

- 2¼ **pounds bone-in chicken thighs, skin removed**
- 2 **pounds sweet potatoes, peeled and diced**
- 1 **3-inch piece ginger, peeled and chopped**
- 2 **cloves garlic, chopped**
- 1½ **cups unsalted chicken stock**
- ½ **cup natural chunky peanut butter**
- 1 **can (14 ounces) diced tomatoes**
- 1 **teaspoon ground coriander**
- ¾ **teaspoon salt**
- ½ **teaspoon black pepper**
- 1 **teaspoon cider vinegar**
  Cilantro and peanuts (optional)

■ Place chicken, sweet potatoes, ginger and garlic in bottom of slow cooker. In a bowl, whisk stock and peanut butter until blended. Stir in tomatoes, coriander, ½ teaspoon of the salt and the black pepper. Pour into slow cooker. Press down until chicken and potatoes are mostly submerged. Cover and cook on HIGH for 4 hours or LOW for 6 hours.

■ Carefully remove chicken to a cutting board. Shred chicken, discarding bones. Stir vinegar and remaining ¼ teaspoon salt into liquid. Stir in shredded chicken.

■ Ladle into bowls and garnish with cilantro and peanuts, if using.

PER SERVING 320 **CAL**; 14 g **FAT** (3 g **SAT**); 24 g **PRO**; 22 g **CARB**; 4 g **FIBER**; 520 mg **SODIUM**; 100 mg **CHOL**

MEXICAN CHIPOTLE SQUASH SOUP

Mexican Chipotle Squash Soup

MAKES 8 servings **PREP** 20 minutes **SLOW COOK** on HIGH for 4 hours or LOW for 6 hours

- 4 **pounds butternut squash, peeled, seeded and cut into 2-inch cubes**
- 1 **medium onion, chopped**
- 2 **cloves garlic**
- 3 **cups unsalted chicken broth**
- 3 **chipotle chiles in adobo, seeded and chopped**
- 2 **teaspoons adobo sauce (from chipotle can)**
- 1 **teaspoon salt**
- ½ **cup sour cream**
  Pepitas (optional)

■ Place squash, onion and garlic in bottom of slow cooker. In a bowl, whisk broth, 2 of the chipotles, 1 teaspoon of the adobo sauce and ½ teaspoon of the salt. Pour over squash. Cook on HIGH for 4 hours or LOW for 6 hours.

■ Puree soup with a hand blender or in batches with a standing blender. Return to slow cooker and stir in remaining ½ teaspoon salt.

■ In a small bowl, blend sour cream with remaining chipotle and 1 teaspoon adobo sauce. Ladle soup into bowls and garnish with a dollop of sour cream and, if using, pepitas.

PER SERVING 130 **CAL**; 3.5 g **FAT** (2 g **SAT**); 5 g **PRO**; 23 g **CARB**; 6 g **FIBER**; 1,070 mg **SODIUM**; 20 mg **CHOL**

Malaysian Pork Noodle Soup

MAKES 8 servings **PREP** 15 minutes
SLOW COOK on HIGH for 6 hours or LOW for 8 hours

3	pounds boneless pork shoulder
1	large yellow onion, diced
1	3-inch piece ginger, peeled and chopped
3	cloves garlic, chopped
2	cups unsalted chicken stock
1	can (13.5 ounces) coconut milk
2	tablespoons lime juice
1	tablespoon curry powder
2	teaspoons sugar
1	teaspoon salt
½	teaspoon red pepper flakes
1	box (8 ounces) pad thai rice noodles
	Scallions and chow mein noodles (optional)

■ Place pork shoulder, onion, ginger and garlic in bottom of slow cooker. In a bowl, whisk stock, coconut milk, lime juice, curry powder, sugar, ½ teaspoon of the salt and the red pepper flakes. Pour over pork. Cover and cook on HIGH for 6 hours or LOW for 8 hours.

■ Using tongs, carefully remove pork to a cutting board and shred. Stir remaining ½ teaspoon salt into liquid and return shredded pork to slow cooker. Meanwhile, prepare rice noodles per package directions.

■ Divide rice noodles among 8 bowls, then ladle some pork and broth on top. Garnish with scallions and chow mein noodles, if using.

PER SERVING 350 **CAL**; 16 g **FAT** (11 g **SAT**); 21 g **PRO**; 30 g **CARB**; 1 g **FIBER**; 400 mg **SODIUM**; 65 mg **CHOL**

Two kinds of noodles means double the deliciousness. This warming bowl features soft rice noodles suspended in a flavorful broth—and a topping of crunchy chow mein noodles too.

BRAZILIAN BLACK
BEAN STEW

Moroccan Beef Chili

MAKES 8 servings **PREP** 10 minutes
SLOW COOK on HIGH for 5 hours or LOW
for 7 hours

- 2 **pounds beef chuck, cut into 1-inch pieces**
- ½ **teaspoons salt**
- ½ **teaspoon ground allspice**
- 3 **medium carrots, sliced on the diagonal into 1-inch pieces**
- 1 **medium yellow onion, diced**
- 3 **cloves garlic, sliced**
- 1 **can (14.5 ounces) diced tomatoes**
- 1 **tablespoon harissa paste**
- 6 **cups cooked pearl couscous**
- ½ **cup plain hummus**
  Chopped parsley (optional)

■ Toss beef with salt and allspice. Place in slow cooker with carrots, onion and garlic. In a bowl, whisk tomatoes and harissa. Pour over beef. Cook on HIGH for 5 hours or LOW for 7 hours.

■ To serve, scoop ¾ cup couscous into each bowl. Spoon stew on top; garnish with 1 tablespoon hummus and, if using, parsley.

PER SERVING 450 **CAL**; 16 g **FAT** (6 g **SAT**); 28 g **PRO**; 43 g **CARB**; 5 g **FIBER**; 370 mg **SODIUM**; 85 mg **CHOL**

MOROCCAN
BEEF CHILI

Brazilian Black Bean Stew

MAKES 10 servings **PREP** 15 minutes **SLOW COOK** on HIGH for 5 hours or LOW for 7 hours

- 2½ **pounds pork spare ribs**
- 3 **ounces diced cured chorizo, casing removed**
- 1 **large yellow onion, diced**
- 4 **cloves garlic, sliced**
- 1 **pound collard greens, large stems discarded, roughly chopped**
- 2 **cups unsalted chicken stock**
- ½ **teaspoon salt**
- ¼ **teaspoon black pepper**
- 2 **cans (15.5 ounces each) black beans, rinsed and drained**
- 1 **tablespoon white vinegar**
- 6 **cups cooked white or brown rice**
- 1 **large orange, peeled and cut into segments**

■ Place ribs, chorizo, onion and garlic in bottom of slow cooker. Place collard greens on top, pressing down firmly. Whisk stock, salt and pepper, then pour on top. Cover and cook on HIGH for 5 hours or LOW for 7 hours.

■ Carefully remove ribs to a cutting board and shred; discard bones. Stir beans and vinegar into liquid. Stir meat back into slow cooker.

■ To serve, scatter about ½ cup rice into each bowl. Ladle some stew on top and garnish with orange segments.

PER SERVING 500 **CAL**; 24 g **FAT** (8 g **SAT**); 25 g **PRO**; 46 g **CARB**; 10 g **FIBER**; 525 mg **SODIUM**; 75 mg **CHOL**

**APPLE CRUMB PIE,
PAGE 287**

NOVEMBER

288

303

305

NATIONAL TREASURES

Travel at the table this Thanksgiving with regional menus from around the country.

Menu

Southern Deep-Fried Turkey

Collard Greens and
Butter Beans

Shrimp and Grits Skewers

Buttermilk Biscuit and Sausage
Dressing

Pimiento Mac and Cheese

Sweet Potato Pie

The South: Spicy, smoky, citrusy and sweet—these down-home flavors are delicious.

Southern Deep-Fried Turkey

MAKES 12 servings **PREP** 45 minutes **COOK** 16 minutes **FRY** 3 to 4 minutes per pound

- 1 **turkey fryer**
  Peanut oil
- 1 **turkey (about 12 pounds)**
- 5 **tablespoons unsalted butter, melted**
- 1½ **cups lemon iced tea (such as Snapple)**
- 2 **tablespoons fresh lemon juice**
- 2 **tablespoons molasses**
- 1 **teaspoon sweet paprika**
- 1 **teaspoon celery salt**
- 1 **teaspoon mustard powder**
- 1 **teaspoon salt**
- ½ **teaspoon plus ⅛ teaspoon black pepper**
- 1 **injector**
- 2 **cloves garlic, chopped**
- 2 **tablespoons all-purpose flour**
- 1¾ **cups unsalted turkey or chicken stock**

■ Follow directions on your turkey fryer for amount of oil (we used a scant 2 gallons). Pour oil into fryer and heat as per manufacturer's directions.

■ Let turkey sit at room temperature for 45 minutes on a rimmed baking sheet. Set aside giblets for gravy. Pat dry (including the cavity) with paper towels.

■ Melt 3 tablespoons of the butter in a microwave-safe bowl. Whisk in 1¼ cups of the tea, the lemon juice, molasses, paprika, celery salt, mustard powder and ½ teaspoon each of the salt and pepper. Inject as much of the mixture as you can into breast, thighs and drumsticks.

■ Place turkey in fryer basket and carefully lower into hot oil as per manufacturer's directions. Cover and fry turkey 3 to 4 minutes per pound, until meat registers 165° on an instant-read thermometer. Let oil drain from turkey for 20 minutes. Carefully remove turkey from fryer basket and transfer to a serving platter.

■ While turkey is frying, prepare gravy. In a medium pot, heat remaining 2 tablespoons butter over medium heat. Stir in giblets; sauté 3 minutes. Stir in garlic and cook 2 minutes. Stir in flour and cook 1 minute. Whisk in stock and remaining ¼ cup tea. Cover, bring to a boil, reduce to a simmer and cook 10 minutes, until thickened. Stir in remaining ½ teaspoon salt and ⅛ teaspoon pepper. Keep covered over very low heat until turkey is ready.

PER SERVING 620 **CAL**; 33 g **FAT** (10 g **SAT**); 70 g **PRO**; 7 g **CARB**; 0 g **FIBER**; 460 mg **SODIUM**; 270 mg **CHOL**

Collard Greens and Butter Beans

MAKES 8 servings **PREP** 15 minutes **COOK** 18 minutes

- 1 **tablespoon unsalted butter**
- 4 **ounces smoked ham shoulder, diced**
- 1 **bunch collard greens (about 1½ pounds), stemmed and chopped**
- 1 **can (15.5 ounces) butter beans, drained and rinsed**
- ¼ **teaspoon salt**
- ¼ **teaspoon black pepper**

■ In large skillet, melt butter over medium heat. Add ham; cook 3 minutes. Stir in greens and sauté 12 minutes. Mix in beans, salt and pepper; cook 2 to 3 minutes, until heated through.

PER SERVING 80 **CAL**; 2.5 g **FAT** (1.5 g **SAT**); 6 g **PRO**; 10 g **CARB**; 4 g **FIBER**; 392 mg **SODIUM**; 10 mg **CHOL**

Shrimp and Grits Skewers

MAKES 8 servings **PREP** 20 minutes
COOK 5 minutes **BROIL** 3 minutes

- 4 slices thick-cut bacon, diced
- 32 small to medium shrimp, peeled and deveined (about 12 ounces)
- 1 tube (about 18 ounces) ready-to-serve polenta, cut into 32 cubes
- 16 6-inch skewers
- ¼ teaspoon salt
- ½ teaspoon freshly cracked black pepper
- 2 scallions, sliced

■ Heat broiler to high. In a large sauté pan, cook bacon over medium heat 3 to 5 minutes, until crispy. Remove bacon to a paper-towel-lined plate with a slotted spoon. Carefully reserve 2 tablespoons of the bacon fat.

■ Thread 2 shrimp and 2 cubes of polenta onto each of the skewers. Place on a baking sheet and brush both sides with reserved bacon fat. Season with salt and pepper.

■ Broil skewers on the highest oven rack 3 minutes, until shrimp are cooked. Garnish with crispy bacon and sliced scallions.

PER SERVING 160 **CAL**; 7 g **FAT** (2.5 g **SAT**); 12 g **PRO**; 10 g **CARB**; 1 g **FIBER**; 440mg **SODIUM**; 80 mg **CHOL**

Buttermilk Biscuit and Sausage Dressing

MAKES 12 servings **PREP** 20 minutes
COOK 13 minutes **BAKE** at 425° for 15 minutes and at 400° for 35 minutes

BISCUITS

- 2 cups all-purpose flour
- 2 teaspoons baking powder
- ½ teaspoon baking soda
- ½ teaspoon salt
- 4 tablespoons unsalted butter, cubed and chilled
- 1 cup buttermilk

DRESSING

- 10 ounces mixed sweet and spicy Italian sausage, casings removed
- 1 tablespoon unsalted butter

- 4 ribs celery, diced
- 1 small yellow onion, diced
- 3 cloves garlic, chopped
- 1 tablespoon chopped fresh thyme
- 1 teaspoon chopped fresh sage
- 3 egg whites
- 2 cups unsalted chicken stock
- ½ cup buttermilk
- ¾ teaspoon salt
- ½ teaspoon black pepper

■ **Biscuits.** Heat oven to 425°. In a bowl, combine flour, baking powder, baking soda and salt. Add butter, mixing with hands until pea size. Make a well and pour in buttermilk. Stir until combined. Let rest 5 minutes.

■ Roll out dough to ¾ inch on a floured surface. Cut out 8 or 9 biscuits with a 2½-inch round cookie cutter, rerolling as necessary (use all the dough). Place on a parchment-lined baking sheet and bake at 425° for 10 to 15 minutes, until browned. Cool completely, then store for at least 1 day before making dressing.

■ **Dressing.** Heat oven to 400°. Cut biscuits into 1-inch cubes; set aside.

■ In a large cast-iron skillet, cook sausage over medium-high heat 6 to 8 minutes, breaking up with a spoon, until browned. Reduce heat to medium and add butter. Stir in celery, onion and garlic. Sauté 3 to 5 minutes, until softened. Stir in thyme and sage. Remove from heat.

■ In a large bowl, whisk egg whites until foamy. Whisk in chicken stock, buttermilk, salt and pepper. Fold biscuits and sausage into egg white mixture. Spray skillet with nonstick cooking spray. Pour stuffing into skillet and press down. Cover with foil and bake at 400° for 25 minutes. Uncover and bake another 10 minutes.

PER SERVING 190 **CAL**; 9 g **FAT** (4.5 g **SAT**); 8 g **PRO**; 20 g **CARB**; 1 g **FIBER**; 591 mg **SODIUM**; 25 mg **CHOL**

Pimiento Mac and Cheese

MAKES 12 servings **PREP** 15 minutes
COOK 8 minutes **BAKE** at 400° for 20 minutes

- 1 pound elbow macaroni
- 4 tablespoons unsalted butter
- 3 cloves garlic, chopped
- 1¼ teaspoons sweet paprika
- 3 tablespoons all-purpose flour
- 2½ cups milk
- 1 pound grated sharp cheddar
- 4 ounces cream cheese
- 2 jars (4 ounces each) sliced sweet pimientos, drained
- ⅓ cup chopped pickled jalapeños
- ¾ teaspoon salt
- ½ cup plain bread crumbs

■ Heat oven to 400°. Bring a pot of salted water to a boil. Add macaroni, return to a boil and cook 6 minutes. Drain.

■ Meanwhile, in a large pot, melt 3 tablespoons of the butter. Add garlic and 1 teaspoon of the paprika; cook 1 minute. Stir in flour; cook 1 minute. Whisk in milk and bring to a simmer. Cook 3 to 5 minutes, until thickened. Stir in cheddar and cream cheese until smooth. Fold in cooked macaroni, pimientos, jalapeños and salt. Transfer mixture to a 13 x 9 x 2-inch baking dish.

■ In a small skillet, melt remaining 1 tablespoon butter over medium heat. Stir in remaining ¼ teaspoon paprika and the bread crumbs; cook 1 minute. Scatter over macaroni. Bake at 400° for 20 minutes or until golden.

PER SERVING 430 **CAL**; 23 g **FAT** (14 g **SAT**); 16 g **PRO**; 37 g **CARB**; 2 g **FIBER**; 580 mg **SODIUM**; 65 mg **CHOL**

SWEET POTATO PIE

Sweet Potato Pie

MAKES 12 servings **PREP** 20 minutes
MICROWAVE 10 minutes **BAKE** at 425° for
15 minutes and at 350° for 45 minutes
CHILL overnight

- 2 **large sweet potatoes (1¼ pounds total), scrubbed**
- 1 **package (14.1 ounces) refrigerated piecrusts**
- 3 **large eggs**
- ¾ **cup half-and-half**
- ¾ **cup plus 1 teaspoon sugar**
- 2 **teaspoons pumpkin pie spice**

■ Heat oven to 425°. Pierce potatoes all over with a fork. Place on a microwave-safe plate and microwave 10 minutes or until tender, turning over halfway through. Peel and mash until completely smooth. Cool slightly.

■ Fit one piecrust into a 9-inch pie dish and form a flat edge. Using a 1-inch acorn- or leaf-shaped cookie cutter, cut out 45 to 50 shapes from second crust; place on a baking sheet and refrigerate until ready to use.

■ Separate 1 egg. In a large bowl, beat cooled sweet potatoes, half-and-half, remaining 2 eggs plus the egg yolk, ¾ cup of the sugar and the pumpkin pie spice. Pour into piecrust.

■ Beat remaining egg white. Brush edge of piecrust with egg white. Overlap pastry shapes around edge, reserving 7 on a small piece of foil. Brush crust edge and extra shapes with egg whites; sprinkle with remaining 1 teaspoon sugar.

■ Bake pie and extra shapes at 425° for 15 minutes. Remove extra dough shapes from oven and reduce temperature to 350°. Carefully cover edge with foil. Bake at 350° for 40 to 45 minutes.

■ Cool pie completely on a wire rack. Refrigerate overnight or until chilled. Garnish with decorative shapes before serving.

The Northeast: Staying true to its origins, this region is all about the best of the harvest.

Maple-Glazed Bacon-Wrapped Turkey

MAKES 12 servings **PREP** 20 minutes **ROAST** at 450° for 30 minutes and at 350° for 2 hours
REST 20 minutes **COOK** 6 minutes

- 2 **teaspoons salt**
- 1 **teaspoon black pepper**
- 1 **teaspoon poultry seasoning**
- 1 **tablespoon olive oil**
- 1 **fresh turkey (about 12 pounds)**
- 8 **sage leaves**
- 1 **cup maple syrup**
- 10 **slices bacon**
- 3 **tablespoons all-purpose flour**
- 2 **cups turkey or chicken broth**
- ¼ **cup flat-leaf parsley, chopped**

■ Heat oven to 450°. Fit a large roasting pan with a rack.

■ In a small bowl, combine salt, pepper and poultry seasoning. Stir in olive oil to form a paste.

■ Remove giblets and neck from cavity of turkey. Rinse turkey and pat dry with paper towels. Place in roasting pan. If desired, tuck wings under turkey and tie legs together with cooking twine.

■ Season turkey with spice rub all over the outside as well as under skin of breast halves. Tuck sage leaves under skin and in cavity. Roast at 450° for 30 minutes.

■ Combine maple syrup with ¼ cup hot water. Reduce oven temperature to 350° and brush turkey with maple syrup glaze. Roast for 1 hour, brushing with maple syrup glaze every 30 minutes. Carefully lay bacon slices over breast in a lattice pattern; roast 1 hour more, until internal temperature reaches 165°. Remove to a cutting board; let rest 20 minutes.

■ Place roasting pan over medium-high heat and whisk in flour; cook 1 minute. Gradually whisk in broth and cook 5 minutes, until gravy thickens. Strain into a gravy boat and stir in parsley.

PER SERVING 680 **CAL**; 29 g **FAT** (9 g **SAT**); 96 g **PRO**; 2 g **CARB**; 0 g **FIBER**; 913 mg **SODIUM**; 358 mg **CHOL**

Chestnut Dressing

MAKES 8 servings **PREP** 15 minutes
COOK 16 minutes **STAND** 5 minutes

- 6 **slices bacon**
- ½ **cup each chopped carrot, celery and onion**
- 2 **cups turkey or chicken broth**
- 4 **tablespoons unsalted butter**
- 4 **cups seasoned stuffing bread cubes**
- 1¼ **cups jarred chestnuts, quartered**
- ¼ **teaspoon salt**
- ¼ **teaspoon black pepper**

■ Heat a large skillet over medium-high heat. Add bacon and cook 8 minutes, turning once, until crispy. Remove to a plate, leaving bacon fat. Chop bacon.

■ Add carrot, celery and onion to skillet and cook 8 minutes, stirring frequently. Add broth and 2 tablespoons of the butter; bring to a simmer. Stir in bread cubes, chestnuts, salt and pepper. Cover, remove from heat and let stand 5 minutes.

■ To serve, fluff with a fork and dot with remaining 2 tablespoons butter.

PER SERVING 591 **CAL**; 26 g **FAT** (8 g **SAT**); 12 g **PRO**; 77 g **CARB**; 2 g **FIBER**; 672 mg **SODIUM**; 119 mg **CHOL**

Mini Crab Cakes with Dijon Thyme Aïoli

MAKES 24 pieces **PREP** 30 minutes
REFRIGERATE 30 minutes **COOK** 12 minutes

AÏOLI

- ½ cup mayonnaise
- 1 tablespoon Dijon mustard
- 1 tablespoon olive oil
- 1 teaspoon fresh thyme leaves

CRAB CAKES

- 1 pound crabmeat
- ½ cup plain dry bread crumbs
- 1 egg, lightly beaten
- 2 tablespoons lemon juice
- 1 tablespoon mayonnaise
- 1 tablespoon Dijon mustard
- 2 teaspoons Old Bay seasoning
- 2 scallions, chopped
- ¼ cup canola oil

■ **Aïoli.** In a small bowl, combine mayonnaise, mustard, olive oil and thyme. Cover and refrigerate until ready to serve.

■ **Crab Cakes.** In a large bowl, combine crabmeat, bread crumbs, egg, lemon juice, mayonnaise, mustard, Old Bay and scallions. Gently mix. Form into 24 small patties, about 2 heaping tablespoons each. Place on a large wax-paper-lined baking sheet and refrigerate 30 minutes.

■ In a large nonstick skillet, heat 2 tablespoons of the oil over medium-high heat. Cook half the crab cakes 2 to 3 minutes per side, until nicely browned. Remove to a plate and repeat with remaining oil and crab cakes. Serve crab cakes with aïoli.

PER PIECE 74 **CAL**; 5 g **FAT** (1 g **SAT**); 4 g **PRO**; 2 g **CARB**; 0 g **FIBER**; 177 mg **SODIUM**; 24 mg **CHOL**

Creamy Succotash

MAKES 8 servings **PREP** 15 minutes
COOK 14 minutes

- 4 tablespoons unsalted butter
- 1 medium zucchini, cut into small dice
- 1 small sweet red pepper, seeded and cut into small dice
- 2 tablespoons dried onion flakes
- 4 cups frozen gold and white corn (such as Birds Eye), thawed
- 1 package (10 ounces) frozen lima beans, thawed
- ½ cup chicken broth
- 6 sage leaves, coarsely chopped
- ¾ teaspoon salt
- ¼ teaspoon black pepper
- ¼ cup heavy cream

■ In a large nonstick skillet, melt 2 tablespoons of the butter over medium-high heat. Add zucchini, red pepper and onion flakes; cook 5 minutes, stirring occasionally.

■ Add corn, lima beans, broth, sage, salt and pepper; simmer 6 minutes, stirring occasionally. Add cream and simmer 3 minutes. Stir in remaining 2 tablespoons butter.

PER SERVING 202 **CAL**; 9 g **FAT** (5 g **SAT**); 6 g **PRO**; 25 g **CARB**; 4 g **FIBER**; 338 mg **SODIUM**; 26 mg **CHOL**

Maple Sweet Potatoes with Toasted Hazelnuts

MAKES 8 servings **PREP** 15 minutes
ROAST at 400° for 30 minutes

- 3 pounds sweet potatoes, peeled and cut into 1-inch pieces
- 3 tablespoons canola oil
- ⅓ cup maple syrup
- 2 tablespoons unsalted butter, cut into small pieces
- ¼ teaspoon salt
- ¼ teaspoon black pepper
- 6 sprigs fresh thyme
- ⅓ cup toasted, skinned hazelnuts, coarsely chopped

■ Heat oven to 400°. Place sweet potatoes on a large rimmed baking sheet and toss with canola oil.

■ Bake at 400° for 20 minutes, turning once. Toss with maple syrup, butter, salt and pepper; scatter thyme over top. Roast for an additional 10 minutes.

■ Top with hazelnuts just before serving.

PER SERVING 236 **CAL**; 11 g **FAT** (2 g **SAT**); 3 g **PRO**; 33 g **CARB**; 4 g **FIBER**; 111 mg **SODIUM**; 8 mg **CHOL**

MINI CRAB CAKES
WITH DIJON
THYME AÏOLI

APPLE CRUMB PIE

Apple Crumb Pie

MAKES 12 servings **PREP** 20 minutes **BAKE** at 425° for 25 minutes and at 375° for 45 minutes **COOL** at least 2 hours

1 **prepared refrigerated piecrust (from a 14.1 ounce package)**

CRUMB TOPPING

1 **cup all-purpose flour**

⅓ **cup packed light brown sugar**

½ **teaspoon ground cinnamon**

⅛ **teaspoon salt**

Pinch ground cloves

6 **tablespoons (¾ stick) unsalted butter, cut into pieces and chilled**

⅓ **cup chopped pecans (optional)**

PIE FILLING

2 **Golden Delicious apples (¾ to 1 pound total), peeled, cored and thinly sliced**

2 **Granny Smith apples (¾ to 1 pound total), peeled, cored and thinly sliced**

2 **cups cranberries, thawed if frozen**

⅔ **cup packed light brown sugar**

¼ **cup all-purpose flour**

½ **teaspoon ground cinnamon**

¼ **teaspoon salt**

Pinch ground cloves

2 **tablespoons fresh lemon juice**

■ Place a rack in the lowest slot of your oven; place foil on bottom of oven to catch drips. Heat oven to 425°. Fit piecrust into a 9-inch pie dish and decoratively crimp edge. Refrigerate until ready to fill.

■ **Crumb Topping.** Combine flour, brown sugar, cinnamon, salt and cloves in a bowl. Rub in butter with fingertips until crumbly. Stir in nuts, if using.

■ **Pie Filling.** In a large bowl, toss apples, cranberries, brown sugar, flour, cinnamon, salt and cloves. Add lemon juice and toss to coat.

■ Spoon filling into pie shell, mounding slightly in center. Cover with foil and bake at 425° for 20 to 25 minutes.

■ Carefully remove pie from oven; reduce oven to 375° and top pie with crumb topping.

■ Return pie to oven and bake at 375° for 45 minutes, until fruit is tender. Let cool at least 2 hours before slicing and serving.

PER SERVING 368 **CAL**; 19 g **FAT** (9 g **SAT**); 3 g **PRO**; 49 g **CARB**; 4 g **FIBER**; 163 mg **SODIUM**; 31 mg **CHOL**

The Midwest: The heartland keeps it real with modern twists on classic crowd-pleasers—glazed turkey, stuffed mushrooms, super-creamy mashed potatoes and a better-than-classic green bean casserole.

Cider-Glazed Turkey

MAKES 12 servings **PREP** overnight **COOK** 8 minutes **MICROWAVE** 1 minute **ROAST** at 450° for 30 minutes and at 350° for 1½ hours **REST** 20 minutes

BRINE AND TURKEY

- 2 gallons plus 1 cup water
- 1 large bottle (1.6 quarts) apple cider
- 1½ cups sugar
- 1 cup kosher salt
- 6 cloves garlic, smashed
- 2 tablespoons whole fresh sage leaves
- 8 cups ice
- 1 fresh turkey (see Note; about 12 pounds), neck and giblets removed
- 2 tablespoons unsalted butter
- 1 tablespoon chopped fresh sage
- ½ teaspoon plus a pinch of table salt
- ½ teaspoon black pepper
- 1 small green apple, cut into wedges
- 1 small onion, cut into wedges

GRAVY

- 2½ cups drippings from roasting pan
- 2 tablespoons unsalted butter
- 2 to 3 tablespoons all-purpose flour
- ¼ teaspoon salt

■ **Brine and Turkey.** In a very large pot, combine 1 gallon of the water, 4 cups of the cider, the sugar, kosher salt, garlic and whole sage leaves. Bring to a boil; reduce heat to medium and simmer 5 minutes. Stir in 1 gallon of the remaining water and the ice. Cool completely.

■ Once brine is cool, transfer it to a turkey roasting bag. Carefully lift bag into pot and add turkey, breast side down, to brine. Seal bag and refrigerate turkey overnight.

■ Heat oven to 450°. Discard brine and place turkey on a rack in a roasting pan. Combine butter, chopped sage, ½ teaspoon of the table salt and the pepper in a small dish. Microwave 1 minute, until butter is melted. Gently lift skin from turkey breast and brush butter mixture under skin. Brush any remaining mixture on top of turkey. Place apple and onion wedges inside cavity. Tie legs together.

■ Roast turkey at 450° for 30 minutes, tenting with foil if it browns too quickly. Reduce oven temperature to 350° and roast for 1 hour, tenting with foil once turkey reaches desired color.

■ Meanwhile, place remaining 2½ cups apple cider and pinch of salt in a medium saucepan. Cook over medium-high heat 25 minutes, until reduced to ½ cup.

■ Uncover turkey and brush with cider glaze. Add remaining 1 cup water to roasting pan. Continue to roast turkey, tented with foil, at 350° for an additional 30 minutes, until temperature registers 165° on an instant-read thermometer. Remove from roasting pan to a board. Let rest, covered with foil, 20 minutes.

■ **Gravy.** Pour pan drippings into a large fat separator. If there's less than 2½ cups liquid, add chicken or turkey stock. Melt butter in a saucepan over medium heat. Whisk in flour and salt. While whisking, add defatted pan drippings. Bring to a boil; boil 3 minutes.

PER SERVING 484 **CAL**; 21 g **FAT** (7 g **SAT**); 66 g **PRO**; 4 g **CARB**; 0 g **FIBER**; 911 mg **SODIUM**; 261 mg **CHOL**

Note: We call for a fresh turkey because most frozen ones are prebrined and would result in a very salty finished bird.

Über-Creamy Mashed Potatoes

MAKES 10 servings **PREP** 20 minutes
COOK 10 minutes
BAKE at 375° for 25 minutes **BROIL** 3 minutes

- 2¾ **to 3 pounds russet potatoes, peeled and cut up**
- ⅔ **cup milk**
- ½ **cup whipped cream cheese with chives**
- ⅓ **cup unsalted butter, cut into pieces**
- 2 **tablespoons chopped fresh parsley**
- ¾ **teaspoon salt**
- ¼ **teaspoon black pepper**
- 2 **to 3 tablespoons grated Parmesan**

■ Heat oven to 375°. Coat a 2-quart baking dish with nonstick cooking spray. Place potatoes in a large pot and add enough cool water to cover by 1 inch. Bring to a boil and lightly season water with salt.

■ Boil potatoes 10 minutes, until fork-tender. Drain and push through a potato ricer (see Note) into a bowl. Alternately, transfer potatoes to a bowl and mash until desired consistency. Stir in milk, cream cheese, butter, parsley, salt and pepper until well combined. Spread into prepared dish and top with grated Parmesan.

■ Bake at 375° for 25 minutes, until top begins to brown. If desired, increase oven temperature to broil and broil potatoes up to 3 minutes, until cheese is golden. To make ahead: Prepare potatoes, top with Parmesan and refrigerate. Bring to room temperature before baking.

PER SERVING 187 **CAL**; 9 g **FAT** (6 g **SAT**); 4 g **PRO**; 23 g **CARB**; 2 g **FIBER**; 258 mg **SODIUM**; 25 mg **CHOL**

Note: We like OXO's ricer ($30).

Stuffed Mushrooms

MAKES 12 servings (2 mushrooms per person)
PREP 20 minutes **BAKE** at 425° for 22 minutes
COOK 7 minutes

- 24 **large stuffing mushrooms (from two 14 ounce package)**
- 1 **tablespoon olive oil**
- ⅛ **plus ¼ teaspoon salt**
- 8 **ounces fresh spicy chicken or pork sausage, casings removed**
- 1 **package (10 ounces) frozen chopped spinach, thawed and squeezed dry**
- 1 **tablespoon fresh sage leaves, chopped**
- ½ **cup dry plain bread crumbs**
- 5 **tablespoons grated Parmesan**
- ¼ **teaspoon black pepper**
- 1 **large egg, lightly beaten**

■ Heat oven to 425°. Remove stems from mushrooms and reserve. Clean mushrooms and place curved side up on 1 large or 2 small baking sheets. Brush with olive oil, sprinkle with ⅛ teaspoon of the salt and bake at 425° for 10 minutes. Drain off any liquid and turn over mushrooms.

■ Chop enough of the stems to equal 1 cup. Heat a large nonstick skillet over medium-high heat. Crumble sausage into skillet and cook 3 minutes, breaking apart with a wooden spoon or silicone spatula. Stir in chopped mushroom stems and cook 3 minutes. Add spinach and sage. Cook 1 minute, remove from heat and transfer to a bowl.

■ Stir in bread crumbs, 4 tablespoons of the Parmesan, remaining ¼ teaspoon salt and the pepper. Mix in egg. Using a spoon and your hands to compress filling slightly, divide filling among mushroom caps. Sprinkle with remaining 1 tablespoon Parmesan and bake at 425° for 10 to 12 minutes, until tops are lightly browned. To make ahead: Prepare filling and stuff mushrooms. Refrigerate, then bake for 20 minutes before serving.

PER SERVING 94 **CAL**; 5 g **FAT** (1 g **SAT**); 7 g **PRO**; 7 g **CARB**; 1 g **FIBER**; 285 mg **SODIUM**; 32 mg **CHOL**

Cheesy Green Bean Casserole

MAKES 10 servings **PREP** 20 minutes
COOK 13 minutes **BAKE** at 375° for 25 minutes

- 1½ **pounds green beans, trimmed and cut into 2-inch pieces**
- 6 **tablespoons unsalted butter**
- 1 **package (10 ounces) brown mushrooms, cleaned, trimmed and sliced**
- 1 **teaspoon garlic salt**
- 3 **tablespoons all-purpose flour**
- 1½ **cups milk**
- ¼ **teaspoon black pepper**
- 1 **package (7 ounces) Swiss cheese, shredded**
- 1 **container (2.8 ounces) French's fried onions**
- ¼ **cup panko bread crumbs**

■ Heat oven to 375°. Coat a baking dish with nonstick cooking spray. Bring a large pot of lightly salted water to a boil. Add green beans and cook 4 minutes. Drain, leaving beans in the colander. Return pot to stove.

■ Melt 3 tablespoons of the butter in a large nonstick skillet set over medium heat. Add sliced mushrooms and cook 5 minutes, until softened and slightly browned. Season with ½ teaspoon of the garlic salt.

■ Add remaining 3 tablespoons butter to pot from green beans. Melt over medium heat and whisk in flour. Cook, whisking, 1 minute. While whisking, add milk. Season with remaining ½ teaspoon garlic salt and the pepper. Bring to a simmer; cook 3 minutes, whisking frequently. Remove from heat and whisk in Swiss cheese. Fold in green beans, mushrooms and ⅓ cup of the fried onions, crushed. Pour into prepared dish.

■ In a small bowl, toss together remaining fried onions and the panko. Sprinkle over casserole and bake at 375° for 25 minutes.

To make ahead: Assemble casserole, but do not sprinkle with crumbs until just before baking. Extend bake time by at least 5 minutes to heat through.

PER SERVING 254 **CAL**; 18 g **FAT** (9 g **SAT**); 10 g **PRO**; 15 g **CARB**; 2 g **FIBER**; 208 mg **SODIUM**; 4 mg **CHOL**

Beer-Brat Dressing

MAKES 10 servings **PREP** 25 minutes
TOAST 8 minutes **COOK** 11 minutes
BAKE at 375° for 30 minutes

- 1 **round loaf (about 1 pound) hearty white bread (unsliced)**
- 2 **tablespoons unsalted butter**
- ¾ **pound fresh bratwurst (such as Johnsonville), casings removed**
- 2 **ribs celery, trimmed and diced**
- 1 **medium onion, chopped**
- 2 **medium carrots, peeled and diced**
- 2 **tablespoons chopped fresh sage**
- 1 **cup amber or dark beer**
- ½ **teaspoon salt**
- ½ **teaspoon black pepper**
- ½ **to ¾ cup unsalted turkey or chicken stock**

■ Heat oven to 375°. Coat a 13 x 9 x 2-inch baking dish with nonstick cooking spray. Set aside. Cut bread into 1-inch slices. Place directly on oven rack and toast 3 to 4 minutes. Flip over and toast an additional 4 minutes, until dry to the touch. Let cool until you can handle slices.

■ Melt butter in a large lidded nonstick skillet set over medium heat. Crumble in bratwurst and cook, breaking apart with a wooden spoon, 4 minutes. Add celery, onion, carrots and sage and cook, covered, 5 minutes. Stir in beer, salt and pepper and cook, uncovered, 2 minutes.

■ Cut toasted bread into 1-inch cubes and place in a large bowl. Carefully pour in contents of skillet and stir to combine. Transfer dressing to prepared baking dish and drizzle with stock (adding more if needed). Bake at 375° for 30 minutes. To make ahead: Prepare dressing and place in prepared dish (don't drizzle with stock). Refrigerate. Bring to room temperature and drizzle with stock. Bake at 375° for 30 minutes or until hot.

PER SERVING 265 **CAL**; 12 g **FAT** (5 g **SAT**); 11 g **PRO**; 26 g **CARB**; 1 g **FIBER**; 625 mg **SODIUM**; 32 mg **CHOL**

French Silk Pie

MAKES 12 servings **PREP** 40 minutes **BAKE** at 450° for 11 minutes **COOL** at least 30 minutes
COOK 15 minutes **REFRIGERATE** at least 5 hours

- 1 **refrigerated rolled piecrust (from a 14.1 ounce package)**
- 1¾ **cups heavy cream**
- 6 **ounces semisweet chocolate, chopped**
- ⅓ **cup unsalted butter**
- ⅓ **cup plus 1 tablespoon sugar**
- 2 **egg yolks, beaten**
- **Chocolate curls (optional)**

■ Heat oven to 450°. Fit piecrust into a 9-inch pie dish and decoratively flute edge. Pierce all over with a fork. Bake crust at 450° for 9 to 11 minutes. Cool at least 30 minutes.

■ In a medium heavy saucepan, combine 1 cup of the cream, the chopped chocolate, butter and ⅓ cup of the sugar. Cook over low heat, stirring constantly, until chocolate is melted, about 10 minutes. Remove from heat. Gradually whisk half the hot mixture into beaten egg yolks. Return egg mixture to chocolate mixture in saucepan. Cook over medium-low heat, stirring constantly, until mixture is slightly thickened and begins to bubble, about 5 minutes. Remove from heat. (Mixture may appear slightly curdled.) Stir in ¼ cup of the remaining cream. Place saucepan in a bowl of ice water, stirring occasionally, until mixture stiffens and becomes hard to stir (about 20 minutes). Transfer chocolate mixture to a medium mixing bowl.

■ Beat cooled chocolate mixture with an electric mixer on medium to high speed 2 to 3 minutes, until light and fluffy. Spread filling in baked pastry shell. Cover and refrigerate pie at least 5 hours. To serve, whip remaining ½ cup heavy cream with remaining 1 tablespoon sugar. Spoon whipped cream into center of pie. Garnish with chocolate curls, if using.

PER SERVING 346 **CAL**; 29 g **FAT** (17 g **SAT**); 3 g **PRO**; 23 g **CARB**; 1 g **FIBER**; 110 mg **SODIUM**; 94 mg **CHOL**

The West Coast: The fresh nature of West Coast cuisine is reflected in this menu: in herb-roasted turkey, sourdough stuffing, marinated olives, artichoke gratin and a pear-topped cheesecake for dessert.

Herb-Roasted Turkey with White Wine Gravy

MAKES 12 servings **PREP** 20 minutes **ROAST** at 425° for 2 hours, 15 minutes **REST** 20 minutes **COOK** 12 minutes

- 1 **turkey (about 12 pounds)**
- 4 **tablespoons olive oil**
- 2 **cloves chopped garlic**
- 3 **tablespoons chopped fresh parsley**
- 1 **tablespoon chopped fresh rosemary**
- 1 **tablespoon chopped fresh thyme**
- 1 **teaspoon chopped fresh sage**
- 1½ **teaspoons kosher salt**
- ½ **teaspoon plus ⅛ teaspoon black pepper**
- 1 **small yellow onion, quartered**
- 1 **head garlic, halved**
- 2 **tablespoons all-purpose flour**
- ½ **cup dry white wine (such as Chardonnay)**
- 1½ **cups unsalted chicken stock**

■ Let turkey sit at room temperature for 45 minutes before placing in oven. Remove giblets and neck (add neck to roasting pan, if desired); pat dry with paper towels. Heat oven to 425°.

■ In a bowl, mix 2 tablespoons of the oil with the chopped garlic, 2 tablespoons of the parsley, the rosemary, thyme, sage, ½ teaspoon of the salt and ¼ teaspoon of the pepper.

■ Place onion and garlic head inside turkey. Tie legs and place on a rack in a roasting pan, tucking wings underneath turkey. Rub herb mixture underneath breast and leg skin. Rub turkey with 1 tablespoon of the olive oil and season with remaining 1 teaspoon salt and ¼ teaspoon of the pepper.

■ Roast at 425° for 1 hour, 45 minutes to 2 hours, 15 minutes, or until temperature reaches 165° in thigh. Transfer turkey to a cutting board and let rest 20 minutes before carving.

■ While turkey is resting, make gravy. Remove onion and garlic from cooked turkey. Dice half the onion and several of the garlic cloves. Place roasting pan over 2 burners on medium heat. Add remaining 1 tablespoon olive oil. Stir in onion and garlic; sauté 2 minutes. Whisk in flour; cook 1 minute. Whisk in wine; bring to a boil and cook until reduced by half, about 2 minutes. Whisk in stock and return to a boil. Reduce to a simmer and cook 7 minutes, until thickened. Season with remaining 1 tablespoon parsley and ⅛ teaspoon pepper.

PER SERVING 480 **CAL**; 19 g **FAT** (4.5 g **SAT**); 70 g **PRO**; 2 g **CARB**; 0 g **FIBER**; 420 mg **SODIUM**; 260 mg **CHOL**

Artichoke Gratin

MAKES 8 servings **PREP** 15 minutes
BAKE at 400° for 50 minutes **REST** 15 minutes

- 1 **cup heavy cream**
- 4 **boxes (9 ounces each) frozen artichoke hearts, thawed**
- 4 **ounces white cheddar, grated**
- 3 **cloves garlic, chopped**
- ¼ **cup chopped parsley**
- 1 **tablespoon chopped fresh thyme**
- 1 **tablespoon all-purpose flour**
- ¾ **teaspoon salt**
- ¼ **teaspoon black pepper**
- ½ **cup shredded Asiago**

■ Heat oven to 400°. In a small pot, heat heavy cream to simmering.

■ In a bowl, combine artichoke hearts, cheddar, garlic, parsley, thyme, flour, salt and pepper. Transfer to a 2-quart baking dish. Pour cream on top. Sprinkle with Asiago.

■ Cover baking dish with foil and bake at 400° for 25 minutes. Uncover and bake an additional 25 minutes, until golden and bubbling. Let rest 15 minutes before serving.

PER SERVING 270 **CAL**; 19 g **FAT** (12 g **SAT**); 8 g **PRO**; 14 g **CARB**; 9 g **FIBER**; 440 mg **SODIUM**; 65 mg **CHOL**

Sourdough, Date and Turkey Sausage Stuffing

MAKES 12 servings **PREP** 20 minutes
COOK 12 minutes **BAKE** at 400° for 35 minutes

- 1 pound sourdough bread, cut into ½-inch cubes
- 1 tablespoon olive oil
- 12 ounces sweet turkey sausage, casings removed
- 1½ cups chopped pitted dates
- 1 cup chopped walnuts
- 1 small yellow onion, diced
- 2 cloves garlic, minced
- 2½ cups unsalted chicken stock
- ½ cup grated Parmesan
- 2 tablespoons chopped fresh parsley
- 1 tablespoon chopped fresh thyme
- ¾ teaspoon salt
- ¼ teaspoon black pepper

■ Heat oven to 400°. Spread bread cubes on 2 baking sheets. Bake at 400° for 5 minutes, toss, then bake another 5 minutes or until lightly browned. Transfer to a large bowl.

■ In a skillet, heat oil over medium-high heat. Add sausage, breaking up with a spoon. Cook 5 to 7 minutes, until browned. Reduce heat to medium. Stir in dates, walnuts, onion and garlic. Cook 5 minutes. Stir in stock, ¼ cup of the Parmesan, the parsley, thyme, salt and pepper. Transfer to a 13 x 9 x 2-inch baking dish and press down with a spatula. Scatter remaining ¼ cup Parmesan over top.

■ Cover dish with foil. Bake at 400° for 20 minutes. Uncover; bake 5 minutes more.

PER SERVING 280 **CAL**; 13 g **FAT** (1.5 g **SAT**); 13 g **PRO**; 31 g **CARB**; 2 g **FIBER**; 600 mg **SODIUM**; 25 mg **CHOL**

Sweet and Spicy Olive Mix

MAKES 12 servings **PREP** 5 minutes
MARINATE 2 hours or overnight

- 2 tablespoons extra-virgin olive oil
- 2 tablespoons honey
- 1 tablespoon lemon juice plus ½ teaspoon lemon zest
- ½ teaspoon chopped fresh rosemary
- ¼ teaspoon red pepper flakes
- ⅛ teaspoon salt
- 2 cups mixed olives with pits (such as niçoise, Castelvetrano, Cerignola, Picholine and Nyon)
- ½ cup Marcona almonds
- ½ cup raisins

■ Whisk oil, honey, lemon juice and zest, rosemary, red pepper and salt. Fold in olives, almonds and raisins. Cover with plastic wrap and allow to marinate at least 2 hours or overnight.

PER SERVING 170 **CAL**; 13 g **FAT** (2 g **SAT**); 1.5 g **PRO**; 12 g **CARB**; 1 g **FIBER**; 470 mg **SODIUM**; 0 mg **CHOL**

Crispy Olive Oil Potatoes

MAKES 12 servings **PREP** 15 minutes
COOK 42 minutes

- 3 pounds small red and yellow potatoes (about 2 inches round)
- 6 tablespoons extra-virgin olive oil
- ¾ teaspoon salt
  Freshly cracked black pepper
- 1 teaspoon chopped fresh thyme
- ½ teaspoon chopped fresh rosemary

■ Place potatoes in a large pot and cover with 2 inches cold water. Bring to a boil and cook 18 minutes. Drain and place on a baking sheet.

■ Allow to cool 5 minutes. Using the back of a measuring cup, press down on each potato to flatten to ½ inch (skin will crack).

■ In a large skillet, heat 2 tablespoons of the olive oil over medium-high heat. Place a third of the potatoes in skillet. Fry 4 minutes on one side, until skin is crispy. Flip and season crispy side with ⅛ teaspoon salt. Fry another 4 minutes. Place on a platter and sprinkle nonseasoned side with ⅛ teaspoon of the salt and freshly cracked pepper. Repeat with 2 more batches, adding 2 tablespoons olive oil per batch. Scatter thyme and rosemary on top of potatoes.

PER SERVING 140 **CAL**; 7 g **FAT** (1 g **SAT**); 2 g **PRO**; 18 g **CARB**; 2 g **FIBER**; 170 mg **SODIUM**; 0 mg **CHOL**

Maple-Pear Cheesecake Pie

MAKES 12 servings **PREP** 25 minutes
COOK 20 minutes **BAKE** at 375° for 20 minutes
REFRIGERATE at least 3 hours

- 12 graham cracker boards (or 1½ cups graham cracker crumbs)
- 4 tablespoons unsalted butter, melted
- ¾ cup plus 1 tablespoon maple syrup, plus more for drizzling
- 2 to 3 pears, peeled, halved and cored
- 2 packages (8 ounces each) cream cheese, at room temperature
- 1 large egg
- 2 teaspoons cornstarch
- ⅛ teaspoon ground cinnamon
  Toasted walnuts (optional)

■ Heat oven to 375°. In a food processor, crush graham crackers until even crumbs are created. Add melted butter and 1 tablespoon of the syrup and pulse until blended. Press into a 9-inch pie dish. Set aside.

■ In a large lidded pot, combine ½ cup of the syrup and 2 cups water and bring to a boil over high heat. Reduce heat to medium and add pear halves. Cover and cook 10 minutes.

■ Meanwhile, in a medium bowl, beat cream cheese until smooth. Add remaining ¼ cup syrup, the egg, cornstarch and cinnamon. Spread into prepared crust.

■ Bake cream cheese layer at 375° for 20 minutes.

■ Uncover pears and turn over. Cover and continue to cook 10 minutes more. Remove to a cutting board and cool slightly.

■ Slice pears into thin wedges. Fan into pie over cream cheese filling. Cool to room temperature, then refrigerate at least 3 hours. Drizzle with additional syrup and sprinkle with toasted walnuts, if using.

PER SERVING 319 **CAL**; 19 g **FAT** (10 g **SAT**); 4 g **PRO**; 36 g **CARB**; 2 g **FIBER**; 251 mg **SODIUM**; 71 mg **CHOL**

MAPLE-PEAR
CHEESECAKE PIE

Menu

Orange Chili-Rubbed Turkey

Cornbread and Chorizo Dressing

Warm Black Bean Dip

Chipotle Smashed
Sweet and White Potatoes

Brussels Sprouts with
Caramelized Shallots and Pepitas

Salted Caramel Pecan Pie

The Southwest: From the region bordering Mexico comes an intensely spiced menu infused with chiles and lime and featuring favorite ingredients that include black beans, cilantro, chorizo and crunchy pepitas.

Orange Chili-Rubbed Turkey

MAKES 12 servings **PREP** 15 minutes **ROAST** at 450° for 30 minutes and at 350° for 2 hours **REST** 20 minutes **COOK** 6 minutes

- 1 tablespoon each chili powder, ground cumin, paprika, garlic powder and dried oregano
- 2 teaspoons salt
- ½ teaspoon cayenne pepper
- 3 tablespoons olive oil
- 1 fresh turkey (about 12 pounds)
- ½ cup frozen orange juice concentrate, thawed
  Juice of 1 lime
- 3 tablespoons all-purpose flour
- 2 cups turkey or chicken broth
- 2 tablespoons chopped cilantro

■ Heat oven to 450°. Fit a large roasting pan with a rack.

■ In a bowl, combine chili powder, cumin, paprika, garlic powder, oregano, salt and cayenne. Stir in olive oil to form a paste.

■ Remove giblets and neck from cavity of turkey. Rinse turkey and pat dry with paper towels. Place in roasting pan. If desired, tuck wings under turkey and tie legs together with cooking twine.

■ Season turkey with spice rub on the outside as well as under skin of breast halves. Roast at 450° for 30 minutes. Combine orange juice concentrate and lime juice. Reduce heat to 350° and brush turkey with juice mixture. Roast for 2 hours, until internal temperature reaches 165°. Brush with juice mixture twice more during the last 2 hours of cooking. If turkey starts getting too dark, tent with foil for last hour of cooking. Remove to a cutting board; let rest 20 minutes.

■ Place roasting pan over medium heat and whisk in flour; cook 1 minute. Gradually whisk in broth and cook 5 minutes, until thickened. Strain gravy and stir in cilantro.

PER SERVING 486 **CAL**; 18 g **FAT** (5 g **SAT**); 70 g **PRO**; 7 g **CARB**; 1 g **FIBER**; 590 mg **SODIUM**; 257 mg **CHOL**

Brussels Sprouts with Caramelized Shallots and Pepitas

MAKES 8 servings **PREP** 15 minutes **COOK** 16 minutes

- 3 tablespoons olive oil
- ½ cup sliced shallots
- 6 cloves garlic, peeled and smashed
- 2 pounds Brussels sprouts, trimmed and quartered
- 1 sweet red pepper, seeded and thinly sliced
- ½ teaspoon salt
- ¼ teaspoon black pepper
- ¼ teaspoon red pepper flakes
- 2 tablespoons roasted pepitas

■ Heat 1 tablespoon of the oil in a large skillet; add shallots and cook on medium-high heat until crispy, about 5 minutes. Remove shallots to a plate.

■ Wipe out skillet and add remaining 2 tablespoons oil. Add garlic and cook 1 minute; add Brussels sprouts and cook, uncovered, 5 minutes, stirring occasionally.

■ Stir in sweet red pepper, salt, black pepper, red pepper flakes and ¼ cup water. Cover and cook 5 minutes, stirring occasionally, until tender.

■ To serve, spoon Brussels sprouts into a serving bowl and top with shallots and pepitas.

PER SERVING 118 **CAL**; 7 g **FAT** (1 g **SAT**); 4 g **PRO**; 13 g **CARB**; 4 g **FIBER**; 461 mg **SODIUM**; 0 mg **CHOL**

Cornbread and Chorizo Dressing

MAKES 8 servings **PREP** 20 minutes
COOK 4 minutes **BAKE** at 350° for 45 minutes

- 4 tablespoons unsalted butter
- 1 green pepper, seeded and chopped
- 1 jalapeño, seeded and chopped
- 1 cup all-purpose flour
- 1 cup coarse cornmeal
- 2 tablespoons sugar
- 2½ teaspoons baking powder
- ¾ teaspoon salt
- ½ teaspoon baking soda
- 1¼ cups buttermilk
- 1 egg, lightly beaten
- 1 tablespoon olive oil
- 3.5 ounces cured chorizo sausage, casing removed, diced
- 1 cup turkey or chicken broth, heated
- ¾ cup shredded Mexican cheese blend

■ Heat oven to 350°. Coat an 8 x 8-inch baking pan with nonstick cooking spray.

■ Heat 2 tablespoons of the butter in a small skillet; add peppers and cook 3 minutes, until softened. Set aside, add remaining 2 tablespoons butter and allow to melt.

■ In a large bowl, whisk flour, cornmeal, sugar, baking powder, salt and baking soda. Make a well in center and add buttermilk, egg and butter-and-pepper mixture. Mix until just combined. Spoon into prepared baking pan and bake at 350° for 35 minutes. Turn out cornbread and cool slightly. With a serrated knife, cut into 1-inch cubes and place in a large bowl.

■ In the same small skillet, heat olive oil. Add chorizo and cook 1 minute, until lightly crisp. Add to cornbread cubes; stir in broth and cheese.

■ Spoon into a baking dish; bake at 350° for 10 minutes until warm and cheese is melted. Serve with turkey and gravy.

PER SERVING 315 **CAL**; 15 g **FAT** (7 g **SAT**); 11 g **PRO**; 33 g **CARB**; 1 g **FIBER**; 713 mg **SODIUM**; 58 mg **CHOL**

WARM BLACK BEAN DIP

Warm Black Bean Dip

MAKES 8 servings **PREP** 10 minutes **BAKE** at 350° for 25 minutes

- 2 cans (15 ounces each) black beans, drained and rinsed
- ½ red onion, chopped
- ⅓ cup cilantro leaves
- 2 tablespoons red wine vinegar
- 2 tablespoons olive oil
- 2 cloves garlic
- ¾ teaspoon ground cumin
- ½ teaspoon salt
- ¼ teaspoon black pepper
- 1 cup (4 ounces) shredded Monterey Jack
- 1 bag (12 ounces) baked tortilla chips

  Lime wedges and cilantro, for garnish

■ Heat oven to 350°. Coat a 1-quart baking dish with nonstick cooking spray.

■ In a food processor, combine 1 can of the beans, the onion, cilantro, vinegar, olive oil, garlic, cumin, salt and pepper. Process until smooth. Remove to a medium bowl and stir in remaining can of black beans and ¾ cup of the Monterey Jack.

■ Spoon mixture into prepared baking dish, top with remaining ¼ cup cheese and bake at 350° for 25 minutes, until bubbly.

■ Serve with chips. Garnish with lime and cilantro, if using.

PER ½ CUP DIP PLUS CHIPS 383 **CAL**; 14 g **FAT** (4 g **SAT**); 13 g **PRO**; 50 g **CARB**; 10 g **FIBER**; 848 mg **SODIUM**; 15 mg **CHOL**

Chipotle Smashed Sweet and White Potatoes

MAKES 8 servings **PREP** 15 minutes **COOK** 16 minutes

- 1½ **pounds sweet potatoes, peeled and cut into 1-inch pieces**
- 1½ **pounds all-purpose potatoes, peeled and cut into 1-inch pieces**
- ¼ **cup unsalted butter**
- 4 **scallions, trimmed and sliced**
- 1 **chipotle pepper in adobo, seeded and chopped; 1 teaspoon adobo reserved**
- ½ **cup heavy cream**
- ¼ **cup cilantro leaves, chopped**
- ¼ **teaspoon salt**

Chopped scallion for garnish (optional)

■ Place sweet potatoes and potatoes in a large pot. Cover with cool water and salt lightly. Bring to a boil; reduce heat to medium and cook, covered, 12 to 15 minutes or until tender. Drain; return to pot.

■ In a small saucepan, melt butter over medium heat. Add scallions, chipotle and reserved adobo; cook 1 minute. Add cream and cook until heated.

■ Mash potatoes with a potato masher to desired consistency. Stir in chipotle and cream mixture. Fold in cilantro and salt; garnish with scallion, if using.

PER SERVING 210 **CAL**; 12 g **FAT** (7 g **SAT**); 2 g **PRO**; 25 g **CARB**; 4 g **FIBER**; 173 mg **SODIUM**; 36 mg **CHOL**

CHIPOTLE SMASHED SWEET AND WHITE POTATOES

SALTED CARAMEL
PECAN PIE

Salted Caramel Pecan Pie

MAKES 12 servings **PREP** 15 minutes **BAKE** at 350° for 1 hour **COOL** at least 2 hours

- 1 **refrigerated piecrust (from a 14.1 ounce package)**
- ½ **cup light corn syrup**
- ½ **cup caramel sauce**
- ¾ **cup sugar**
- 4 **large eggs**
- 1 **teaspoon vanilla extract**
- ½ **teaspoon kosher salt**
- 1 **cup coarsely chopped pecans**
- 1 **cup whole pecan halves**
  Whipped cream (optional)

■ Heat oven to 350°. Coat a 9-inch pie dish with nonstick cooking spray. Fit piecrust into prepared dish, fluting edge.

■ In a bowl, whisk corn syrup, caramel sauce, sugar, eggs, vanilla and salt. Stir in chopped pecans. Carefully pour pecan mixture into crust; scatter pecan halves evenly over top.

■ Bake at 350° for 55 minutes to 1 hour, covering crust with foil if browning too quickly. Cool at least 2 hours, then refrigerate until serving. Garnish with whipped cream, if using.

PER SERVING 348 **CAL**; 20 g **FAT** (3 g **SAT**); 5 g **PRO**; 40 g **CARB**; 2 g **FIBER**; 235 mg **SODIUM**; 62 mg **CHOL**

CONDIMENT DELUXE

Next-day turkey sandwiches rise above mere leftovers with these easy-to-make spreads.

SPICY SWEET PEPPER RELISH

TRUFFLE MAYO

CHESTNUT AND THYME MUSTARD

Spicy Sweet Pepper Relish

MAKES 1¼ cups **START TO FINISH** 10 minutes

- 1 cup jarred roasted red peppers, diced
- 1 jalapeño, seeded and diced
- 1 teaspoon sugar
- 1 teaspoon cider vinegar
- ¼ teaspoon salt

■ In a small bowl stir together roasted red peppers, jalapeño, sugar, cider vinegar and salt.

Truffle Mayo

MAKES ½ cup **START TO FINISH** 5 minutes

- ½ cup mayonnaise
- 1 teaspoon truffle oil
- ⅛ teaspoon freshly cracked black pepper

■ In a small bowl stir together mayonnaise, truffle oil and black pepper.

Chestnut and Thyme Mustard

MAKES about ½ cup
START TO FINISH 10 minutes

- 3 tablespoons finely chopped chestnuts
- ⅓ cup Dijon mustard
- 1 teaspoon chopped fresh thyme

■ In a small bowl stir together chestnuts, mustard and thyme.

TURKEY-TIME TREATS

When pumpkin pie seems too serious, try one of these whimsical sweets.

TURKEY
CUPCAKES

CRISPY
PUMPKIN
TREATS

NUTTY
OWLS

Guests will gobble up these fall-theme treats made with easy-to-find decorating ingredients such as candy corn, M&M's, Twizzlers, candy-coated sunflower seeds and edible candy eyes.

Nutty Owls

MAKES 16 (2½-inch) cookies **PREP** 15 minutes
REFRIGERATE at least 2 hours
BAKE at 350° for 15 minutes

- ½ cup whole natural (skin-on) almonds plus 8, halved lengthwise
- 1½ cups all-purpose flour
- ⅓ cup confectioners' sugar
- ¼ teaspoon salt
- ¾ cup (1½ sticks) unsalted butter, at room temperature
- 1 teaspoon vanilla extract
- 1 teaspoon almond extract
- 36 brown M&M's

■ Place ½ cup of the almonds in a food processor and pulse until finely ground. Add flour, confectioners' sugar and salt and pulse to blend. Spoon butter, vanilla and almond extract into food processor and process until dough begins to hold together. Remove dough from processor, flatten into 2 discs and wrap in plastic. Refrigerate at least 2 hours.

■ Heat oven to 350°. On floured wax paper, roll out dough to ³⁄₁₆- to ¼-inch thickness. Cut out circles with a 2½-inch round cookie cutter. Transfer circles to 2 large baking sheets. Use cutter to mark "wings" on cookies, pressing down but not all the way through dough. Using ¼ teaspoon dough for each, form 2 balls. Affix balls to a cookie as eyes and press gently to flatten. Place a brown M&M's on each eye, and press half an almond between eyes to resemble a beak. Use a fork to add "feet" between wings.

■ Repeat with remaining dough, M&M's and almond halves, rerolling scraps as needed. If dough becomes too soft, refrigerate until firm, about 1 hour. Bake cookies at 350° for 15 minutes. Let cool on baking sheets on a wire rack 2 minutes, then transfer directly to rack to cool completely.

Crispy Pumpkin Treats

MAKES 12 pumpkins **PREP** 5 minutes
COOK 5 minutes **STAND** 3 hours

- 3 tablespoons unsalted butter
- 1 bag (10 ounces) marshmallows
- 1 tablespoon orange gel food coloring
- 6 cups Rice Krispies cereal
- 12 Tootsie Rolls Midgees

■ In a large saucepan, heat butter over low heat until melted. Add marshmallows, stirring occasionally until completely melted. Add food coloring and stir until orange is spread throughout.

■ Remove from heat and stir in Rice Krispies cereal.

■ Grease a bowl and pour mixture into bowl. Coat your hands or food-safe plastic gloves with nonstick cooking spray. Form pumpkin shapes using ⅔ cup of the mixture for each pumpkin. Roll and shape Tootsie Rolls to resemble stems. Add stems to pumpkins. Let stand 3 hours before serving.

Turkey Cupcakes

MAKES 24 cupcakes **ASSEMBLE** 1 hour

- 24 Nutter Butter cookies
- 3 strawberry Twizzlers
- 1 cup confectioners' sugar
- 48 Wilton edible candy eyes
- 24 orange candy-coated sunflower seeds
- 24 baked jumbo chocolate cupcakes
- Canned chocolate frosting
- Candy corn (about 190 pieces)

■ Using a serrated knife, cut off about one-fourth from a short side of each Nutter Butter cookie.

■ With scissors, cut Twizzlers into pieces measuring about ½ x ⅓ inch.

■ In a small bowl, whisk confectioners' sugar and 4 teaspoons water, creating a thick frosting.

■ Using sugar frosting, attach eyes, a candy-coated sunflower seed for the beak and a Twizzlers piece for the wattle to each Nutter Butter.

■ Spread cupcakes with chocolate frosting, stick a decorated Nutter Butter into each cupcake and add candy corns as tail feathers (7 or 8 per cupcake).

HEALTHY FAMILY DINNERS

Family-friendly favorites get a healthy makeover with these slow cooker recipes.

CHICKEN AND CORN CHILI,
PAGE 308

Harvest Pork Chops

MAKES 4 servings **PREP** 30 minutes **COOK** 5 minutes **SLOW COOK** on HIGH for 2 hours or LOW for 4 hours

- 3 cups ¾-inch cubes peeled butternut squash
- 1 cup sliced celery
- 1 large onion, cut into wedges
- 4 bone-in pork chops (6 ounces each)
- 1 cup apple cider
- 1 tablespoon chopped chipotle pepper in adobo
- ½ teaspoon dried basil
- ¼ teaspoon salt
- ¼ teaspoon garlic powder
- ¼ cup plain low-fat yogurt
- 3 cups cooked brown rice

■ In a 4-quart slow cooker, layer butternut squash, celery and onion.

■ Generously coat a large skillet with nonstick cooking spray. Heat over medium heat. Add chops to skillet; cook 5 minutes, turning once. Place chops on top of vegetables in slow cooker.

■ In a small bowl, combine cider, chipotle, basil, salt and garlic powder. Pour over chops. Cover and cook on HIGH for 2 hours or LOW for 4 hours.

■ Using a slotted spoon, transfer chops and vegetables to a serving platter. Discard cooking liquid. Spoon yogurt over chops. Serve with brown rice.

PER SERVING 320 **CAL**; 4 g **FAT** (1 g **SAT**); 13 g **PRO**; 59 g **CARB**; 7 g **FIBER**; 225 mg **SODIUM**; 19 mg **CHOL**

Skip soaking and scrubbing the usual baked-on mess in the lasagna pan by placing a slow cooker liner (such as Reynolds) in the crock before you add any ingredients. Made of a special heat-resistant material, the bag won't break and makes cleanup simple.

TURKEY LASAGNA

Spicy-Sweet Pot Roast

MAKES 8 servings **PREP** 15 minutes
SLOW COOK on HIGH for 5 hours or
LOW for 10 hours **COOK** 3 minutes

- 2½ **pounds boneless beef chuck roast, trimmed**
- 2 **teaspoons garlic-pepper seasoning**
- 1 **package (7 ounces) dried fruit mix**
- 1 **tablespoon chopped chipotle pepper in adobo**
- 2 **teaspoons cornstarch**
  Fresh cilantro sprigs (optional)

■ Season meat with garlic-pepper seasoning and place in slow cooker. Add dried fruit, ½ cup water and chipotle.

■ Cover and cook on HIGH for 5 hours or LOW for 10 hours. Transfer meat and fruit to a serving platter; thinly slice meat. Keep meat and fruit warm.

■ Pour cooking liquid into a bowl and skim off fat. In a medium saucepan, combine 1 tablespoon water and cornstarch. Add cooking liquid and simmer over medium heat until thickened, about 3 minutes.

■ Serve meat and fruit with sauce. Garnish with cilantro, if using.

PER SERVING 351 **CAL**; 18 g **FAT** (7 g **SAT**);
27 g **PRO**; 18 g **CARB**; 1 g **FIBER**; 302 mg **SODIUM**;
107 mg **CHOL**

Turkey Lasagna

MAKES 8 servings **PREP** 10 minutes **COOK** 10 minutes **SLOW COOK** on HIGH for 4 hours or
LOW for 5 hours

- 1 **tablespoon canola oil**
- 1 **medium onion, chopped**
- 2 **cloves garlic, chopped**
- 1¼ **pounds ground turkey**
- 1 **teaspoon dried oregano**
- ½ **teaspoon salt**
- ¼ **teaspoon black pepper**
- 1 **container (15 ounces) low-fat ricotta**
- 1 **cup Italian blend shredded cheese**
- 12 **lasagna noodles, broken in half**
- 1 **package (10 ounces) frozen chopped broccoli, thawed and squeezed dry**
- 1 **jar (26 ounces) chunky tomato sauce**

■ In a large nonstick skillet, heat oil over medium-high heat. Cook onion and garlic 4 minutes or until softened. Add turkey and cook 6 minutes, breaking up with a wooden spoon; season with oregano, salt and pepper. Set aside.

■ In a small bowl, combine ricotta and ½ cup of the shredded cheese.

■ Line a 5- to 6-quart slow cooker with a slow cooker liner. Layer half the uncooked noodles into slow cooker, overlapping as necessary. Spread half the turkey mixture and broccoli over noodles; top with half the tomato sauce and ¼ cup water. Gently spread ricotta mixture on top. Continue layering with remaining noodles, turkey mixture, broccoli, sauce and an additional ¼ cup water.

■ Cover and cook on HIGH for 4 hours or LOW for 5 hours. Sprinkle remaining ½ cup shredded cheese on top during last 15 minutes of cooking. Use liner to lift lasagna from slow cooker; slice and serve.

PER SERVING 418 **CAL**; 13 g **FAT** (4 g **SAT**);
32 g **PRO**; 44 g **CARB**; 4 g **FIBER**;
706 mg **SODIUM**; 68 mg **CHOL**

CHICKEN AND CORN CHILI

Chicken with Figs and Blue Cheese

MAKES 6 servings **PREP** 20 minutes
COOK 13 minutes
SLOW COOK on LOW for 5 hours

1½	cups low-sodium chicken broth
¼	cup balsamic vinegar
1	tablespoon grated orange zest
½	teaspoon black pepper
2	tablespoons vegetable oil
2	pounds boneless, skinless chicken thighs
1	large onion, thinly sliced
½	teaspoon salt
2	tablespoons all-purpose flour
1	package (8 ounces) dried Mission figs, stems removed and coarsely chopped
1	tube (16 ounces) prepared polenta
⅔	cup crumbled blue cheese

■ In a small bowl, combine broth, vinegar, orange zest and ¼ teaspoon of the pepper; set aside.

■ Heat oil in a large nonstick skillet over medium-high heat. Add chicken to skillet and cook 5 minutes per side or until browned. Remove chicken to slow cooker. Add onion to skillet and season with ¼ teaspoon each of the salt and pepper; cook 2 minutes. Stir in flour and cook 1 minute. Pour in broth mixture and bring to a boil. Pour contents of skillet into slow cooker; add figs.

■ Cover and cook on LOW for 5 hours.

■ Meanwhile, prepare polenta following package directions. Season chicken mixture with remaining ¼ teaspoon salt.

■ Serve chicken and figs with polenta; crumble blue cheese over each serving.

PER SERVING 473 **CAL**; 17 g **FAT** (6 g **SAT**); 33 g **PRO**; 43 g **CARB**; 6 g **FIBER**; 698 mg **SODIUM**; 150 mg **CHOL**

Chicken and Corn Chili

MAKES 6 servings **PREP** 10 minutes **SLOW COOK** on HIGH for 4 hours or LOW for 6 hours

1	large onion, chopped
1	pound boneless, skinless chicken breasts
2	cups low-sodium chicken broth
1	green pepper, seeded and chopped
1	jalapeño, seeded and chopped
1¾	teaspoons ground cumin
½	teaspoon cayenne pepper
¾	teaspoon salt
1	can (14.5 ounces) diced tomatoes with jalapeños, drained
1½	cups frozen corn, thawed
2	cans (15 ounces each) cannellini beans, drained and rinsed
2	tablespoons stone-ground cornmeal
	Shredded Monterey Jack (optional)

■ In a 5- to 6-quart slow cooker, combine onion, chicken, broth, green pepper, jalapeño, 1½ teaspoons of the cumin and ¼ teaspoon each of the cayenne and salt. Cover and cook on HIGH for 4 hours or LOW for 6 hours.

■ During the last 30 minutes of cooking, remove chicken to a cutting board and shred. Return chicken to slow cooker with remaining ¼ teaspoon each of the cumin and cayenne, the tomatoes, corn and beans. Gently mash some of the beans against side of bowl to thicken chili. Stir in cornmeal and remaining ½ teaspoon salt.

■ Sprinkle with Monterey Jack, if using.

PER SERVING 287 **CAL**; 3 g **FAT** (1 g **SAT**); 27 g **PRO**; 38 g **CARB**; 9 g **FIBER**; 736 mg **SODIUM**; 45 mg **CHOL**

CHICKEN WITH FIGS
AND BLUE CHEESE

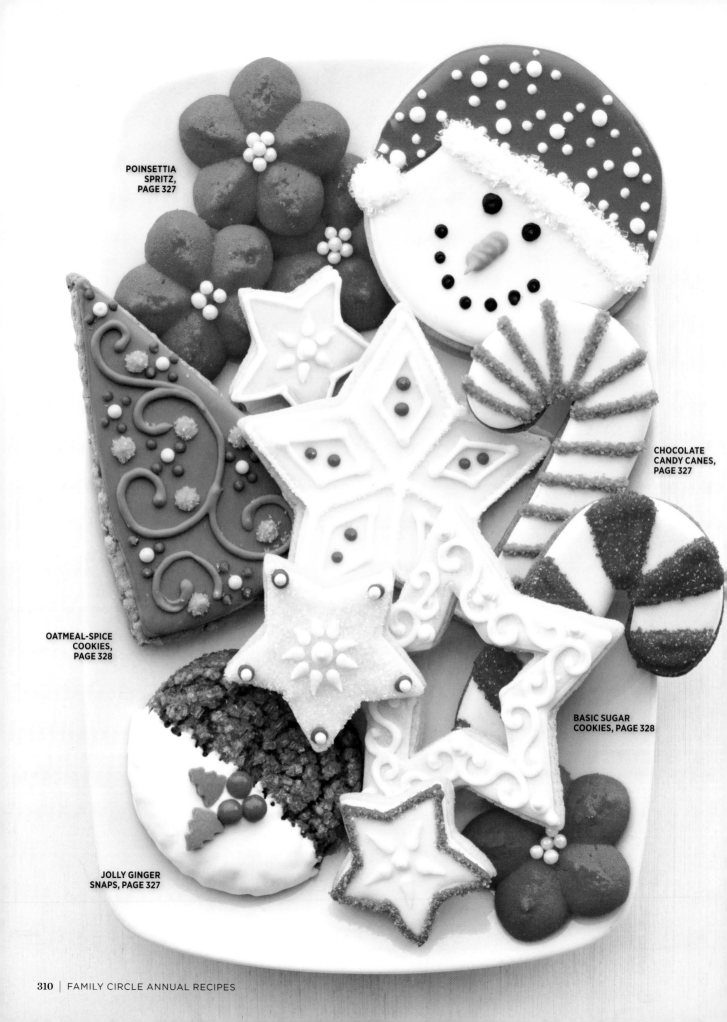

POINSETTIA
SPRITZ,
PAGE 327

CHOCOLATE
CANDY CANES,
PAGE 327

OATMEAL-SPICE
COOKIES,
PAGE 328

BASIC SUGAR
COOKIES, PAGE 328

JOLLY GINGER
SNAPS, PAGE 327

DECEMBER

316

320

329

GET THE PARTY STARTED

Whatever the occasion, there's an app for that! These crowd-pleasers take 15 minutes of prep, max.

CHICKEN TIKKA MASALA WINGS, PAGE 314

WEDGE SALAD STACKS, PAGE 314

ZA'ATAR NUT MIX,
PAGE 315

SPANAKOPITA CUPS,
PAGE 315

CRAB-STUFFED
MINI PEPPERS,
PAGE 315

POMEGRANATE
GUACAMOLE

MEATBALL PARM
MUSHROOMS

KOREAN BEEF
SKEWERS

SAUSAGE-BACON
WRAPS

Chicken Tikka Masala Wings

MAKES 24 wings PREP 10 minutes
BAKE at 400° for 55 minutes

- **3 pounds drummettes and wings (about 24 pieces)**
- **2 tablespoons vegetable oil**
- **2 tablespoons unsalted butter plus 3 tablespoons unsalted butter**
- **1 teaspoon garam masala plus another ½ teaspoon garam masala**
- **1 teaspoon salt**
- **⅓ cup tomato sauce**
- **Cilantro for garnish**

■ Coat a large rimmed baking sheet with nonstick cooking spray. In a bowl, toss drummettes and wings with 2 tablespoons each vegetable oil and melted unsalted butter and 1 teaspoon each garam masala and salt. Spread wings in a single layer on prepared sheet. Bake at 400° for 45 to 55 minutes, until crispy. Meanwhile, stir tomato sauce, 3 tablespoons unsalted butter and ½ teaspoon garam masala in a small skillet over medium heat until simmering. Toss cooked wings with sauce in a clean bowl, transfer to a serving platter and garnish with chopped cilantro.

PER SERVING 90 CAL; 7 g FAT (3 g SAT); 5 g PRO; 0 g CARB; 0 g FIBER; 135 mg SODIUM; 35 mg CHOL

Wedge Salad Stacks

MAKES 16 servings PREP 15 minutes
MICROWAVE 3 minutes

- **8 thick-cut bacon slices cut into quarters (32 pieces total)**
- **1 head of iceberg lettuce**
- **8 grape or cherry tomatoes**
- **Bottled blue cheese salad dressing**
- **¼ cup crumbled blue cheese (if desired)**

■ Cut bacon slices into quarters (32 pieces total). Stack on layers of paper towels and microwave 3 minutes until cooked but still pliable. Cut a 1-inch slice from a head of iceberg lettuce. Cut slice crosswise into 1-inch squares (you'll need a total of 16 squares, so you may have to cut another slice from the head of lettuce). Using 6-inch bamboo skewers, begin making stacks: On each skewer, slide 1 lettuce square, 2 bacon pieces and half a grape or cherry tomato. Place on a platter and drizzle stacks with a few tablespoons bottled blue cheese salad dressing. Sprinkle with crumbled blue cheese (if desired). Serve alongside ⅓ cup additional bottled dressing for dipping.

PER STACK 80 CAL; 7 g FAT (2 g SAT); 3 g PRO; 1 g CARB; 0 g FIBER; 202 mg SODIUM; 9 mg CHOL

Pomegranate Guacamole

MAKES 12 servings PREP 10 minutes

- **3 peeled and pitted avocados**
- **¾ cup pomegranate seeds**
- **½ cup chopped cilantro**
- **2 tablespoons lime juice**
- **½ teaspoon salt**
- **Sliced jicama or tortilla chips**

■ In a bowl, mash avocados. Stir in pomegranate seeds, chopped cilantro, lime juice and salt. Serve with sliced jicama or tortilla chips.

PER SERVING 100 CAL; 8 g FAT (1 g SAT); 1 g PRO; 9 g CARB; 6 g FIBER; 354 mg SODIUM; 3 mg CHOL

Meatball Parm Mushrooms

MAKES 24 servings PREP 15 minutes
BAKE at 375° for 25 minutes

- **2 packages (14 ounces) large stuffing mushrooms (about 24)**
- **12 fully cooked Italian-style beef or chicken meatballs (thawed if frozen)**
- **1½ cups jarred spicy or traditional marinara sauce**
- **¾ cup shredded Asiago cheese**
- **¼ cup grated Parmesan**

■ Heat oven to 375°. Clean mushrooms and remove and discard stems. Place mushrooms curved side up on a large rimmed baking sheet. Bake at 375° for 10 minutes. Remove tray from oven and carefully flip mushrooms over. Cut meatballs in half. Fit a meatball half into each mushroom cap and spoon 1 tablespoon marinara sauce over mushrooms. Sprinkle mushrooms with Asiago cheese and grated Parmesan. Bake stuffed mushrooms at 375° for 15 minutes, until tops are lightly browned.

PER SERVING 57 CAL; 3 g FAT (1 g SAT); 5 g PRO; 4 g CARB; 4 g FIBER; 100 mg SODIUM; 0 mg CHOL

Korean Beef Skewers

MAKES 24 skewers PREP 15 minutes
BROIL on HIGH for 4 minutes

- 1 **pound shell steak (1½ to 2 inches thick)**
- ⅓ **cup Korean barbecue sauce (such as Sky Valley)**
- **Sliced scallions (for garnish)**

■ Slice steak on the bias into ¼-inch-thick slices. Toss with barbecue sauce. Thread on twenty-four 6-inch bamboo skewers (soaked in water) and place on a nonstick foil-lined baking sheet in a single layer. Broil on HIGH for 2 minutes; flip and broil another 2 minutes. Garnish with sliced scallions.

PER SKEWER 35 CAL; 1 g FAT (1 g SAT); 4 g PRO; 1 g CARB; 0 g FIBER; 90 mg SODIUM; 10 mg CHOL

Sausage-Bacon Wraps

MAKES 16 servings PREP 12 minutes
BAKE at 400° for 24 minutes
MICROWAVE 45 seconds

- 4 **center-cut bacon slices**
- 2 **tablespoons apricot preserves plus another ⅓ cup**
- 1 **package (12 ounces) spicy mango with jalapeño smoked chicken sausage**
- 1 **tablespoon Dijon mustard**

■ Heat oven to 400°. Line a large baking sheet with parchment. Spread center-cut bacon slices on a cutting board, long edges touching. Spoon 2 tablespoons apricot preserves into a small bowl. Spread about ½ teaspoon preserves over each slice of bacon. Cut slices in half. Cut smoked chicken sausage into 16 pieces (4 pieces per link). Roll up a sausage piece in a half slice of bacon. Secure with a toothpick and place cut side down on prepared baking sheet. Repeat with 4 more center-cut bacon slices, remaining apricot preserves and remaining sausage. Bake at 400° for 12 minutes. Flip over and bake for another 12 minutes. Meanwhile, blend ⅓ cup apricot preserves with Dijon mustard. Microwave 45 seconds to heat. Serve with sausage-bacon wraps.

PER SERVING 81 CAL; 4 g FAT (1 g SAT); 4 g PRO; 9 g CARB; 0 g FIBER; 250 mg SODIUM; 21 mg CHOL

Spanakopita Cups

MAKES 30 pieces PREP 15 minutes
BAKE at 350° for 15 minutes

- 1 **package (10 ounces) thawed frozen spinach (squeezed dry)**
- 1 **large chopped scallion**
- 1 **tablespoon olive oil**
- 1 **teaspoon dry minced onion**
- ½ **teaspoon garlic powder**
- 1 **cup crumbled herb-flavored feta**
- 2 **eggs**
- 30 **mini phyllo shells (two 1.9 ounce packages)**

■ Heat oven to 350°. In a large skillet, cook spinach and scallion in olive oil 4 minutes. Stir in onion and garlic powder. In a large bowl, combine spinach mixture with feta and lightly beaten eggs. Spoon mixture into shells. Place on a baking sheet and bake at 350° for 15 minutes.

PER MINI CUP 39 CAL; 2 g FAT (1 g SAT); 2 g PRO; 3 g CARB; 0 g FIBER; 78 mg SODIUM; 16 mg CHOL

Crab-Stuffed Mini Peppers

MAKES 24 pieces PREP 15 minutes
BAKE at 300° for 15 minutes

- 12 **ounces lump crabmeat**
- 2 **tablespoons mayonnaise**
- 2 **tablespoons finely chopped sweet red pepper**
- 2 **tablespoons Dijon mustard**
- ¼ **cup snipped dill plus additional for garnish (if desired)**
- 2 **tablespoons olive oil**
- ¼ **teaspoon salt**
- ¼ **teaspoon pepper**
- 12 **mini sweet peppers**

■ Heat oven to 300°. Combine crabmeat, mayonnaise, red pepper, Dijon mustard, dill, olive oil, salt and pepper. Slice sweet peppers in half horizontally and fill with crab mixture. Place on a baking sheet and bake at 300° for 15 minutes. Garnish with additional fresh dill, if desired.

PER PIECE 27 CAL; 1 g FAT (0 g SAT); 3 g PRO; 0 g CARB; 0 g FIBER; 175 mg SODIUM; 10 mg CHOL

Za'atar Nut Mix

MAKES 5 cups PREP 10 minutes
BAKE at 300° for 15 minutes

- 2 **cups shelled pistachios**
- 2 **cups cashews**
- 1 **cup golden raisins**
- 1 **tablespoon olive oil**
- 2 **tablespoons Za'atar seasoning**
- ½ **teaspoon salt**
- ¼ **teaspoon black pepper**

■ Heat oven to 300°. In a large bowl, combine shelled pistachios, cashews, raisins, olive oil, Za'atar seasoning, salt and pepper. Spread mixture on a rimmed baking pan and bake at 300° for 15 minutes.

Tip Any extra nut mix can be packed into ¼-cup servings for snacking.

PER 1/4 CUP 176 CAL; 13 g FAT (2 g SAT); 5 g PRO; 14 g CARB; 2 g FIBER; 62 mg SODIUM; 0 mg CHOL

MINI CHICKEN AND WAFFLES

PEAR, GOAT CHEESE AND HAZELNUT CROSTINI

COCKTAIL SHRIMP WITH COCONUT CHUTNEY

Mini Chicken and Waffles

MAKES 16 servings **PREP** 10 minutes
BAKE at 425° for 20 minutes **BROIL** 1 minute

- **16** pieces popcorn chicken
- **32** mini Eggo waffles
- **3** tablespoons peach preserves
- **3** tablespoons honey mustard

■ Heat oven to 425°. Spread popcorn chicken on a large rimmed baking sheet. Bake at 425° for 20 minutes, turning once. During the last 5 minutes, add mini Eggo waffles directly to oven rack. Remove chicken from oven and increase temperature to broil. Broil waffles 1 minute to toast until lightly browned. Spread ½ teaspoon peach preserves on 16 of the waffles and ½ teaspoon honey mustard on each of the 16 remaining waffles. Place each chicken piece between a preserves- and a mustard-coated waffle. Secure each with a toothpick.

PER SERVING 94 **CAL**; 4 g **FAT** (1 g **SAT**); 3 g **PRO**; 12 g **CARB**; 0 g **FIBER**; 180 mg **SODIUM**; 12 mg **CHOL**

Pear, Goat Cheese and Hazelnut Crostini

MAKES 24 crostini **PREP** 15 minutes
BROIL on HIGH for 2 minutes

- **1** French baguette (about ¾ pound)
- **8** ounces semi soft goat cheese
- **3** tablespoons heavy cream or milk
- **1½** ripe pears
- **2** tablespoons honey
- **⅓** cup toasted chopped hazelnuts
  Freshly cracked black pepper

■ Slice French baguette on the bias into 24 slices. Using a hand mixer or spatula, combine goat cheese with heavy cream or milk until smooth. Spread 2 teaspoons of the goat cheese mixture on each crostino. Cut pears into 24 ¼-inch-thick slices; place 1 slice on top of each crostino. Drizzle honey over all the crostini. Broil on HIGH for 2 minutes on the top rack. Top with hazelnuts and season with black pepper.

PER CROSTINO 110 **CAL**; 5 g **FAT** (3 g **SAT**); 4 g **PRO**; 12 g **CARB**; 1 g **FIBER**; 115 mg **SODIUM**; 10 mg **CHOL**

Cocktail Shrimp with Coconut Chutney

MAKES 12 servings **PREP** 10 minutes

- **¾** cup shredded unsweetened coconut
- **¾** cup coconut milk
- **1** inch piece peeled, roughly chopped ginger
- **2** roughly chopped scallions
- **1** tablespoon lime juice
- **2** teaspoons sugar
- **¼** teaspoon salt
- **⅛** teaspoon cayenne
- **1** pound cold cooked peeled and deveined shrimp

■ In a food processor, combine shredded coconut, coconut milk, ginger, scallions, lime juice, sugar, salt and cayenne. Process until combined but still slightly chunky. Serve with shrimp.

PER SERVING 120 **CAL**; 7 g **FAT** (6 g **SAT**); 9 g **PRO**; 9 g **CARB**; 1 g **FIBER**; 410 mg **SODIUM**; 80 mg **CHOL**

Greek Flatbread

MAKES 24 servings **PREP** 15 minutes
BAKE at 425° for 13 minutes

- **1** cup artichoke tapenade
- **4** 8 × 8-inch flatbreads (such as Toufayan lavash)
- **1½** cups shredded Fontina cheese
- **¼** cup halved, pitted Kalamata olives
- **¼** cup thinly sliced red onion
- **2** tablespoons chopped fresh parsley

■ Heat oven to 425°. Spread artichoke tapenade onto flatbreads. Top with cheese, Kalamata olives and red onion. Transfer to baking sheets and bake at 425° for 10 minutes. Carefully slide flatbreads from sheets directly to oven racks and bake at 425° for an additional 3 minutes, until crisp. Sprinkle with parsley and cut each square into 6 pieces.

PER SERVING 35 **CAL**; 6 g **FAT** (2 g **SAT**); 4 g **PRO**; 6 g **CARB**; 2 g **FIBER**; 178 mg **SODIUM**; 8 mg **CHOL**

Mini Smoked Salmon Tostadas

MAKES 24 tostadas **PREP** 10 minutes

8	ounces soft cream cheese
2	tablespoons snipped fresh chives
2	tablespoons chopped pimientos
24	small, flat, round tortilla chips
	Smoked salmon
	Fresh cilantro sprigs

■ Combine cream cheese, snipped fresh chives, chopped pimientos. Spread mixture over tortilla chips. Top with a small piece of smoked salmon and a fresh cilantro sprig.

PER SERVING 49 **CAL**; 4 g **FAT** (2 g **SAT**); 2 g **PRO**; 2 g **CARB**; 0 g **FIBER**; 75 mg **SODIUM**; 11 mg **CHOL**

Roasted Ratatouille Bites

MAKES 16 servings **PREP** 15 minutes
ROAST at 400° for 25 minutes

1	medium eggplant
	Olive oil
	Balsamic vinegar
	Salt
	Herbs de Provence seasoning
16	grape tomatoes
½	teaspoon black pepper
	Large pitted green olives
	Bite-size pieces of fresh mozzarella

■ Heat oven to 400°. Cut eggplant into 1-inch pieces and spread on a baking sheet; toss with 2 tablespoons each olive oil and balsamic vinegar and 1 teaspoon each salt and herbs de Provence seasoning. Roast at 400° for 15 minutes. Toss 16 grape tomatoes with eggplant and black pepper; roast for an additional 10 minutes. On each of 16 wood skewers, thread 2 pieces of eggplant, 1 tomato, 1 large pitted green olive and 1 bite-size piece of fresh mozzarella. Place on a serving platter and drizzle with 1 tablespoon each olive oil and balsamic vinegar.

PER SERVING 102 **CAL**; 8 g **FAT** (3 g **SAT**); 4 g **PRO**; 2 g **CARB**; 1 g **FIBER**; 191 mg **SODIUM**; 18 mg **CHOL**

MINI SMOKED SALMON TOSTADAS

ROASTED RATATOUILLE BITES

GREEK FLATBREAD

RULE THE ROAST

Pick any main and a side or two—every combination is a guaranteed winner. *A few suggestions:* Pork Loin Roast with Warm Farro Salad, Beef Tenderloin and Taleggio Sweet Potato Gratin, Leg of Lamb alongside Spinach Salad with Dates and Pine Nuts.

MAINS

PORK LOIN ROAST WITH TWO SAUCES

HERB-ROASTED LEG OF LAMB

BEEF TENDERLOIN WITH HORSERADISH SAUCE

SIDES

SWEET-TART RED CABBAGE WITH ROASTED PEARS

FINGERLING POTATOES WITH CHIVE VINAIGRETTE

TALEGGIO SWEET POTATO GRATIN

ORECCHIETTE WITH BROCCOLI RABE

SPINACH SALAD WITH DATES AND PINE NUTS

WARM FARRO SALAD

Pork Loin Roast with Two Sauces

MAKES 8 servings **PREP** 15 minutes **ROAST** at 450° for 20 minutes and at 325° for 80 to 90 minutes **REST** 10 minutes **COOK** 3 minutes

- 4 cloves garlic, chopped
- 1 tablespoon lemon juice
- 1 tablespoon coarsely chopped sage
- 1 teaspoon coarsely chopped savory or oregano
- 1 teaspoon chopped thyme
- ½ teaspoon salt
- ¼ teaspoon black pepper
- 1 center-cut pork loin roast with 6 ribs (about 4½ pounds)
- 1 tablespoon olive oil
- 3 tablespoons flour
- 2 cups vegetable broth
  Fig and Port Sauce (recipe follows)

■ Heat oven to 450°. Fit a large roasting pan with a rack.

■ In a small bowl, combine garlic, lemon juice, sage, savory, thyme, salt and pepper. Brush pork roast with olive oil and rub with garlic-and-herb mixture.

■ Place pork in prepared pan and roast at 450° for 20 minutes. Lower oven heat to 325° and roast an additional 80 to 90 minutes or until internal temperature reaches 145°. Let rest 10 minutes.

■ While pork is resting, prepare gravy. Pour off all but 2 tablespoons of the fat from roasting pan. Place pan over medium heat and sprinkle with flour. Cook 1 minute, scraping up any browned bits from bottom of pan. Gradually whisk in vegetable broth and 1 cup water. Bring to a boil and cook 2 minutes, whisking constantly. Strain into a small saucepan and keep warm. Slice pork and serve with gravy and Fig and Port Sauce.

PER SERVING 398 **CAL**; 24 g **FAT** (8 g **SAT**); 40 g **PRO**; 4 g **CARB**; 0 g **FIBER**; 515 mg **SODIUM**; 115 mg **CHOL**

Fig and Port Sauce

MAKES 1¼ cups **PREP** 5 minutes **COOK** 9 minutes

- 2 sliced shallots
- 1 tablespoon plus another 2 tablespoons butter
- 1 tablespoon flour
- 1 cup ruby port
- 6 quartered dried figs
- ⅛ teaspoon salt
- ⅛ teaspoon pepper

■ Cook shallots in 1 tablespoon butter 3 minutes. Add flour and cook 1 minute. Whisk in port; simmer 3 minutes. Add figs and cook 2 minutes. Stir in 2 tablespoons water and 2 tablespoons butter. Season with salt and pepper.

HERB-ROASTED
LEG OF LAMB

BEEF TENDERLOIN WITH
HORSERADISH SAUCE

Herb-Roasted Leg of Lamb

MAKES 12 servings **PREP** 45 minutes
ROAST at 400° for 1 hour, 30 minutes to 1 hour, 45 minutes **REST** 15 minutes

- 1 boneless leg of lamb (4 to 5 pounds), butterflied
- ¼ cup extra-virgin olive oil
- 4 cloves garlic, minced
- 2 tablespoons chopped fresh mint
- 1 tablespoon chopped fresh rosemary
- 1 tablespoon lemon zest
- 2 teaspoons kosher salt
- ¾ teaspoon black pepper
  Mint Pesto (optional; recipe follows)

■ Let lamb sit at room temperature for 45 minutes before placing in oven. Heat oven to 400°.

■ Combine 3 tablespoons of the oil, the garlic, mint, rosemary, lemon zest, 1 teaspoon of the salt and ½ teaspoon of the pepper in a bowl. Place lamb on a cutting board, butterflied side up. Rub mixture on entire inside surface of the lamb. Roll lamb tightly and tie several times crosswise and once lengthwise with butcher string to secure.

■ Place lamb on a rimmed baking sheet fitted with a wire rack. Rub lamb with remaining 1 tablespoon oil and season with remaining 1 teaspoon salt and ¼ teaspoon pepper. Roast at 400° for 1 hour, 30 minutes to 1 hour, 45 minutes or until temperature reaches 145° on an instant-read thermometer. Let rest 15 minutes, then slice crosswise. Serve with Mint Pesto, if desired.

PER SERVING 270 **CAL**; 13 g **FAT** (4 g **SAT**); 35 g **PRO**; 1 g **CARB**; 0 g **FIBER**; 460 mg **SODIUM**; 110 mg **CHOL**

Mint Pesto

MAKES ¾ cup **PREP** 10 minutes

- 2 cups packed mint
- ¼ cup toasted walnuts
- 1 garlic clove
- 2 tablespoons lemon juice plus ½ teaspoon zest
- ⅓ cup olive oil
- ½ teaspoon kosher salt
- ⅛ teaspoon black pepper

■ In a food processor, combine mint, walnuts, garlic clove and lemon juice and zest. Pulse until roughly chopped. Stream in olive oil with processor running; blend until smooth. Transfer to a bowl and stir in salt and pepper.

PER SERVING 70 **CAL**; 8 g **FAT** (1 g **SAT**); 1 g **PRO**; 1 g **CARB**; 1 g **FIBER**; 100 mg **SODIUM**; 0 mg **CHOL**

Beef Tenderloin with Horseradish Sauce

MAKES 8 servings **PREP** 15 minutes
ROAST at 425° for 40 minutes **REST** 5 minutes

- 1 **beef tenderloin roast (about 3 pounds), tied**
- 2 **tablespoons instant espresso powder**
- 1 **teaspoon salt**
- ½ **teaspoon ground cinnamon**
- ½ **teaspoon chili powder**
- ½ **teaspoon ground black pepper**
- ⅓ **cup sour cream**
- ⅓ **cup light mayonnaise**
- 2 **tablespoons creamy horseradish**
- 1 **tablespoon chopped chives or parsley**

■ Heat oven to 425°. Fit a roasting pan with a rack. Let beef sit at room temperature while oven heats.

■ In a small bowl, stir instant espresso powder, salt, cinnamon, chili powder and pepper. Rub all over beef tenderloin and place roast on rack in pan.

■ Roast at 425° for 40 minutes or until meat registers 135° to 140° for medium on an instant-read thermometer. Let rest, covered with foil, 5 minutes.

■ Meanwhile, prepare sauce: In a bowl, whisk sour cream, mayonnaise, horseradish and chives. Refrigerate until serving.

■ Remove string from roast. Slice beef into ½-inch slices and serve with sauce.

PER SERVING 294 **CAL**; 15 g **FAT** (5 g **SAT**); 38 g **PRO**; 2 g **CARB**; 0 g **FIBER**; 467 mg **SODIUM**; 114 mg **CHOL**

SWEET-TART RED CABBAGE WITH ROASTED PEARS

Sweet-Tart Red Cabbage with Roasted Pears

MAKES 8 servings **PREP** 20 minutes **BAKE** at 450° for 25 minutes **COOK** 35 minutes

- 4 **firm pears**
- 1 **tablespoon canola oil plus another 1 tablespoon**
- 1 **tablespoon sugar**
- 12 **cups sliced red cabbage**
- ⅓ **cup white vinegar**
- ¼ **cup granulated sugar**
- ¼ **cup packed brown sugar**
- 1 **sliced onion**
- ½ **teaspoon salt**
- ¼ **teaspoon black pepper**
- ¼ **teaspoon ground ginger**
  A pinch of ground cloves

■ Peel, halve and core pears; place cut side down on a baking sheet. Brush with 1 tablespoon canola oil and sprinkle with sugar. Bake at 450° for 25 minutes, turning after 15 minutes. Toss red cabbage with white vinegar, granulated sugar and brown sugar. In a large skillet cook onion in 1 tablespoon canola oil 5 minutes. Add cabbage and ⅓ cup water; cook 25 minutes, covered, stirring occasionally. Season with salt, pepper, ginger and cloves; cook 5 minutes, uncovered. Place pears over cabbage and serve.

PER SERVING 205 **CAL**; 4 g **FAT** (0 g **SAT**); 3 g **PRO**; 43 g **CARB**; 7 g **FIBER**; 185 mg **SODIUM**; 0 mg **CHOL**

FINGERLING
POTATOES WITH
CHIVE VINAIGRETTE

One potato, two potato. Choose between crisp roasted fingerlings dressed in an herbed vinaigrette and creamy and indulgent sweet potatoes baked until bubbly in cheese and cream.

TALEGGIO SWEET POTATO GRATIN

Fingerling Potatoes with Chive Vinaigrette

MAKES 8 servings **PREP** 15 minutes
ROAST at 400° for 20 minutes

- 1¾ **pounds fingerling potatoes**
- 2 **tablespoons extra-virgin olive oil plus another 2 tablespoons**
- ½ **teaspoon kosher salt plus another ¼ teaspoon**
- ¼ **teaspoon black pepper plus another ⅛ teaspoon**
- 2 **tablespoons white wine vinegar**
- ½ **teaspoon Dijon mustard**
- 3 **tablespoons chopped fresh chives**

■ Slice potatoes in half lengthwise, then, if necessary, in half crosswise into 3-inch pieces. Toss in 2 tablespoons extra-virgin olive oil, ½ teaspoon salt and ¼ teaspoon pepper. Roast on a rimmed baking sheet at 400° for 20 minutes. Meanwhile, prepare vinaigrette: In a large bowl, whisk 2 tablespoons extra-virgin olive oil, white wine vinegar, mustard, ¼ teaspoon salt and ⅛ teaspoon pepper. Stir in chives. Toss hot potatoes in vinaigrette and serve warm.

PER SERVING 140 **CAL**; 7 g **FAT** (1 g **SAT**); 2 g **PRO**; 18 g **CARB**; 2 g **FIBER**; 190 mg **SODIUM**; 0 mg **CHOL**

Taleggio Sweet Potato Gratin

MAKES 8 servings **PREP** 25 minutes **COOK** 5 minutes **BAKE** at 375° for 90 minutes

- 1 **large leek**
- 2 **tablespoons butter**
- 4 **large peeled sweet potatoes**
- 6 **ounces Taleggio cheese cut into small cubes**
- 4 **teaspoons chopped fresh sage**
- 1 **teaspoon chopped fresh thyme**
- 1½ **cups heavy cream**
- 1 **teaspoon salt**
- 1 **teaspoon garlic powder**
- ¼ **teaspoon black pepper**

■ Slice leek and cook in butter 5 minutes. Cut potatoes into ⅛-inch slices. In a 2-quart baking dish, layer one-third of the sweet potatoes, half the leek slices, 2 ounces Taleggio, 2 teaspoons chopped fresh sage and ½ teaspoon chopped fresh thyme. Repeat layering. Top with remaining third of the potatoes and Taleggio. In a small saucepan, combine cream, salt, garlic powder and pepper; bring to a simmer. Pour over potatoes and down sides of baking dish. Bake at 375°, covered, for 45 minutes, then uncovered for 45 minutes. Cool 10 minutes before serving.

PER SERVING 337 **CAL**; 27 g **FAT** (17 g **SAT**); 6 g **PRO**; 19 g **CARB**; 2 g **FIBER**; 462 mg **SODIUM**; 96 mg **CHOL**

ORECCHIETTE WITH
BROCCOLI RABE

SPINACH SALAD WITH
DATES AND PINE NUTS

Orecchiette with Broccoli Rabe

MAKES 8 servings **PREP** 10 minutes
COOK 19 minutes

- 1 bunch broccoli rabe
- 1 box (1 pound) orecchiette pasta
- 1 package (10 ounces) baby bella mushrooms
- 2 tablespoons unsalted butter
- 2 tablespoons olive oil
- 4 sliced garlic cloves
- ½ cup heavy cream
- ½ teaspoon salt
- 2 tablespoons grated Parmesan
    Freshly ground black pepper

■ Bring a large pot of lightly salted water to a boil. Trim tough stems from broccoli rabe and cut into 2-inch pieces. Add broccoli rabe to boiling water and cook 1 minute. Scoop out to a bowl and return water to a boil. Add orecchiette pasta and cook 9 minutes. Meanwhile, clean, trim and slice mushrooms. Melt butter with olive oil in a large skillet. Add mushrooms and cook 3 minutes. Add garlic cloves and cook 1 minute. Drain pasta and set aside. Add broccoli rabe to mushrooms in skillet, along with heavy cream. Simmer 5 minutes. Season with salt and stir in orecchiette. Transfer to a serving bowl and toss with Parmesan. Sprinkle with pepper and serve warm.

PER SERVING 335 **CAL**; 13 g **FAT** (6 g **SAT**); 11 g **PRO**; 45 g **CARB**; 4 g **FIBER**; 192 mg **SODIUM**; 29 mg **CHOL**

Spinach Salad with Dates and Pine Nuts

MAKES 8 servings **PREP** 15 minutes

- 3 tablespoons balsamic vinegar
- 3 tablespoons extra-virgin olive oil
- 1 teaspoon Dijon mustard
- ½ teaspoon salt
- ¼ teaspoon black pepper
- 1 package (10 ounces) baby spinach
- 1 cup chopped pitted dates
- ⅓ cup toasted pine nuts
- ¼ cup thinly sliced shallots

■ In a large bowl, whisk balsamic vinegar, olive oil, mustard, salt and pepper. Toss with spinach, dates, pine nuts and shallots.

PER SERVING 170 **CAL**; 9 g **FAT** (1 g **SAT**); 2 g **PRO**; 23 g **CARB**; 4 g **FIBER**; 220 mg **SODIUM**; 0 mg **CHOL**

Warm Farro Salad

MAKES 8 servings **PREP** 20 minutes
COOK 15 minutes

- 1½ **cups quick-cook farro**
- ¾ **teaspoon salt plus another
  ¼ teaspoon**
- 3 **tablespoons red wine vinegar**
- 2 **tablespoons chopped fresh
  parsley**
- 2 **teaspoons honey Dijon mustard**
- ¼ **teaspoon pepper**
- ¼ **cup olive oil**

- 2 **packages (9 ounces each) fresh
  Brussels sprouts**
- 4 **ounces diced pancetta**
- 2 **minced garlic cloves**
- ⅓ **cup crumbled blue cheese**

■ Combine farro with 5 cups water and ¾ teaspoon salt. Bring to a boil, cover and reduce heat to medium-low. Simmer 15 minutes, then drain. Meanwhile, make dressing: Whisk red wine vinegar, parsley, mustard, ¼ teaspoon salt and pepper. Add olive oil in a thin stream, whisking constantly. Trim stem ends from Brussels sprouts. Peel apart sprouts into individual leaves. Heat a large stainless skillet over medium-high heat. Add pancetta and cook over medium heat 5 minutes, until crisp. Add garlic cloves and Brussels sprout leaves. Cook 2 to 3 minutes, until leaves are bright green. Remove from heat and add drained farro and dressing. Transfer to a serving bowl and toss with blue cheese. Serve warm.

PER SERVING 292 **CAL**; 15 g **FAT** (4 g **SAT**); 10 g **PRO**; 32 g **CARB**; 5 g **FIBER**; 493 mg **SODIUM**; 14 mg **CHOL**

WARM FARRO SALAD

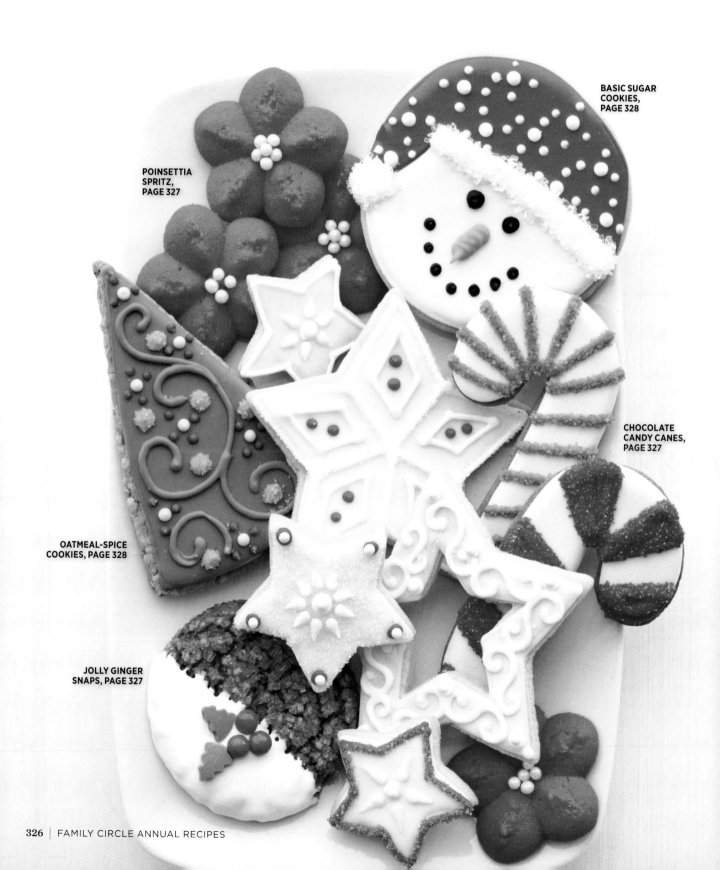

COOKIES FOR SANTA

Set out your best for the jolly man in the red suit—and for friends and family too.

POINSETTIA SPRITZ, PAGE 327

BASIC SUGAR COOKIES, PAGE 328

CHOCOLATE CANDY CANES, PAGE 327

OATMEAL-SPICE COOKIES, PAGE 328

JOLLY GINGER SNAPS, PAGE 327

Poinsettia Spritz

MAKES 11½ dozen **PREP** 10 minutes
BAKE at 375° for 12 minutes per batch

- 3½ cups all-purpose flour
- 1 teaspoon baking powder
- ½ teaspoon salt
- 1½ cups unsalted butter, softened
- 1 cup sugar
- 1 large egg
- 1 teaspoon vanilla extract
- Red paste food coloring
- Small yellow sprinkles

■ Heat oven to 375°. In a medium bowl, combine flour, baking powder and salt.

■ In a large bowl, beat butter and sugar until light and fluffy, about 5 minutes. Add egg and vanilla and beat until well blended. Gradually add flour mixture and beat until just blended. Tint dough red with paste food coloring.

■ Fit a flower disk (with diamond-shape openings) into a cookie press. Add dough, packing it slightly to remove any air bubbles. Press cookie dough shapes, about 1½ inches apart, on a cookie sheet, adding more dough when necessary. Place several yellow sprinkles in center of each flower. Bake at 375° until set and lightly golden, 10 to 12 minutes. Transfer to a wire rack to cool. Repeat with remaining dough.

Jolly Ginger Snaps

MAKES 2½ dozen cookies **PREP** 15 minutes
BAKE at 350° for 10 minutes per batch
MICROWAVE 1 minute **REFRIGERATE** 5 minutes

- 1 cup coarse white decorating sugar
- 2 cups all-purpose flour
- 1 tablespoon ground ginger
- 2 teaspoons baking soda
- 1 teaspoon ground cinnamon
- ½ teaspoon salt
- ½ cup unsalted butter, softened
- ¼ cup plus 1 tablespoon shortening
- 1 cup granulated sugar
- 1 large egg
- ¼ cup molasses
- 1½ cups Wilton white melting wafers
- Wilton small green tree sprinkles
- Red M&M's minis or small red candies (such as SweetWorks pearls)

■ Heat oven to 350°. Line several cookie sheets with parchment paper. Place decorating sugar in a pie dish and set aside.

■ In a medium bowl, combine flour, ginger, baking soda, cinnamon and salt. In a large bowl, beat butter, ¼ cup of the shortening and the granulated sugar until light and fluffy, about 3 minutes. Add egg and molasses and beat until blended. Gradually add flour mixture and beat until just combined.

■ Shape dough into 1½-inch balls. Roll dough balls in decorating sugar to coat. Arrange on prepared cookie sheets about 2 inches apart. Bake in batches at 350° until flattened, about 8 to 10 minutes. Transfer to a wire rack to cool completely. Repeat with remaining dough.

■ Place white melting wafers in a medium bowl with remaining 1 tablespoon shortening.

■ Microwave candy wafers, stirring until smooth, about 1 minute. Dip a cookie halfway into melted candy, remove any excess and transfer to a wax-paper-lined cookie sheet. While wafers are still wet, add candy trees and red candies to resemble holly. Refrigerate until set, 5 minutes.

Chocolate Candy Canes

MAKES 3 dozen **PREP** 15 minutes
REFRIGERATE 4 hours
BAKE at 350° for 12 minutes per batch

- 1 cup all-purpose flour
- ½ cup cocoa powder
- ½ teaspoon baking powder
- ⅛ teaspoon salt
- ½ cup (1 stick) unsalted butter, softened
- ¾ cup sugar
- 1 large egg
- ¾ teaspoon vanilla extract
- Royal Icing (recipe on page 328), nonpareils, coarse sugar and crushed candy canes

■ In a medium bowl, whisk flour, cocoa powder, baking powder and salt. Set aside.

■ In a large bowl, beat butter and sugar until smooth, 2 minutes. Beat in egg and vanilla. On low speed, beat in flour mixture until just combined. Divide dough in half and form each half into a disk. Wrap in plastic wrap and refrigerate 4 hours or overnight.

■ Heat oven to 350°. On a lightly floured surface, roll out one disk to ¼-inch thickness. Using a 3¼-inch candy cane–shape cookie cutter, cut out shapes.

■ Place shapes on an ungreased baking sheet. Bake at 350° for 10 to 12 minutes, until lightly golden around edges. Remove to wire racks to cool completely.

■ Repeat with remaining dough. Gather scraps and refrigerate. Reroll and cut into additional shapes. Bake and cool on wire racks; decorate with white Royal Icing, sugar and crushed candy canes as desired. When dry, store in an airtight container up to 2 weeks.

Basic Sugar Cookies

Use this recipe for stars and snowmen.

MAKES 3 dozen **PREP** 15 minutes
REFRIGERATE 4 hours
BAKE at 350° for 12 minutes per batch

- 1½ cups all-purpose flour
- ½ teaspoon baking powder
- ⅛ teaspoon salt
- ½ cup (1 stick) unsalted butter, softened
- ¾ cup sugar
- 1 large egg
- ¾ teaspoon vanilla extract
  Royal Icing (recipe right), silver or white luster dust, nonpareils and coarse sugar

■ In a medium bowl, whisk flour, baking powder and salt. Set aside.

■ In a large bowl, beat butter and sugar until smooth, about 2 minutes. Beat in egg and vanilla. On low speed, beat in flour mixture until just combined. Divide dough in half and form each half into a disk. Wrap in plastic wrap and refrigerate 4 hours or overnight.

■ Heat oven to 350°. On a lightly floured surface, roll out one disk to ¼-inch thickness. Using a 3¼-inch round cookie cutter (for snowmen) or 3½-, 2- and 1¾-inch star cookie cutters, cut out shapes. Place on an ungreased baking sheet. Bake at 350° for 10 to 12 minutes, until lightly golden around edges. Remove cookies to wire racks to cool completely.

■ Repeat with remaining half of dough. Gather scraps and refrigerate. Reroll and cut into additional shapes. Bake and cool on wire racks; decorate as desired. For stars, once base frosting is dry, brush with luster dust. For snowmen, add hat and face embellishments after base coat has dried completely. When dry, store in an airtight container up to 2 weeks.

Oatmeal-Spice Cookies

Use this recipe for Christmas trees.

MAKES 4 dozen **PREP** 30 minutes
REFRIGERATE 1 hour
BAKE at 350° for 15 minutes per batch

- 1 cup unsalted butter
- 1 cup packed brown sugar
- ½ cup granulated sugar
- 1 teaspoon baking soda
- 1 teaspoon pumpkin pie or apple pie spice
- ½ teaspoon salt
- 2 eggs
- 1 teaspoon vanilla extract
- 2¾ cups all-purpose flour
- 1½ cups regular or quick-cooking rolled oats
  Royal Icing (recipe right), coarse decorating sugar and nonpareils

■ In a large mixing bowl, beat butter with an electric mixer on medium to high speed 30 seconds. Add brown sugar, granulated sugar, baking soda, pumpkin pie spice and salt. Beat until combined, scraping sides of bowl. Beat in eggs and vanilla. Beat in as much flour as you can with mixer (dough will be stiff). Stir in any remaining flour and the oats. Divide dough into 6 pieces, wrap in plastic wrap and refrigerate 1 hour to firm.

■ Heat oven to 350°. Roll out 1 piece of dough to an 8-inch circle. Cut into 8 wedges, leaving pieces touching. Repeat with 2 more disks. Bake at 350° for 12 to 15 minutes until lightly browned and centers are set. Cool on cookie sheets 2 minutes, then recut and separate wedges. Remove with spatula and cool completely on wire racks. Repeat with remaining 3 dough disks. Decorate with green, white and red Royal Icing and assorted decorating sugars and nonpareils.

Royal Icing

MAKES 3 cups **PREP** 5 minutes

- 1 box (16 ounces) confectioners' sugar
- 6 tablespoons warm water
- 3 tablespoons powdered egg whites (such as Just Whites)
  Red, green, orange and black gel food coloring, piping bags and writing tips

■ In a large bowl, combine confectioners' sugar, warm water and powdered egg whites. Beat with an electric mixer on medium speed until smooth and fluffy, about 5 minutes.

■ Keep covered with plastic wrap until ready to use; divide and tint to desired colors for each recipe. Transfer some of the tinted icing into piping bags fitted with small writing tips.

SHAKE IT UP

Liven up the holiday season with this trio of festive cocktails.

Sparkling Pear Cocktail

MAKES 1 drink **PREP** 5 minutes

- **1** slice pear
- **2** ounces chilled pear nectar
- **3** ounces chilled sparkling wine

■ Place a pear slice inside a Champagne flute. Pour in pear nectar, then top with sparkling wine.

Hot Brown Buttered Rum

MAKES 4 drinks **PREP** 15 minutes

- **1** stick unsalted butter
- **½** cup packed dark brown sugar
- **½** teaspoon ground cinnamon
- **¼** teaspoon nutmeg
- **⅛** teaspoon ground cardamom
- **2** cups boiling water
- **6** ounces spiced rum
- **4** cinnamon sticks

■ Melt butter over medium heat and cook several minutes, until it starts to brown (be careful not to burn). Stir in sugar, ground cinnamon, nutmeg and cardamom. Transfer mixture to a 4-cup heatproof measuring cup. Stir in 2 cups boiling water and mix until most of the sugar is dissolved. Stir in rum. Pour into 4 glasses and serve warm. Garnish with a cinnamon stick.

Blood Orange Whiskey Sour

MAKES 1 drink **PREP** 5 minutes

- Ice
- **2** ounces bourbon
- **1** ounce blood orange juice, freshly squeezed or bottled, such as Italian Volcano
- **1** teaspoon sugar
- **1** pasteurized egg white
- Blood orange slice

■ Fill a cocktail shaker with ice. Pour in bourbon, blood orange juice, sugar and egg white. Shake 15 seconds, until cold and foamy. Pour through a strainer into a glass. Garnish with a blood orange slice.

INDEX

IN-A-PINCH SUBSTITUTIONS

It can happen to the best of us: Halfway through a recipe, you find you're completely out of a key ingredient. Here's what to do:

When the Recipe Calls For:	You May Substitute:
1 square unsweetened chocolate	3 tbsp. unsweetened cocoa powder + 1 tbsp. butter/margarine
1 cup cake flour	1 cup less 2 tbsp. all-purpose flour
2 tbsp. flour (for thickening)	1 tbsp. cornstarch
1 tsp. baking powder	¼ tsp. baking soda + ½ tsp. cream of tartar + ¼ tsp. cornstarch
1 cup corn syrup	1 cup sugar + ¼ cup additional liquid used in recipe
1 cup milk	½ cup evaporated milk + ½ cup water
1 cup buttermilk or sour milk	1 tbsp. vinegar or lemon juice + enough milk to make 1 cup
1 cup sour cream (for baking)	1 cup plain yogurt
1 cup firmly packed brown sugar	1 cup sugar + 2 tbsp. molasses
1 tsp. lemon juice	¼ tsp. vinegar (not balsamic)
¼ cup chopped onion	1 tbsp. dried minced onion
1 clove garlic	¼ tsp. garlic powder
2 cups tomato sauce	¾ cup tomato paste + 1 cup water
1 tbsp. prepared mustard	1 tsp. dry mustard + 1 tbsp. water

HOW TO KNOW WHAT YOU NEED

Making a shopping list based on a recipe can be tricky if you don't know how many tomatoes yields 3 cups chopped. Our handy translations:

When the Recipe Calls For:	You Need:
4 cups shredded cabbage	1 small head cabbage
1 cup grated raw carrot	1 large carrot
2½ cups sliced carrots	1 pound raw carrots
4 cups cooked cut fresh green beans	1 pound green beans
1 cup chopped onion	1 large onion
4 cups sliced raw potatoes	4 medium-size potatoes
1 cup chopped sweet pepper	1 large pepper
1 cup chopped tomato	1 large tomato
2 cups canned tomatoes	16-oz. can
4 cups sliced apples	4 medium-size apples
1 cup mashed banana	3 medium-size bananas
1 tsp. grated lemon rind	1 medium-size lemon
2 tbsp. lemon juice	1 medium-size lemon
4 tsp. grated orange rind	1 medium-size orange
1 cup orange juice	3 medium-size oranges
4 cups sliced peaches	8 medium-size peaches
2 cups sliced strawberries	1 pint
1 cup soft bread crumbs	2 slices fresh bread
1 cup bread cubes	2 slices fresh bread
2 cups shredded cheese	8 oz. cheese
1 cup egg whites	6 or 7 large eggs
1 egg white	2 tsp. egg white powder + 2 tbsp. water
4 cups chopped walnuts or pecans	1 pound shelled